ABE LINCOLN LAUGHING

Abe Lincoln Laughing

Humorous Anecdotes from Original Sources by and about Abraham Lincoln

Edited with an introduction by P.M. Zall

Foreword by Ray Allen Billington

The University of Tennessee Press
Knoxville

Paper: 1st printing, 1995; 2nd printing, 1997; 3rd printing, 2001.

The paper use in this book meets the minimum requirements of ANSI/
NISO Z39.48-1992 (R 1997) (Permanence of Paper). The binding
materials have been chosen for strength and durability.

Library of Congress Cataloging-in-Publication Data

Abe Lincoln laughing: humorous anecdotes from original sources by
and about Abraham Lincoln / edited with an introduction by P. M. Zall;
foreword by Ray Allen Billington.
        p.   cm.
    Includes index.
    ISBN 0-87049-889-4 (pbk.: alk. paper)
    1.Lincoln, Abraham, 1809–1865—Anecdotes. I. Lincoln, Abraham,
1809–1865. II. Zall, Paul M.
E457.15.A13   1995
973.7'092–dc20   94-45374

For Marissa and Regina

Contents

Foreword

Here is an oft-told Lincoln story that is *not* in this book:

A Mississippi River barge rammed the abutment of a newly built railroad bridge spanning the river, causing such damage that the railroad brought suit to recover. Because the barge's owner questioned the whole right of railroads to interfere with navigation, a battery of high-powered lawyers was imported from the East to present the railroad's case, while the barge owner retained Abraham Lincoln as his sole counsel. The trial was long and tedious, with evidence piled on evidence, but at last the time arrived for the summation speeches by the attorneys. Those for the railroad spoke eloquently, summarizing the evidence, advancing watertight arguments, and clearly impressing the jurors. Then came Lincoln's turn. He rose, strode to the jury box, smiled, and made a single statement: "My learned opponents," he said, "have presented an impressive case. There is no question that they have their facts absolutely right. But they have drawn completely wrong conclusions." The jurors laughed uproariously, adjourned to their deliberations, and after only a few moments returned with a verdict favoring Lincoln's client.

As soon as court adjourned, the railroad attorneys besieged Lincoln with questions. "We had that case won," they told him. "Then you simply tell the jurors that our facts are right and our conclusions wrong, and they decide in your favor. Why? What did you do to them?"

"Well, boys," Lincoln replied, "it just happened that when the court had adjourned for lunch today, I happened into a saloon where the jurors were eating, and told them a little story. A story about a farmer who was working in his barnyard one day when his ten-year-old boy came rushing up to him, all excited. 'Paw,' said the boy. 'Come quick. The hired man and Sis are up in the haymow, and he's a-pullin' down his pants and she's a-liftin' up her skirts. Paw, they're gettin' ready to pee all over our hay.' 'Son,' said the farmer, 'you've got your facts absolutely right, but you've drawn a completely wrong conclusion.' "

That anecdote has the ring of a perfect Abraham Lincoln story; it is plausible, appealing, earthy, and just the sort of thing that he might have said. Why, then, did Paul Zall not include it in the excellent collection that he has assembled in this book? Certainly moralistic standards did not demand its exclusion, for others that appear are far bawdier. And it is, to today's reader, far funnier than a good many others that have been judged worthy.

The answer to those questions is important if we are to appreciate the true purpose of this book. For this is no uncritical, helter-skelter assembling of Lincoln yarns, selected indiscriminately from the thousands that have been attributed to the Great Emancipator. It is, true, rich in humor, invaluable for its insights into the life of nineteenth-century America, and an uproarious delight to read. But it's also a work of impeccable scholarship, designed with one basic purpose: to separate the authentic from the apocryphal Lincoln stories. It is a book that will please the meticulous scholar no less than the casual reader. Each anecdote that Zall has included has passed the test of his own scholarly scrutiny. "The present edition," he tells us, "is designed to resolve some of the confusion [in Lincoln scholarship] by providing reliable texts along with the alternative choices from credible witnesses." So it does. The story of the railroad bridge trial, plausible though it may be, cannot be authenticated as ever told by Lincoln. Hence it is one of hundreds that have been eliminated.

To apply such exacting standards has required the use of a variety of scholarly tools, searching insights—and a vast amount of hard work. Paul Zall has combed manuscript depositories as far apart as the Huntington Library of San Marino, California and the Library of Congress in the national capital; he has read, and critically read, every Lincoln jokebook published in the nineteenth and twentieth centuries; he has pored over the books and manuscripts written by or about each of Lincoln's friends or acquaintances; he has spent weeks and months searching contemporary magazines and newspapers for Lincoln anecdotes. He has, in other words, searched out every single bit of writing that seemed likely to contain a true and authentic tale.

No one could have been better equipped for this rigorous task. A well-known student of English literature with a special interest in Anglo-American humor, he is the author and editor of a number of standard books essential for the background information needed in writing this volume: *A Hundred Merry Tales, and Other English Jestbooks of the Fifteenth and Sixteenth Centuries* (1963), *A Nest of Ninnies, and Other English Jestbooks of the Seventeenth Century* (1970), and in the American field, *Comical Spirit of Seventy-Six: The Humor of Francis Hopkinson* (1976), and *Ben Franklin Laughing: Anecdotes from Original Sources By and About Benjamin Franklin* (1980), these in addition to several works on English literature and criticism.

This background has given Zall a body of information which he has used well in this book. His vast knowledge of past humor has allowed him to trace the origins of many jokes that Lincoln told, and that were centuries old when he told them. His carefully wrought notes enrich the volume, and greatly enhance its scholarly usefulness.

Yet no one should be misled into thinking this a volume useful to dry-as-dust scholars alone. Lincoln was a superb raconteur; his wit was spontaneous, his store of anecdotes formidable, his ability to apply exactly the right story to each situation phenomenal. And what rib-tickling tales he could tell: of the woman whose drowned husband's body was brought home full of eels and who ordered that "They take the eels out and set him again"; of the two drunks who fought so furiously that each fought himself out of his own coat and into his opponent's; of the boy who had a bear by the hind legs and shouted to a companion: "Bill, for God's sake, come down and help me let this darned bear go"; of the girl who had inquired in vain of a wounded soldier where he had been hit being told by Lincoln, "My dear girl, the ball that hit *him*, would not have injured *you*"; of the man whose legs were so short that when he walked in the snow the seat of his trousers wiped out his footprints; of the farmer who nested his hen on forty-three eggs because "I wanted to see her spread herself"; of the young man told by his father to take a wife asking whose wife he should take; of the scarecrow so ugly that crows brought back the corn they had taken two days before.

Yes, Lincoln was a formidable yarn-spinner, so famed for his prowess in his own day that (as he tells it), a Quaker lady once voiced the opinion that he must be a praying man, and was told by her companion, "Yes, but the Lord will think Abraham is joking."

Anecdotes such as these may not seem as funny to today's sophisticated readers as they seemed in the 1850s and 1860s, but they mirror the times in which Lincoln lived, and they shed light on Lincoln as a warm, compassionate, witty, and earthy human being—a man who possessed that greatest of all virtues: the ability to laugh at himself. This is a fun book to chuckle over, and a revealing book to contemplate. Read and profit and enjoy.

Ray Allen Billington

The Huntington Library

Introduction: Lincoln's Stories and "Lincoln Stories"

This edition of humorous anecdotes by and about Abraham Lincoln does not pretend to be exhaustive. On the contrary, it represents only those sayings and stories having some semblance of authenticity along with a mere sampling of apochryphal "Lincoln stories" that have been attached to his name because of his reputation as a funny fellow. Drawn from manuscript as well as printed material, all the entries are given in the earliest form available in order to reduce the odds that they were simply copied from some suspect source. At the same time, the notes indicate earlier sources that Lincoln himself could have known. Whether he actually used those sources is not at issue, but they are included to show that he habitually told stories that must have been already familiar to those who heard them. It was because of this practice that his name became a lodestone for the hundreds of old jokes that expanded in time to become the mass of "Lincoln stories" now embedded in our national heritage. The trouble with such stories, however, is that they distort our vision of Lincoln's own humor.

Today's fashion is to analyze his humor as a key to his personality. Keith Jennison's *The Humorous Mr. Lincoln* (1965) pretty well summarizes the consensus: In his youth Lincoln told jokes because they came naturally to him. When he practiced law, he employed them as tools of the trade; and when he entered politics, he wielded them as a weapon for satire and ridicule. In the early presidency, they provided a roundabout way of saying "no," and later, as the responsibilities of the office became almost "unendurable," they provided therapy "to lessen the tensions in himself and those around him" (p. i). The mystical view from this position is that Lincoln's storytelling became the salvation of his sanity in the dark night of our national soul. But there is also a pragmatic view that Lincoln practiced storytelling as he practiced law or politics, as an art designed to move men's minds and hearts. It is the latter view that is obscured by the "Lincoln stories" because they make his storytelling appear uncontrolled, unrestrained, and artless, when in fact as lawyer, as politician, and as president Lincoln was master of the art.

The task in clarifying that view is to separate his own stories from the mass of apochrypha and then to make a selection from multiple versions of the same story provided by witnesses of equal credibility. Jennison, for instance, enters a disclaimer: "There being a confusion of final authorities as to the precise text of the anecdotes, I have chosen simply the versions that pleased me the most and for which there appeared to be *enough* authority" (ibid.). While not intended to be a "final authority," the present edition is designed to resolve some of the confusion by providing probably reliable texts along with alternative choices from credible witnesses.

This seems the best we can do under the handicap of history. For the confusion surrounding Lincoln's stories developed in his own time, partly from his own practice. His reputation as a legendary raconteur on the Illinois circuit preceded him to the presidency, causing sobersided citizens considerable anxiety for the dignity of the office. By the time of the second inaugural he was being blamed for more bad jokes than anyone since Joe Miller. Both parties capitalized on his fame for funny stories—Democrats in mockery, Republicans in praise of his homely humanity. Thus the pro-Lincoln *Old Abe's Jokes* of 1864 countered the anti-Lincoln *Old Abe's Joker* of 1863. Not even the shock of assassination could suppress the stream of stories advertised as having originated from the White House. From London, the *Legacy of Fun* (1865) accumulated a century's old jokes, attaching them to Lincoln's name. Sample: When a busybody complained that General Grant drank twelve bottles at one sitting, Old Abe replies, "That's more than I can swallow" (p. 3). But even friendly humorists such as Robert H. Newell would associate him with such similar stories as the one about Dr. Dobbs testifying that anyone who doubts the world goes round has never been drunk (New York *Mercury*, 27 December 1864).

In the confusion resulting from such crossfire, Lincoln himself had been unsure just what he had or had not said. Asked about the stories in the friendly *Old Abe's Jokes*, he acknowledged responsibility for "only about half a dozen."[1] Respecting the stories generally assigned to him, he said he was responsible for "about half,"[2] but told another reporter, his friend Noah Brooks, that he was responsible for "about one-sixth."[3] In any case, he was clearly concerned about the fame or infamy accruing to him, and tried to clarify what he meant by being "responsible" for these stories.

He did not mean that he originated them. He explained to Brooks: "You speak of Lincoln stories. I don't think that is the correct phrase. I don't make the stories mine by telling them." This was not false modesty, for as the notes in this edition show, about sixty percent of the stories assigned to him during his lifetime can be linked to previously printed sources, a surprising number of them contemporary; for example, the writings of Joseph G. Baldwin, Charles F. Browne ("Artemus Ward"), David R. Locke ("Petroleum V. Nasby"), and Charles Halpine ("Private Miles O'Reilly"). These were in addition to such sources as *Joe Miller's Jest-Book* and similar collections of stories, jokes, and sayings which competed with almanacs for popular readers.

More timely still were the humor columns in newspapers and magazines generally, but particularly *Harper's Monthly*. Its "Editor's Drawer" was sustained by readers' contributions from across the nation: "good things that are flying around generally in the lips and ears of its readers."[4] This was the source even of such celebrated figures of speech as the "homeopathic soup that was made by boiling the shadow of a pigeon that had starved to death," which he used in a speech of October 1858.[5] It had appeared in "Editor's Drawer" only a few years earlier, March 1853: "The learned Dr. Francis once made himself 'memorable' by a remark which he made in a Homeopathic discussion; namely, the boiling of the *shadow* of a pigeon in a bottle of water, and dividing the fluid into infinitesimal quantities, and administering this powerful 'concentrated medicine to the patient once every six months,' at night, before going to bed."[6] Thus, far from being "original," Lincoln cultivated such sayings and stories as would be familiar to his audience.

This kind of open borrowing must amaze us moderns but, as many of the early entries below indicate, reporters needed only to allude to a story and would be confident that their readers could flesh it out for themselves. Again, Lincoln himself explained what he was doing: "It is not the story itself, but its purpose, or effect, that interests me."[7] By analogy, he was a performer rather than a playwright. In the forties and fifties, the whole Eighth Judicial Circuit was his stage. After court business concluded for the day, everyone moved to the local tavern where star storytellers performed to standing-room-only crowds —as described by his partner William Herndon:

> The barroom, windows, halls, and all passageways would be filled
> to suffocation by the people eager to see the "big ones" and to
> hear their stories told by them. Lincoln would tell his story in his
> very best style. The people, all present, including Lincoln, would
> burst out in a loud laugh and a hurrah at the story. The listeners
> . . . would cry out: "Now, Uncle Billy (William Engle), you must
> beat that or go home." Engle would clear his throat and say:
> "Boys, the story just told by Lincoln puts me in mind of a story
> I heard when a boy." . . . Lincoln would tell his story and then
> followed Engle and then came Murray and thus this story-telling,
> joking, jesting, would be kept up till one or two o'clock in the
> night, and thus night after night till the court adjourned for that
> term.[8]

Night after night for six months out of year after year in county seat
after county seat across eight counties, Lincoln performed this way,
honing his craft.

This kind of performing meant more than mere fun and
games. Lincoln and the others were circuit-riding lawyers whose business was establishing rapport with unfamiliar juries, persuading judges
with whom they were all too familiar, ridiculing one another's forensic
arguments, and clarifying complex issues. They employed stories as
Daniel Webster used eloquence, practicing in or out of court. When
one lawyer visiting from the East opined that Lincoln was wasting
time telling stories to the jury, his host had to educate him to the ways
of the West by explaining that Lincoln, like a good race horse, "breaks
to win."[9] The art of his storytelling lay in its seeming artlessness.

In fact, when he tried transferring the same kind of performance to the political stage, he met unkind criticism. The *Illinois State
Register* for 23 November 1839, reviewing a speech, warned him against
"a sort of assumed *clownishness*" that was neither natural to him nor
effective for the audience: "Mr. Lincoln will sometimes make his language correspond with this clownish manner, and he can thus frequently raise a loud laugh among his Whig hearers; but this entire
game of buffoonery convinces the *mind* of no man, and is utterly lost
on the majority of his audience." The *Register* seriously advised him
"to correct this clownish fault before it grows upon him."[10]

Ten years later, by the time of the Lincoln-Douglas debates,
he had learned to control rather than "correct" this fault. When friends
urged him to play for audience support with his stories, he felt the
occasion was too serious: "I do not seek applause . . . nor to amuse the
people, I want to convince them."[11] Yet his reputation posed a con-

stant threat. Douglas was apprehensive: "Every one of his stories seems like a whack upon my back. . . . Nothing else— not any of his arguments or any of his replies to my questions— disturbs me. But when he begins to tell a story, I feel that I am to be overmatched."[12] Clearly his storytelling had been polished into a potent political weapon.

But he would still tell stories at the law office just for fun. He would drop his pen or lay down his book in a burst of spontaneous storytelling, sending his apprentices into convulsions: "with their hands on their sides, their heads thrown back, their mouths open, and the tears coursing down their cheeks, laughing as if they would die."[13] Nevertheless, Herndon, like other biographers, sought deeper motives. He thought that Lincoln's storytelling compensated for a weakness in expressing himself: "He was often perplexed to give proper expression to his ideas; first, because he was not master of the English language; and secondly, because there were, in the vast store of words, so few that contained the exact coloring, power, and shape of his ideas."[14] The stories thus, like pictures, spoke a thousand words.

Whatever their psychological basis, there can be no doubt about their rhetorical effectiveness. We can see this in a description of his platform manner during the Whig Convention of 1844: "He commenced his speech in a rather diffident manner, even seemed for a while at a loss for words, his voice was irregular, a little tremulous, as at first he began his argument by laying down his propositions."[15] This would lend credence to Herndon's theory, except that the description goes on to hint at the seemingly artless art noted earlier: "As he proceeded he seemed to gain more confidence, his body straightened up, his countenance brightened, his language became free and animated, as, during this time he had illustrated his argument by two or three well-told stories, that drew the attention of the thousands of his audience to every word he uttered."

By the time of his presidency he had broadened rather than changed the application of his art. One of his old apprentices visiting in Washington was saddened to see that the President now told stories seldom for fun, rather "for business, to give a hint or enforce an argument."[16] While early biographers concur that he continued to tell stories for fun, they also agree that more often he had ulterior motives: "If a man broached a subject which he did not wish to discuss, he told a story which changed the direction of the conversation. If he was called upon to answer a question, he answered it by telling a story."[17]

He himself confessed that he would tell stories to save time and temper in the routine of his office: "I often," he said, "avoid a long and useless discussion by others or a laborious explanation on my own part by a short story that illustrates my point of view. So, too, the sharpness of a refusal or the edge of a rebuke may be blunted by an appropriate story, so as to save wounded feeling and yet serve the purpose." In this respect storytelling, as "an emollient," he said, "saves me much friction and distress."[18]

Even more compelling, however, was the need to sustain national morale. Responding to criticism that storytelling "lowers the dignity of the presidential office," Lincoln rejected that complaint: "I have found that common people (repeating with emphasis common people), take them as you find them, are more easily influenced by a broad and humorous illustration than in any other way."[19] And to a visitor noting his weariness, the President explained that " 'his ear bones ached' to hear a good peal of honest laughter," because he had just about used up his stock of stories "that were good to cheer up people in this hard world."[20] He added that "he had been giving out so much cheer to the generals and Congressmen that he had pumped himself dry and must take in a new supply from some source at once." The stock accumulated in a lifetime of storytelling was not, after all, inexhaustible especially when drained by the demands of those dark days.

The currently fashionable view that sees him using stories in those days to salvage his sanity seems based largely on a scene reconstructed a quarter-century afterward by the former Congressman James Ashley. A leader among those demanding decisive action, the young congressman from Ohio approached the president on a matter of grave urgency:

> "You have come up to see me about McClellan?"
> "Yes, sir."
> "Well," said he, "that reminds me of a story."
> I was determined to have a solid talk with him. So I said, rising to my feet: "Mr. President, I beg your pardon, but I didn't come this morning to hear a story."
> He looked at me and said, with such a sad face: "Ashley, I have great confidence in you, and great respect for you, and I know how sincere you are. But if I didn't tell these stories, I would die. Now you sit down!"[21]

Even allowing for the fact that Lincoln could have been exercising his rhetorical art on Ashley, the pathos of this scene, with the wise old chief taming the lusty young warrior, seems too appealing to discard.

Yet its sentimentality ("such a sad face") makes it suspect. The scene seems bathed in the aura of a mythology developing since Lincoln's tragic death, best described by historian David Donald as the reconciliation of two opposing views of his personality.[22] After the trauma of the assassination, with the nation badly needing a hero, two mythological creations emerged. One was the Emancipator-Martyr deriving from literary myths about the demigod rising from obscurity to lead his people, then dying at the height of his power to expiate their sins. The other was the folklore Frontier Hero of humble but honest origin, supreme in mother wit, physical prowess, and moral fiber, but given to rough living and telling jokes.

Donald points out the difficulty in fitting Lincoln with a demigod image, since a demigod who told jokes was "a thing unprecedented in the record of mythology" (p. 384). But this was no real obstacle to biographers. They suggested he told jokes either to confound his enemies or to release internal stresses that would have murdered a mere mortal. Congressman Ashley chose the second option for his portrait, achieving a compromise between the folklore hero and the demigod current even today. The composite image embodies what Donald calls "the central symbol in American democratic thought," reinforcing our faith that a poor boy can make good, and at the same time reinforcing "the incurable romanticism of the American spirit" (p. 396).

If Lincoln's storytelling did contribute to creating that image, so the image in turn colored the stories that came to be attributed to him. Consider the claims once made for his love of earthy stories. An unfriendly writer says contemporaries called him "the foulest in his jests and stories of any man in the country."[23] Even an old friend said his love of smut was "something akin to lunacy,"[24] while an expert like David Donald speaks of "an extensive cycle of ribald and Rabelaisian stories" circulating in folklore but "for the most part unprintable and unfortunately gradually becoming lost" (p. 390). A half-dozen may still be found interred in manuscripts (196-197, for example), but who can say how many were suppressed.

Such suppression must have been as pragmatic as moral. Leonard Swett, among Lincoln's closest friends, refused to allow Herndon's using allusions to the President's "swearing"—"The reason is that I am satisfied the public does not want to hear them. . . . If I should say Mr. Lincoln ever swore and you were to publish it, the public would believe I lied about it. It would damage your book."[25] Swett was aware of how the popular imagination was shaping his old friend. Heroes, he said, are the standards of history and "in time, all faults and all bad or common humanities are eliminated, and they become clothed with imaginary virtues. Thus, for instance, the hatchet story of George Washington."

The emerging demigod-folkhero image of Lincoln attracted its own share of "hatchet stories." Jokes that in earlier times had gravitated to Til Eulenspiegel, Joe Miller, and Ben Franklin, now appeared recycled as Lincoln's. One biographer popular in the last century explained why he knowingly included such switches as the one about a stranger asking Lincoln if a well-to-do neighbor was a man of means and being told that he was the meanest man around. "This may or may not be authentic," confessed Charles Leland, "but it is eminently Lincolnian."[26] Given this attitude, recycling "Lincoln stories" grew to be a cottage industry, with hundreds of homegrown Parson Weemses eager to supply a hungry press. Again, because of his own practice of retelling such stories, only the most foolhardy would dismiss the whole mass of "Lincoln stories" as counterfeit.

We have the enormous scholarship of the past fifty years as a check against total anecdotal anarchy. A case in point is the popular story about Douglas accusing Lincoln of having tended bar. In 1965, Keith Jennison gave this polished version of Lincoln's supposed reply: "He says that I sold liquor over a counter. He forgot to tell you that while I was on one side of the counter, the Judge was always on the other."[27] Now, exhaustive research of the debates shows that Lincoln merely denied the charge without alluding to the Judge's drinking habit.[28] It would seem, then, that even when facts are available, a kind of Gresham's Law functions to suppress them when they subvert the folklore. Why not? The popular imagination would be as impoverished without such stories as without Washington's hatchet. But perhaps this auditing of the record will help prevent utter bankruptcy by showing that, unlike Washington, Lincoln himself helped create the folklore.

What we cannot recreate, alas, is the way Lincoln told his stories. A few entries may hint of his manner as old friends remind one another of "a good one" he told (e.g., 98). Otherwise we must rest satisfied with such general descriptions as this from *Harper's Weekly*, 26 May 1860, in announcing his nomination:

> His manner before a popular assembly is as he pleases to make it, being either superlatively ludicrous or very impressive. He employs but little gesticulation, but when he desires to make a point

produces a shrug of his shoulders, an elevation of his eyebrows, a depression of his mouth, and a general malformation of countenance so comically awkward that it never fails to "bring down the house."[29]

There is simply no way to recapture what the *Weekly* called "the remarkable mobility of his features, the frequent contortions of which excite a merriment his words could not produce."

Nor can we recapture the pacing of his delivery or the elaboration he would bring to the same story under differing circumstances. Once he advised the family preacher on two ways of telling a story: "If you have an auditor who has the time," he said, "and is inclined to listen, lengthen it out slowly as if from a jug. If you have a poor listener, hasten it, shorten it, shoot it out of a pop-gun."[30] Lacking further analysis, perhaps we can apply Mark Twain's essay, "How to Tell a Story," which shows how to tell the same story in a witty, or comic, manner and in a humorous manner. The witty delivery, for Twain as for Lincoln, is shot out of a popgun. But the humorous story is a work of art: the teller "is innocent and happy and pleased with himself, and has to stop every little while to hold himself in and keep from laughing outright; and does hold in, but his body quakes in a jelly-like way with interior chuckles; and at the end of the ten minutes the audience have laughed until they are exhausted, and the tears are running down their faces."[31]

Perhaps we can apply, too, Twain's description of a master storyteller elaborating a humorous story:

> He tells it in the character of a dull-witted old farmer who has just heard it for the first time, thinks it is unspeakably funny, and is trying to repeat it to a neighbor. But he can't remember it; so he gets it all mixed up and wanders helplessly round and round, putting in tedious details that don't belong in the tale and only retard it; taking them out conscientiously and putting in others that are just as useless; making minor mistakes now and then and stopping to correct them and explain how he came to make them; remembering things which he forgot to put in their proper place and going back to put them in there. (Page 7)

Such lengthy description, needful for generations unfamiliar with the art even when Twain wrote it in 1895, might aid our imagination now.

For we are at the mercy of cold print. The stories given below are stripped of their essence—the dramatic pose or character,

the improvisational tone and timing, the comical gestures, all inter-
acting with audience response. It would be best to think of each entry
as a scenario for performance. Some of the early ones are mere notes
or allusions where this is obvious. Many later ones are quite elaborate,
but the elaboration might not be Lincoln's. Still, taken all together,
these stories are the only heritage we have of Lincoln's humor.

This does not pretend to be a complete collection of "Lincoln stories." It is meant merely to represent the mass of those
apocrypha while emphasizing the stories he most likely told. In view
of the problems reviewed earlier, selecting these reliable stories relies
on educated guesses. The few appearing in his own work are of course
above suspicion. But those reported by even his closest friends are suspect. Manuscripts, for instance, show that his bodyguard, Ward
Lamon, chose to print Lincoln stories from previously printed sources
rather than from his own notes (23n.). Herndon's manuscripts contain
interview notes pursued with extraordinary zeal, often double-checked
for "accuracy." His witnesses, however, were recalling events thirty
years or more in the past which had been colored by subsequent events
and Lincoln's fame. For this reason, the selection is perhaps overcautious as opposed to "comprehensive," but it is meant to be reliable.

Notes following the entries identify the source of the written
text and, in many instances, a source or analogue that could have been
familiar to Lincoln. Because some of these analogues appeared in ancient Greece does not mean that he could read Greek, only that he
could have been familiar with the more modern versions of the same
stories. As his favorite reporter, Noah Brooks, said: "Probably many
people who heard him during the war repeat long passages from
stories, or comical articles, which he had seen in print, wondered how
he ever found time to commit such trifles to memory. The truth was
that anything that he heard or read fastened itself into his mind, if it
tickled his fancy."[32] Another reporter claimed that Lincoln "committed
almost every good story he heard to writing,"[33] and others mention
his carrying written slips that he would read from, apparently until
the stories were memorized. Thus, we know that he did use sources
but we can only guess at which ones he used. Again, my identifications
are overcautious, simply pointing out the existence of probable sources
and analogues for about half the entries.

The stories themselves are presented in order of the earliest
written version I could find. If later versions of the same story reveal
anything about the reliability of the earlier version, they are included
in the notes. Information about the context, including names of par-

ticipants, is incorporated into the text in brackets, while information about earlier compilers is included in the headnotes or in the appendix listing the full titles of my sources.

My basic resource has been the magnificent Judd Stewart collection of Lincoln materials at the Huntington Library. Consisting of manuscripts and scrapbooks as well as printed matter, that collection has made this edition possible. For identification of people and events in the anecdotes I have relied on the chronology, *Lincoln Day by Day*, ed. Earl Schenck Miers (Washington: Lincoln Sesquicentennial Commission, 1960), and John Carroll Power, *History of the Early Settlers of Sangamon County, Illinois* (Springfield: E. A. Wilson, 1876). For many other kinds of help I am indebted to the expert staff of the Huntington Library, especially Fred Perez, Martin Ridge, Elsa Sink, Leona Schonfeld, Doris Smedes, James Thorpe, and Lee Zall. My colleague Addison Potter also helped and the California State University Los Angeles Foundation funded my travel to the Library of Congress. But my deepest debt is to Ray Allen Billington who died a few weeks after he wrote the Foreword—a good friend, wise counselor, marvelous storyteller.

NOTES TO INTRODUCTION

1. Joseph H. Barrett, *Life of Lincoln* (1904), 2:337.

2. *Century Magazine*, 74 (September 1907), 809.

3. *Scribner's Monthly*, 15 (March 1878), 679.

4. Vol. 19 (June 1859), 133.

5. *Collected Works*, ed. Roy P. Basler (1953–1955), 3:279; hereafter cited as *W*.

6. Vol. 6, p. 565.

7. *Century Magazine*, 73 (February 1907), 502.

8. Emanuel Hertz, *Lincoln Talks* (1938), p. 101.

9. Osborne H. Oldroyd, *Lincoln Memorial: Album Immortelles* (1882), p. 151.

10. Herbert Mitgang, *Abraham Lincoln, a Press Portrait* (1971), pp. 17–18.

11. Isaac N. Arnold, *Reminiscences of the Illinois Bar Forty Years Ago* (1881), p. 26.

12. Interview with Robert Hitt, shorthand reporter, in unidentified newspaper article, copyright 1911, in Stewart scrapbook, Huntington Library accession 151179, 5:64.

13. Roy P. Basler, *The Lincoln Legend* (1935), p. 125.

14. *Herndon's Lincoln*, ed. Paul M. Angle (1949), p. 477.

15. Jeriah Bonham, *Fifty Years' Recollections* (1883), pp. 159–160.

16. *Beacon Magazine,* 1 (January 1892), 52.

17. Josiah Holland, *Life of Lincoln* (1866), pp. 74–75.

18. *Century Magazine,* 73 (February 1907), 499–502.

19. Chauncey Depew in R. T. Rice, *Reminiscences of Abraham Lincoln by Distinguished Men of His Time* (1886), p. 427. In retelling the story for *Scribner's,* 70 (November 1921), 528, Depew used the term "plain people" in place of "common people."

20. Russell H. Conwell, *Why Lincoln Laughed* (1922), pp. 73, 115.

21. *Reminiscences of the Great Rebellion* (1890), p. 39.

22. "The Folklore Lincoln," *Illinois State Historical Society Journal,* 40 (1947), 377–396.

23. Letter, 30 August 1887, in Herndon-Weik papers, Library of Congress microfilm, reel 10, frames 2198–2199.

24. Charles Minor, *The Real Lincoln* (1904), pp. 29–30.

25. Donald, p. 381.

26. *Abraham Lincoln* (1879), p. 238.

27. *The Humorous Mr. Lincoln,* p. 57.

28. See, for example, Paul M. Angle, ed., *Created Equal?* (1958), p. 118.

29. Vol. 4, p. 321.

30. Diary of P. D. Gurley in Ervin Chapman, *New Light on Lincoln* (1917), 2:502.

31. *How to Tell a Story and Other Essays* (1897), pp. 7–8.

32. *Scribner's Monthly,* 15 (February 1878), 563.

33. Conwell, p. 122.

Anecdotes
By & About
Abraham Lincoln

The entries appear in order of the earliest written version available. Headnotes introduce groups of three or more from the same source, with page numbers referring to that source appended to each entry in the series. Otherwise, each entry is followed by a short reference to sources listed in more complete form in the bibliographical lists headed "Sources" and "Resources." Along with such textual references, notes contain information about multiple versions, possible sources available to Lincoln, and contemporary analogues that would have been familiar to his public. When entries consist of mere hints or allusions, the notes may also contain expanded versions of the stories intended. Unless otherwise noted, ellipses (. . .) in the entries or notes indicate editorial deletions. Two abbreviations are used throughout the entries and notes: *AL* referring to Abraham Lincoln, and *W* referring to his *Collected Works*, ed. Roy P. Basler (1953–1955).

1839

1.   [During a speech in Springfield, Illinois, 26 December 1839, alluding to Democrats who absconded with public funds:] They are most distressingly affected in their *heels* with a species of "*running itch.*" It seems that this malady of their heels, operates on these *sound-headed* and *honest-hearted* creatures, very much like the cork-leg, in the comic song, did on its owner: which, when he had once got started on it, the more he tried to stop it, the more it would run away. At the hazard of wearing this point thread bare, I will relate an anecdote, which seems too strikingly in point to be omitted. A witty Irish soldier,

who was always boasting of his bravery, when no danger was near, but who invariably retreated without orders at the first charge of an engagement, being asked by his Captain why he did so, replied: "Captain, I have as brave a *heart* as Julius Caesar ever had; but some how or other, whenever danger approaches, my *cowardly* legs will run away with it."

> *Speech of Mr. Lincoln* (1840), rpt. *W* 1:177–178. The comic song, "The Cork Leg," is reproduced in L. S. Levy, *Flashes of Merriment* (1971), pp. 19–21. In "Sam Weller," *Pickwick Jest-Book* (1837), p. 186, the Irish soldier says "he had as bold a *heart* as any man in the army, but his cowardly *legs* always ran away with it." In *Harper's Weekly*, 1 (27 June 1857), 414, the soldier says his cowardly legs "always run away with me body."

1841

2.   [Replying to objections by Representative Wickliffe Kitchell against an amendment in the Illinois legislature, 26 February 1841:] He begged leave to tell an anecdote. The gentleman's course the past winter reminded him of an eccentric old bachelor who lived in the Hoosier State. Like the gentleman from Montgomery, he was very famous for seeing *big bugaboos* in every thing. He lived with an older brother, and one day he went out hunting. His brother heard him firing back of the field, and went out to see what was the matter. He found him loading and firing as fast as possible in the top of a tree.

Not being able to discover any thing in the tree, he asked what he was firing at. He replied a squirrel— and kept on firing. His brother believing there was some humbug about the matter, examined his person, and found on one of his eye lashes a *big louse* crawling about. It is so with the gentleman from Montgomery. He imagined he could see squirrels every day, when they were nothing but lice.

> *Sangamo Journal*, 5 March 1841, rpt. *W* 1:244. *Lincoln's Anecdotes* (1867), p. 24, gives this version of the speech: "Mr. Speaker, the attack of the member from Wabash on the constitutionality of this measure reminds me of an old friend of mine. He's a peculiar looking old fellow, with shaggy, overhanging eye-brows, and a pair of spectacles under them. (Everybody turned to the member from Wabash and recognized a personal description.) One morning just after the old man got up, he imagined, on looking out of his door, that he saw rather a lively squirrel on a tree near his house. So he took down his rifle and fired at the squirrel, but the

squirrel paid no attention to the shot. He loaded and fired again, and again, until the thirteenth shot, he set down his gun impatiently, and said to his boy, who was looking on, 'boy there's something wrong about this rifle.' 'Rifle's all right, I know 'tis,' replied the boy, 'but where's your squirrel?' 'Don't you see him, humped up about half way up the tree,' inquired the old man, peeping over his spectacles, and getting mystified. 'No, I don't,' responded the boy; and then turning and looking into his father's face, he exclaimed, 'I see your squirrel! You've been firing at a louse on your eyebrow!' "

Jeriah Bonham, *Fifty Years' Recollections* (1883), pp. 172–173, gives virtually the same speech as from the Lincoln-Douglas debates of 1858. But *Harper's Monthly*, 16 (May 1858), 856–857, tells the story and attributes it to "the late Roger Barton" of Mississippi, "a popular orator of great power and influence over the masses," who told it about his friend Tom Martin in 1840.

1842

3.   [Addressing the Temperance Society, Springfield, Illinois, 22 February 1842:] There is something so ludicrous in *promises* of good, or *threats* of evil, a great way off, as to render the whole subject with which they are connected, easily turned into ridicule. "Better lay down that spade you're stealing, Paddy,— if you don't you'll pay for it at the day of judgment." "By the powers, if ye'll credit me so long, I'll take another jist."

> *Sangamo Journal*, 25 March 1842, rpt. W 1:275–276. During the previous century, this story had an Irish soldier stealing a shirt from a farmer's clothesline: "Well, (said the farmer) if you keep it, you will pay for it in this world or in the next—" "Faith, (replied the soldier) if you will trust me so long, I will take another" (*Funny Stories* [Worcester, Mass., 1795], p. 40).

1848

4.   [Speaking in Congress, 27 July 1848] I have heard some things from New-York; and if they are true, one might well say of your party [Democrats] there, as a drunken fellow once said when he heard the reading of an indictment for hog-stealing. The clerk read on till he got to, and through the words "did steal, take, and carry away, ten boars, ten sows, ten shoats, and ten pigs," at which he exclaimed — "Well, by golly, that is the most equally divided gang of hogs, I ever

did hear of." If there is any *other* gang of hogs more equally divided than the democrats of New York are about this time, I have not heard of it.

> *Congressional Globe*, 30th Congress, 1st Session, Appendix, p. 1043; also in *W* 1:516.

1849

5.   [Congressman Moses Hampton, Pittsburgh, Pa., in a letter of 30 March 1849, reminds him of having told two stories:] Do you remember the story of the old Virginian stropping his razor on a certain *member* of a young negro's body which you told and connected with my mission to Brazil—

> *Lincoln Papers*, ed. D. C. Means, 2 vols. (1948), 1:169.

6.   I want this application to be like your story of the old womans *fish*— get *larger*, the more it is handled—

> Ibid.

1852

7.   [Answering Stephen A. Douglas's opposition to Winfield Scott's campaign for President at the Springfield Scott Club, Springfield, 22 September 1852. Douglas had expressed faith in Providence:] Let us stand by our candidate as faithfully as he has always stood by our country, and I much doubt if we do not perceive a slight abatement in Judge Douglas' confidence in Providence, as well as in the people. I suspect that confidence is not more firmly fixed with the Judge than it was with the old woman, whose horse ran away with her in a buggy. She said she trusted in Providence till the britchen broke; and then she didn't know what on airth *to* do.

> *Illinois Weekly Journal*, 24, 26 September 1852; rpt. *W* 2:150–151. The allusion is to "an excellent woman" who dated everything from the time "when their horses ran away," celebrated by Henry W. Griffith in *A Lift for the Lazy* (1849) and, more recently, Samuel P. Avery, *Mrs. Partington's Carpet-Bag of Fun* (1854), p. 195: "She put the firmest reliance on Providence till the breeching broke, and then she gave up."

1856

8.   [Writing for a pass to Richard P. Morgan, superintendent of the railroad at Bloomington, Illinois, 13 February 1856:] Says Tom to John "Heres your old rotten wheelbarrow" "I've broke it, usin on it" "I wish *you* would mend it, case I shall want to borrow it this arter-noon."

Acting on this as a precedent, I say "Heres your old "chalked hat" [railroad pass] "I wish you would take it, and send me a new one, case I shall want to use it the first of March."

> W 2:330. In William E. Burton, *Cyclopaedia of Wit & Humor* (1858), 1:434, the story is told about a neighbor borrowing not a wheelbarrow but an axe.

9.   [Addressing the Anti-Nebraska Editors' Convention, Decatur, Illinois, 22 February 1856:] Mr. L. said, that he was very much in the position of the man who was attacked by a robber, demanding his money, when he answered, "my dear fellow, I have no money, but if you will go with me to the light, I will give you my note."

> *Decatur State Chronicle*, 28 February 1856; rpt. W 2:333.

10.   [At the same convention, Benjamin F. Shaw recording another story:] He felt like the ugly man riding through a wood who met a woman, also on horseback, who stopped and said:

"Well, for land sake, you are the homeliest man I ever saw."

"Yes, madam, but I can't help it," he replied.

"No, I suppose not," she observed, "but you might stay at home."

> Quoted in Otto R. Kyle, "Mr. Lincoln Steps Out," *ALQ*, 5 (1948), 37. It is also reported by a Bloomington, Illinois, lawyer, Ezra M. Prince, in Isaac N. Phillips, *AL by Some Men Who Knew Him*, ed. Paul Angle (1969), p. 51.

11.   [Responding to a toast at the Republican banquet, Chicago, 11 December 1856, chiding Democrats:] Their conduct reminded him of the darky who, when a bear had put its head into the hole and shut out the daylight, cried out, "What was darkening de hole?" "Ah," cried the other darky, who was on to the tail of the animal, "if de tail breaks you'll find out."

> Chicago *Democratic Press*, 11 December 1856; rpt. W 2:384.

12.   · [At the same banquet:] The speaker referred to the anecdote of the boy who was talking to another as to whether Gen[eral
Andrew] Jackson could ever get to Heaven. Said the boy, "He'd get
there if he had a mind to."

Ibid.

1858

13.   [At the Illinois State House, talking over recent politics in
Congress:] "It reminds me," said [AL], "of a case I once had up at
Bloomington."

"Let's hear it!" all said.

"Two old farmers living in the vicinity of Bloomington,
had, from time immemorial, been at loggerheads. They could never
agree, except to disagree; wouldn't build division fences; and, in short,
were everlastingly quarreling. One day, one of them got over on the
land of the other; the parties met, and a regular pitched battle between
them was the consequence. The one who came out second best sued
the other for assault and battery, and I was sent for to come up and
defend the suit.

"Among the witnesses for the plaintiff was a remarkably
talkative old fellow, who was disposed to magnify the importance of
the affair to my client's disadvantage. It came my turn to question
him:

"Witness," said I, "you say you saw this fight."

"Yes, stranger; I reckon I did."

"Was it much of a fight?" said I.

"I'll be darned if it wasn't, stranger; a right smart fight."

"How much ground did the combatants cover?"

"About an acre, stranger."

"About an acre," I repeated, musingly.

"Well, now, witness, just tell me, wasn't that just about the
smallest crop of a fight off of an acre of ground that ever you heard of?"

"That's so, stranger; I'll be gol darned if it wasn't!"

"The jury," added [AL], giving his legs an additional twist,
after the crowd had finished laughing at the application of the anecdote—"the jury fined my client just ten cents!"

If there is a better illustration of the result of the memorable
conflict in Congress than the case above, we should like to hear of it.
In order to be appreciated, however, one should hear [AL] tell it. No
man can "get off" a thing of the kind with more comical effect.

Illinois Journal, 26 February 1858, rpt. Herbert Mitgang, *AL, a Press Portrait* (1971), pp. 88–89. AL was identified only as "a well known ex-Congressman—the one who is to be elected to the U.S. Senate next winter," with dashes in place of his name. He told the same story to W. M. Dickson—"AL at Cincinnati," *Harper's Monthly*, 69 (June 1884), 63—and to Alban J. Conant whose "Painter's Reminiscence of AL," *McClure's*, 32 (March 1909), 516, includes AL's statement on it: "Some of my friends said it was Yankee wit, but that was the only time I ever got credit for it. I wish I had it."

14.   [During the first debate with Stephen A. Douglas, Ottawa, Illinois, 21 August 1858:] As the Judge had complimented me with these pleasant titles, (I must confess to my weakness,) I was a little "taken," [laughter] for it came from a great man. I was not very much accustomed to flattery, and it came the sweeter to me. I was rather like the Hoosier, with the gingerbread, when he said he reckoned he loved it better than any other man, and got less of it. [Roars of laughter.]

"Debates Scrapbook," Library of Congress; rpt. *W* 3:20. Carl Sandburg, *AL: The Prairie Years* (1926), 2:290 provides the enlargement: "When we lived in Indiana," [AL] said, "once in a while my mother used to get some sorghum and ginger and make some gingerbread. It wasn't often, and it was our biggest treat. One day I smelled the gingerbread and came into the house to get my share while it was still hot. My mother had baked me three gingerbread men. I took them out under a hickory tree to eat them. There was a family near us poorer than we were, and their boy came along as I sat down. 'Abe,' he said, 'gimme a man?' I gave him one. He crammed it into his mouth in two bites and looked at me while I was biting the legs off the first one. 'Abe,' he said, 'gimme that other'n.' I wanted it myself, but I gave it to him and as it followed the first, I said to him, 'You seem to like gingerbread.' 'Abe,' he said, 'I don't s'pose anybody on earth likes gingerbread better'n I do— and gets less'n I do.' " This enlargement is hardly faithful to the original, where the Hoosier seems to have been a man rather than a hungry boy, and where there is no self-serving sentimentality about his own impoverished boyhood, exceptional generosity, etc. It may thus serve as an example of how a story by Lincoln could be transformed into a romantic "Lincoln Story."

15.   [During the fifth debate with Douglas, Galesburg, 7 October 1858, arguing that Douglas and Thomas L. Harris have been using

forged documents against him:] The fraud having been apparently successful upon the occasion, both Harris and Douglas have more than once since then been attempting to put it to new uses. As the fisherman's wife, whose drowned husband was brought home with his body full of eels, said when she was asked, "What was to be done with him?" "*Take the eels out and set him again.*" [Great laughter.]

> "Debates Scrapbook," Library of Congress; rpt. *W* 3:228, which notes that AL at first had written a more mild description, "with the pockets full of eels," in place of "with his body full of eels."

16.   [During the seventh debate, Alton, 15 October 1858, observing that Douglas and the Administration were engaged in mutual recriminations:] All I can say now is to recommend to him and to them what I then commended—to prosecute the war against one another in the most vigorous manner. I say to them again—"Go it, husband!—Go it, bear!"

> "Debates Scrapbook," Library of Congress; rpt. *W* 3:298. The allusion is to a jestbook favorite: In *The Humourist's Own Book* (Philadelphia, 1834), pp. 159–160, the long-suffering Kentucky wife stands by as her husband struggles with a bear—"standing by and hallooing, 'Fair play! fair play!' " The company runs up and tries to part the combatants, but she objects: " 'No— no— let them fight! for it is the first fight I ever saw, that I did not care which whipped."

17.   [After describing AL's appearance in Mt. Sterling, Illinois, on 19 October 1858, a young telegrapher, William L. Gross, adds in his journal:] It is true that I have before now heard the story said to have been related by Lincoln himself on himself as follows, "When I was down in the southern part of the state once, to be more plane, down in Egypt where there is plenty of timber and game, I resolved to myself that if I ever found a man that was homelier looking than I was that I would shoot him.

["]I was out gunning one day and was walking moodily along in not a very pleasant mood when I met a man evidently out upon the same business that I was for he had his gun upon his shoulder. I stopped when I saw the man there was evidently something peculiar about him as well as myself for he almost as soon stopped and began eyeing me. We looked at one another in this way for a moment or two and then stepped up to one another.

["]After we had passed the usual ceremonies I turned to him and said I to him. My friend you are evidently a stranger to me as I am to you, but sir, I have this to say to you, you had better be settleing with your maker and that very quick. The man began to show symptoms of fright and urged me to explain. Gladly my friend: I have taken an oath, and certainly if you are a man and an american you cannot ask me to violate my sacred oath, that if I ever in any one of my travels found a man that was Homlier than I was that I would shoot him. And now my friend I have met you and I must say laying all joking aside that I think you are a little the worst looking man I ever met with. And further, in accordance with my oath, it becomes my duty to warn you to prepare to meet your God. You have five minutes to make his peace. Lose not a moment.

["]The man was in a quandery for a few moments and did not know whether to take it as a joke or in earnest. The sober earnest countenance of Lincoln assured him and for a few moments he stood in the most profound attitude eyeing Lincoln something with eyes of a Lynx. After a brief space he spoke, slowly at first but more hurried at the last:

["]'Well sir: you are evidently a gentleman & not as I at first supposed some escaped lunatic & sir, you look as if you might put your threat into execution; but sir, all that I have got to say is, If I am any worse looking than you are, for *God's sake shoot me* and git me out of the way!'["]

Rpt. Harry E. Pratt, *Concerning Mr. Lincoln* (1944), pp. 18-20. This early example of a "Lincoln story"—"said to have been related by himself on himself"—reverses the roles in the more common version found in William Herndon's mss. at the Huntington Library (LN 2328): "A yarn is told of him that on one occasion he was splitting rails, with only shirt and breeches on collar open and in that plight was not very likely to look at a man happened to be passing with a gun, called to Lincoln to look up, which he did. The man raised his gun in a attitude to shoot. Says Lincoln: What do you mean? The man replied that he had promised to shoot the first man he meet who was uglier than himself. Lincoln asked to see the man's face and after taking a look remarked, If I am uglier than you, then blaze away, opening his shirt bosom" (letter to Herndon from ?Samuel Haycroft, 5 July 1861). William Gross's version must also have been common, however, for the incident seems taken as fact (unless a little playful irony) by George W. Shaw, *Personal Reminiscences of L* (1924), p. 9, who concludes:

"The homicide must have been considered justifiable, for Mr. Lincoln was not indicted."

1859

18.   [In a letter, 6 April 1859, observing that the two major parties have reversed their principles since the days of Adams and Jefferson:] I remember once being much amused at seeing two partially intoxicated men engage in a fight with their great-coats on, which fight, after a long, and rather harmless contest, ended in each having fought himself *out* of his own coat, and *into* that of the other.

> W 3:375.

19.   After fiercely contesting the election with *Douglas*, and affecting confidence that he would have a Legislature favourable to his election over his formidable competitor, that body met, and the result was considerably against him. A gentleman, when the election was announced, queried with *Lincoln* how he felt? Said *Abe:* "Well, I feel just like the boy who stubbed his toe— *too d——d badly hurt to laugh and too d——d proud to cry!*"

> *Cincinnati Enquirer*, 16 September 1859; rpt. Herbert Mitgang, *AL, a Press Portrait* (1971), p. 138. *Lincolniana* (1864), p. 12, gives this fuller reply: "I feel a good deal like a big boy I knew in Kentuck. After he'd got a terrible pounding by the school master, some one asked him how he felt? 'Oh! said he, it hurt so awful bad I couldn't laugh, and I was too big to cry over it' "—which lacks the epigrammatic punch of the *Enquirer*'s version, and therefore seems less authentic.

1860

20.   [During a speech at Hartford, Connecticut, 5 March 1860, commenting on the South's sallies into "sectional warfare":] It reminded him of the man who had a poor old lean, bony, spavined horse, with swelled legs. He was asked what he was going to do with such a miserable beast— the poor creature would die. "Do?" said he. "I'm going to fat him up; *don't you see that I have got* him seal fat as high as the knees?" (Roars of laughter.) Well, they've got the Union dissolved up to the ankle, but no farther!

> Hartford *Evening Press*, 6 March 1860; rpt. W 4:13.

21.   [In "Humors of the Day," *Harper's Weekly*, 28 April 1860:] Lincoln, of Illinois, is famous for his quick wit and good jokes. The following struck us as rather amusing. The other day, when he was up not far from Kansas, with a friend or two, they saw a small stream, and inquired its name. One of the passengers said, "It is called 'The Weeping Water.' "

Lincoln's eyes twinkled. "You remember," said he, "the laughing water up in Minnesota, called Minnehaha. Now, I think, this should be Minneboohoo."

There was a roar; and "Minneboohoo" will probably be the name of the stream henceforth.

> Vol. 4:259. If we take "the other day" literally, this story is un-
> likely, because AL spent the spring in the East or in Chicago.

1861

22.   [A contributor to "The Editor's Drawer," *Harper's Monthly* (March 1861), tells how the President-elect once declined election to the legislature to run for the United States Senate. Having a majority of one in the legislature, his friends expected to replace him with another anti-Democrat, but their candidate lost.] This was a terrible blow to Mr. Lincoln's friends, who "took on" terribly; but "Old Abe," when he heard the result, *te-hee'd* one of his peculiar laughs, and, of course, "told a story." He said, the result reminded him of one of the camp-followers of General [Zachary] Taylor's army, who had secured a barrel of cider, erected a tent, and commenced dealing it out to the thirsty soldiers at twenty-five cents a drink; but he had sold but little before another sharp one set up another tent at his back, and tapped the barrel so as to flow on his side, and peddled out No. 1 cider *at five cents a drink!* of course getting the latter's trade entire on the borrowed capital.

> Vol. 22:566.

1863

23.   [A contemporary observer commenting on AL's being "too well informed to believe that the South could be conciliated":] The following anecdote, which he once narrated with great effect, proves that he well understood the deadly nature of the conflict.

"I once knew," he said, "a good sound churchman, whom we will call Brown, who was in a committee to erect a bridge over a very dangerous and rapid river. Architect after architect failed, and, at last, Brown said, he had a friend named Jones, who had built several bridges, and could build this. 'Let us have him in,' said the committee. In came Jones. 'Can you build this bridge, sir?' 'Yes,' replied Jones. 'I could build a bridge to the infernal regions if necessary.' The sober committee were horrified. But when Jones retired, Brown thought it but fair to defend his friend. 'I know Jones so well,' said he, 'and he is so honest a man, and so good an architect, that if he states, soberly and positively, that he can build a bridge to Hades, why, I believe it. But I have my doubts about the abutment on the infernal side.' " So Mr. Lincoln added, "When politicians said they could harmonize the northern and southern wings of the democracy [Democratic party], why, I believed them. But I had my doubt about the abutment on the southern side."

> John S. C. Abbott, *History of the Civil War in America* (1863–1866), 1:87. While Ward Lamon uses different names, his version in "Administration of L" (1886), pp. 128–129, has verbal echoes suggesting copying.

24.   [A New York newspaper commenting on current events:] The President looks haggard and careworn— who wonders at it?— yet he preserves his goodnature, and some story or *bon mot* from him is always in circulation. The last was uttered on Saturday at the public reception, when a Western Paymaster, in full Major's attire, was introduced, and said:

"Being here, Mr. Lincoln, I thought I'd call and pay my respects."

"From the complaints of the soldiers," responded the President, "I guess that's about all any of you do pay."

> *Frank Leslie's Illustrated Newspaper*, 15 (28 February 1863), 355.

25.   [A correspondent in the same newspaper reports how during a trip to Mount Vernon, William H. Seward praised the President's storytelling:] Mr. Lincoln never tells a joke for the joke's sake, they are like the parables of old—lessons of wisdom. Let me give you an instance. When he first came to Washington he was inundated with office-seekers. There was Jem Lane, Jack Street, Joe Avenue and Gus Swamp. One day he was particularly afflicted; about twenty place-hunters from all parts of the Union had taken possession of his room with bales of credentials and self-recommendations ten miles long. After a time the President said:

"Gentlemen, I must tell you a little story I read one day when I was minding a mudscow in one of the bayous near the Yazoo. A certain king had a minister upon whose judgment he always depended, just as I do upon my friend here," pointing to me, said Seward, blushing.

"Now it happened that one day the king took it into his head to go a hunting, and after summoning his nobles and making the necessary preparations, he summoned the minister and asked him if it would rain. The minister told him it would not, and he and his nobles departed.

"While journeying along they met a countryman on a jackass. He advised them to return. 'For,' said he, 'it will certainly rain.' They smiled contemptuously upon him and passed on. Before they had gone many miles, however, they had reason to regret not having taken the rustic's advice, as a heavy shower coming up, they were drenched to the skin.

"When they had returned to the palace the king reprimanded the minister severely.

" 'I met a countryman,' said he, 'and he knows a great deal more than you, for he told me it would rain, whereas you told me it would not.'

"The king then gave him his walking papers, and sent for the countryman, who made his appearance.

" 'Tell me,' said the king, 'how you knew it would rain?'

" 'I didn't know,' said the rustic, 'my jackass told me.'

" 'And how, pray, did he tell you?' asked the king.

" 'By pricking up his ears, your majesty,' returned the rustic.

"The king sent the countryman away, and procuring the jackass of him, put him (the jackass) in the place the minister had filled.

"And here," observed Mr. Lincoln, looking very wise, "is where the king made a great mistake."

"How so?" inquired his auditors eagerly.

"Why, ever since that time," said Mr. Lincoln, with a grin, "every jackass wants an office!"

Ibid., 16 (31 October 1863), 87. Despite the wry satire of Seward, AL could have told the same story in other circumstances. Its nucleus appears in the earliest English jestbook, *A Hundred Merry Tales* (1526); ed. P. M. Zall (1963), p. 136; and a modern version in "The Editor's Drawer," *Harper's Monthly*, 14 (May 1857), 859, where it concludes, "now every donkey wants an office," and where it is said to have been told by Jake Denton "in a village tavern."

26.   [John Hay, young secretary of AL's, responding to a request from New York columnist Charles Graham Halpine ("Miles O'Reilly") for the latest White House jokes, 22 November 1863:] Ever since I got your letter I have been skulking in the shadow of the Tycoon, setting all sorts of dextrous traps for a joke, telling good stories myself to draw him out and suborning [John] Nicolay to aid in the foul conspiracy. But not a joke has flashed from the Tycoonial thundercloud. He is as dumb as an oyster. Once or twice a gleam of hope has lit up my soul as he would begin "That puts me in mind of Tom Skeeters out in Bourbon County" but the story of Skeeters would come out unfit for family reading; and the dawning promise of a reminiscence of Menard County would turn to ashes as it developed a feeble personality which would move rage and not laughter if repeated.

        By the way, an infernal nuisance named Lincoln Postmaster at Brooklyn fastened himself to the Tycoon the other day and tried to get into conversation on the subject of the succession. The Honest Abraham quickly put him off with a story of his friend Jesse Dubois, who, being State Auditor, had control of the State House at Springfield, Ill. An itinerant quack preacher wanted the use of the Representatives Hall to deliver a religious lecture. "What's it about" said Jesse. "The Second Coming of Christ" said the parson. "Nonsense" roared Uncle Jesse, "If Christ had been to Springfield once, and got away, he'd be damned clear of coming again." This won't do for you to repeat, being blasphemous & calculated to hurt the "Quaker vote." I charge you not to use it.

> Huntington Library ms. HP 119. Halpine did use it for his column in the New York *Post*, 17 February 1864, but changed "Christ" to "Saviour," concluding: "he'd be too smart to think of coming back again."

> The next five entries are samples from *Old Abe's Joker, or, Wit at the White House*, a cheap jokebook published by Robert DeWitt, New York, in 1863. The preface says, "What could be more natural than to associate with 'quips and cranks and wanton wiles' the name of one who so greatly enjoys and successfully perpetrates the fine old, full-flavored joke."

27.   The other day, as the President and a friend were sitting on the House of Representatives steps, the last session closed, and the members filed out in a body. Abraham looked after them with a sardonic smile.

"That reminds me," said he, "of a little incident. When I was quite a boy, my flat-boat lay up at Alton, on the Mississippi, for a day, and I strolled about the town. I saw a large stone building with massive walls, not so handsome, though, as this; and while I was looking at it, the iron gateway opened, and a great body of men came out. 'What do you call that?' I asked a by-stander. 'That,' said he, 'is the State Prison, and those are all thieves, going home. Their time is up.'" (Page 21)

> This is a mere switch, or assigning AL's name to an old joke common in such jestbooks as *The Court Jester* (179-), p. 3, where a host tells a visiting countryman that the House of Commons is Bedlam, and as the Members of Parliament come out, the countryman takes fright: "All the madmen are loose!"

28.   "There was a man down in Maine," said the President, "who kep' a grocery-store, and a lot of fellows used to loaf around thar for their toddy. Well, he only gave 'em New–England rum, and they drinked a pretty considerable of it. But after a while they began to get tired of that, and kep' asking for something New— something New; all the time. Well, one night, when the whole crowd was around, the grocer he sot out his glasses, and says he, 'I've got something New for you to drink, boys.' 'Honor bright,' says they. 'Honor bright,' says he; and with that he sot out a jug. 'Thar,' says he, 'that's something New; it's *New*–England rum!' says he. Now," remarked Abraham, shutting one eye, "I guess we're a good deal like that crowd, and Congress is a good deal like that store-keeper!" (Page 49)

29.   "How many legs would a dog have, if you called his tail one?"

"Five, of course."

"No, only four. It wouldn't make his tail a leg to call it one." (Page 54)

> This is not attributed to AL, but in 1866 George W. Julian reported him making a similar remark when discussing whether he had executive power to free the slaves: "He used to liken the case to that of the boy who, when asked how many legs his calf would have if he called its tail a leg, replied, 'Five,' to which the prompt response was made that *calling* the tail a leg would not make it a leg" (*Reminiscences of AL*, ed. A. T. Rice [1886], p. 62).

30.   Old Abe was once canvassing for himself, for a local office, when he came to a blacksmith's shop.

"Sir," said he to the blacksmith, "will you vote for me?"

"Mr. Lincoln," said the son of Vulcan, "I admire your head, but damn your heart!"

"Mr. Blacksmith," returned Abe, "I admire your candor, but damn your manners!" (Page 49)

> Another simple switch. The jestbooks commonly assign the solicitor's role to Charles James Fox, as in the *New Ben Johnson's Jester* (London, ?1800), p. 39.

31.   One terribly stormy night in bleak December, a United States vessel was wrecked off the coast of Jersey, and every soul save one, went down with the doomed craft. This one survivor seized a floating spar and was washed toward the shore, while innumerable kind-hearted tools [laborers] of the Camden and Amboy railroad clustered on the beach with ropes and boats. Slowly the unhappy mariner drifted to land, and as he exhaustedly caught at the rope thrown to him, the kindly natives uttered an encouraging cheer.

"You are saved!" they shouted. "You are saved, and must show the conductor your ticket!"

With the sea still boiling about him, the drowning stranger resisted the efforts to haul him ashore.

"Stop!" said he, in faint tones. "Tell me where I am! What country is this?"

They answered, "New Jersey."

Scarcely had the name been uttered when the wretched stranger let go the rope, ejaculating as he did so, "I guess I'll float a little farther!"

He was never seen again. (Page 63)

> Although not attributed to AL, this was copied by *Old Abe's Jokes* (1864), p. 46, as "Old Abe's Story of New Jersey" and thereafter continued to appear as such in collections down to Emanuel Hertz, *Lincoln Talks* (1939), pp. 287–288.

 The next ten entries are from the diaries of John Hay, AL's secretary, here from *Lincoln and the Civil War in Diaries and Letters of John Hay*, ed. Tyler Dennett (1939), except where indicated.

32.   The President said the Army dwindled on the march like a shovelfull of fleas pitched from one place to another. (Page 53)

Various collections apply this to General George B. McClellan's frequent calls for reinforcements. Emanuel Hertz, *Lincoln Talks* (1939), p. 459, gives the most common variant: "Sending men to that army is like shoveling fleas across a barnyard—half of them never get there."

33.   The Presidential aspirations of Mr. [Salmon P.] Chase are said to have been compared by the President to a horsefly on the neck of a plowhorse—which kept him lively about his work. (Page 54)

> F. B. Carpenter, *Six Months at the White House* (1866), pp. 129–130, reports that AL told this story to Henry J. Raymond: "My brother and I . . . were once ploughing corn on a Kentucky farm, I driving the horse, and he holding the plough. The horse was lazy; but on one occasion rushed across the field so that I, with my long legs, could scarcely keep pace with him. On reaching the end of the furrow, I found an enormous *chin fly* fastened upon him, and knocked him off. My brother asked me what I did that for. I told him I didn't want the old horse bitten in that way. 'Why,' said my brother, *'that's all that made him go!'* Now," said Mr. Lincoln, "if Mr. [Chase] has a presidential *chin fly* biting him, I'm not going to knock him off, if it will only make his department [the Treasury] *go*."

34.   [Diary entry, 18 July 1863:] He told one good story about U[sher] F. Linder getting a fellow off who had stolen a hog, by advising him to go and get a drink, suggesting that the water was better in Tennessee.

> Omitted by Tyler Dennett but reprinted in the Brown University Commemorative catalogue, *Life and Works of John Hay* (1961), p. 14.

35.   [29 September 1863:] Today came to the Executive Mansion an assembly of cold-water men & cold-water women to make a temperance speech at the Tycoon . . . in which they called Intemperance the cause of our defeats. He could not see it, as the rebels drink more & worse whisky than we do. (Page 96)

> His speech to the "Sons of Temperance," 29 September 1863, put the same point more subtly: "You have suggested that in an army — our army— drunkenness is a great evil, and one which, while it exists to a very great extent, we cannot expect to overcome so entirely as to leave [have?] such successes in our arms as we might

have without it. This undoubtedly is true, and while it is, perhaps, rather a bad source to derive comfort from, nevertheless, in a hard struggle, I do not know but what it is some consolation to be aware that there is some intemperance on the other side, too, and that they have no right to beat us in physical combat on that ground" (*W* 6:487). Still, Hay repeated his own version to William Herndon in a letter, 5 September 1866: "Once in rather dark days early in the war, a Temperance committee came to him and said the reason we did not win was because our army drank so much whiskey as to bring down the curse of the Lord upon them. He said drily that it was rather unfair on the part of the aforesaid curse, as the other side drank more and worse whiskey than ours did" (Huntington ms. LN 2408, 2:462–3). And this was the version perpetuated in the various collections.

36.   [24 November 1863:] Tonight the President said he was much relieved at hearing from [General John] Foster that there was firing at Knoxville yesterday. He said anything showing [General Ambrose] Burnside was not overwhelmed was cheering: "Like Sally Carter when she heard one of her children squall would say, 'There goes one of my young 'uns, not dead yet, bless the Lord.' " (Page 127)

> An enlarged version appeared as "in a letter from Washington" in *Old Abe's Jokes* (1864), p. 105, where it concludes: "It reminds me of Mistress Sallie Ward, a neighbor of mine, who had a very large family. Occasionally some of her numerous progeny would be heard crying in some out-of-the-way place, upon which Mrs. Sallie would exclaim, 'There's one of my children that isn't dead yet.' "

37.   [10 December 1863:] Tonight the President, talking with [Isaac N.] Arnold and me, told a magnificent Western law story about a steam doctor's bill. (Page 134)

> "Steam doctor" was synonymous with "quack," so I suspect the allusion is to a story told in David Paul Brown, *The Forum* (1856), 2:375–376. In a group of "Anecdotes and Wit of the Bench and Bar," one tells of a quack suing for surgical fees who is being cross-examined by the defending attorney:
> *Counsel.*— "Did you treat the patient according to the most approved principles of surgery?"
> *Witness.*— "By all means— certainly I did."
> *Counsel.*— "Did you decapitate him?"
> *Witness.*— "Undoubtedly I did— that was a matter of course."
> *Counsel.*— "Did you perform the Caesarean operation upon him?"

Witness.— "Why, of course, his condition required it, and it was attended with great success."

Counsel.— "Did you, now Doctor, subject his person to an autopsy?"

Witness.— "Certainly, that was the last remedy adopted."

Counsel.— "Well, then, Doctor, as you performed a *post mortem* operation upon the defendant, and he survived it, I have no more to ask, and if your claim will survive it, quackery deserves to be immortal."

38.   [23 December 1863:] The President last night had a dream. He was in a party of plain people and as it became known who he was they began to comment on his appearance. One of them said, "He is a very common-looking man." The President replied, "Common looking people are the best in the world: that is the reason the Lord makes so many of them." (Page 143)

> The more common version of this comment appeared in the New York *Tribune*'s Sunday Illustrated Supplement, 20 December 1903, p. 13: "A Congressman from a Western district approached him during his term as President and apologized for presenting a petition from his constituents, because they were very common people.
>
> " 'Well,' said Mr. Lincoln pleasantly, 'God must love the common people, He's made so many of 'em.' "
>
> This paraphrased a story told by A. K. McClure in a symposium for *Success Magazine*, February 1904: "I once heard him rebuke a western congressman who was in Washington, and who felt that, in making some request of the President, he had to apologize for the want of intelligence of his far-away constituency, by saying: 'I have always felt that God must love common people, or He wouldn't have made so many of them' " (Huntington Library scrapbook 15, p. 174).

1864

39.   [28 April 1864:] Granville Moody was here this evening & told a good story about Andy Johnson & his fearful excitement when [General D. C.] Buell was proposing to give up Nashville to the enemy. He found him walking up & down the room supported by two friends. "Moody, I'm glad to see you," he said. The two friends left & he & Moody were alone. "We're *sold*, Moody, we're *sold*," fiercely reiterating. "He's a traitor, Moody," and such. At last suddenly, "Pray! Moody!" And they knelt down & prayed, Andy joining in the responses like a

Methodist. After they had done he said, "Moody, I feel better. Moody I'm not a Christian— no church,— but I believe in God, in the Bible, all of it, Moody, but *I'll be damned if Nashville shall be given up.*" (Pages 176–177)

> Ward Hill Lamon, "Administration of Lincoln" (1886), p. 453, says evangelist Moody vouched for this story which AL used to tell.

40.   [22 May 1864:] I said to the President today . . . [about rumors that a contender for the Republican presidential nomination would be General John C. Fremont] Fremont would be dangerous if he had more ability & energy.

"Yes," says the Ancient, "he is like Jim Jett's brother. Jim used to say that his brother was the damndest scoundrel that ever lived, but in the infinite mercy of Providence he was also the damndest fool." (Page 183)

41.   [1 July 1864:] This evening I referred to [Washington correspondent Samuel] Wilkeson's blackguardly misstatements in today's [New York] *Tribune* & asked if I might not prepare a true statement of facts to counteract the effects of these falsehoods. He answered, "Let 'em wriggle." (Page 203)

> F. B. Carpenter, *Six Months at the White House* (1866), p. 145, enlarges the episode and explains the allusion: "It is not worth fretting about," said the President; "it reminds me of an old acquaintance, who, having a son of a scientific turn, bought him a microscope. The boy went around, experimenting with his glass upon everything that came in his way. One day, at the dinner-table, his father took up a piece of cheese. 'Don't eat that, father,' said the boy; 'it is full of *wrigglers*.' 'My son,' replied the old gentleman, taking, at the same time, a huge bite, 'let 'em *wriggle*; I can stand it if they can.' "

> The story, not assigned to AL, is in *Porter's Spirit of the Times*, 1 (29 November 1856), 210; copied by *Harper's Weekly*, 4 (5 May 1860), 283: "A collegian, enlightening a farmer upon animalculae, applied his microscope in the cheese, saying, 'Now, look and see them wiggle.'— 'Well,' said the farmer, placing the cheese in his mouth, 'let them wiggle. I can stand it as long as they can.' "

 Entries 42–60 are from the New York *Post*, 17 February 1864, where, filling almost two columns on page 1, they

are headed, "Several Little Stories by or about President Lincoln." Many were conceivably supplied by John Hay (see 26). They provided the New York *Herald* a chance to satirize the *Post* which, though Republican, was lukewarm on AL's candidacy for reelection. Thus the *Herald* pretended that the jokes were part of the *Post*'s campaign to reelect him. In reprinting the series, 19 February, p. 5, the *Herald* merely added the new headline: "The Presidential Campaign: The First Electioneering Document. The Evening Post Out in Favor of 'Old Abe.'"

42.   Mr. Lincoln, in his happier moments, is not always reminded of a "little story," but often indulges in a veritable joke. One of the latest reported is his remark when he found himself attacked by the varioloid. He had been recently very much worried by people asking favors. "Well," said he, when the contagious disease was coming upon him, "I've got something now that I can give to everybody."

> The previous December, he had come down with a light case, according to Gideon Welles, *Diary*, 1:480.

43.   It is told by a general correspondent, who is probably "reliable," that Mr. Lincoln was walking up Pennsylvania avenue the other day relating "a little story" to Secretary [W. H.] Seward, when the latter called his attention to a low sign bearing the name of T. R. Strong. "Ha!" says Old Abe, his countenance lighting up with a peculiar smile. "T. R. Strong, but coffee are stronger." Seward smiled, but made no reply. We don't see how he could reply after so atrocious a thing as that.

> The tone of this entry implies its incredibility.

44.   As a further elucidation of Mr. Lincoln's estimate of Presidential honors, a story is told of how a supplicant for office of more than ordinary pretensions called upon him, and, presuming on the activity he had shown in behalf of the Republican ticket, asserted, as a reason why the office should be given to him, that he had made Mr. Lincoln President. "You made me President, did you," said Mr. Lincoln with a twinkle of his eye. "I think I did," said the applicant. "Then a precious mess you've got me into, that's all," replied the President, and closed the discussion.

45.   The story will be remembered, perhaps, of Mr. Lincoln's reply to a Springfield (Illinois) clergyman, who asked him what was to be his policy on the slavery question.

"Well, your question is rather a cool one, but I will answer it by telling you a story. You know Father B., the old Methodist preacher? and you know Fox river and its freshet. Well, once in the presence of Father B., a young Methodist was worrying about Fox river, and expressing fears that he should be prevented from fulfilling some of his appointments by a freshet in the river. Father B. checked him in his gravest manner. Said he:—'Young man I have always made it a rule in my life not to cross Fox river till I get to it!' And," said the President, "I am not going to worry myself over the slavery question till I get to it!" A few days afterwards a Methodist minister called on the President, and on being presented to him, said simply: "Mr. President, I have come to tell you that I think we have got to Fox river." Mr. Lincoln thanked the clergyman and laughed heartily.

46.   One day, it is said, a distinguished New York official was at Washington, and in an interview with the President, introduced the question of Emancipation. "Well, you see," said Mr. Lincoln, "we've got to be mighty cautious how we manage the negro question. If we're not, we shall be like the barber out in Illinois, who was shaving a fellow with a hatchet face and lantern jaws like mine. The barber put his finger in his customer's mouth, to make his cheek stick out; but while shaving away he cut through the fellow's cheek and cut off his own finger. If we don't play smart about the negro we shall do as the barber did."

> In the New Haven jestbook, *Joke Upon Joke* (1818), pp. 95–96, the barber's victim is a French immigrant just landed at Dover. Addressing the Lincoln Day dinner in New York, 1889, Horace Porter said AL told this story as a comment on England's relations with the Confederacy. Porter's version in *Addresses Delivered at the Lincoln Dinners* (1909), pp. 30–31, concludes: "Finally he cut clear through the cheek and into his own finger. He pulled the finger out of the man's mouth, snapped the blood off it, glared at him and said, 'There, you lantern-jawed cuss, you've made me cut my finger.' "

47.   Mr. Lincoln, as the highest public official of the nation, is necessarily very much bored by all sorts of people calling upon him. An officer of the government called one day at the White House, and

introduced a clerical friend. "Mr. President," said he, "allow me to present to you my friend, the Rev. Mr. F. of ———. Mr. F. has expressed a desire to see you and have some conversation with you, and I am happy to be the means of introducing him." The President shook hands with Mr. F. and, desiring him to be seated, took a seat himself. Then— his countenance having assumed an expression of patient waiting— he said, "I am now ready to hear what you have to say." "O bless you, sir," said Mr. F., "I have nothing especially to say. I merely called to pay my respects to you, and, as one of the million, to assure you of my hearty sympathy and support." "My dear sir," said the President, rising promptly— his face showing instant relief, and with both hands grasping that of his visitor, "I am very glad to see you; I am very glad to see you indeed! *I thought you had come to preach to me!*"

48.   Another member of Congress was conversing with the President, and was somewhat annoyed by the President's propensity to divert attention from the serious subject he had on his mind by ludicrous allusions.

          "Mr. Lincoln," said he, "I think you would have your joke if you were within a mile of hell."

          "Yes," said the President, "that is about the distance to the Capitol."

49.   When informed that General [E. H.] Stoughton had been captured by the rebels at Fairfax [8 March 1863], the President is reported to have said that he did not mind the loss of the brigadier as much as he did the loss of the horses. "For," said he, "I can make a much better brigadier in five minutes, but the horses cost a hundred and twenty-five dollars a piece."

> The allusion is to the scandalous capture of Stoughton by Captain John Mosby's raiders. He was leading a unit searching for Mosby when the raiders took Stoughton prisoner as he lay abed on a Sunday morning at Fairfax Courthouse.

50.   Mr. Lincoln has a very effective way sometimes of dealing with men who trouble him with questions. Somebody asked him how many men the rebels had in the field. He replied very seriously, "Twelve hundred thousand, according to the best authority." The interrogator blanched in the face, and ejaculated, "My God!" "Yes, sir, twelve hundred thousand— no doubt of it. You see, all of our Generals, when

they get whipped, say the enemy outnumbers them from three or five to one, and I must believe them. We have four hundred thousand men in the field, and three times four make twelve. Don't you see it?" The inquisitive man looked for his hat soon after "seeing it."

51.   When the [General Thomas] Sherman expedition which captured Port Royal [October 1861] was fitting out, there was great curiosity to learn where it had gone. A person visiting the Chief Magistrate at the White House importuned him to disclose the destination to him. "Will you keep it entirely secret?" asked the President. "Oh, yes, upon my honor." "Well," said the President, "I'll tell you." Assuming an air of great mystery, and drawing the man close to him, he kept him a moment awaiting the revelation with an open mouth and great anxiety. "Well," said he in a loud whisper, which was heard all over the room, "the expedition has gone to— sea!"

52.   A Virginia farmer, not over patriotic, probably, importuned the President to use his influence to have a claim for damage done to his farm by soldiers considered immediately. "Why, my dear sir," replied Mr. Lincoln blandly, "I couldn't think of such a thing. If I considered individual cases, I should find work for twenty Presidents!" "But," said the persevering sufferer, "couldn't you just give me a *line* to Colonel ——— about it, *just one line?*" "Ha, ha, ha!" responded Old Abe, "you remind me of old Jock Chase, out in Illinois." At this the crowd huddled forward to listen. "You see Jock— I knew him like a brother— used to be a lumberman on the Illinois, and he was steady and sober, and the best raftsman on the river. It was quite a trick, twenty-five years ago to take the logs over the rapids; but he was skilful with a raft and always kept her straight in the channel. Finally a steamboat was put on, and Jock— he's dead now, poor fellow!— was made captain of her. He always used to take the wheel going through the rapids. One day, when the boat was plunging and wallowing along the boiling current, and Jock's utmost vigilance was being exercised to keep her in the narrow channel, a boy pulled at his coat tail and hailed him with, 'Say, Mister captain! I wish you would jest stop your boat a minute— *I've lost my apple overboard!*' "

> In both *Old Abe's Jokes* (1864) and *Lincolniana* (1864) "Jock Chase" is "Jack Chase," the name appearing in subsequent collections (pp. 77 and 61 respectively).

53.   One day when Mr. [Attorney General Edward] Bates was remonstrating with Mr. Lincoln against the appointment of some indifferent lawyer to a place of judicial importance, the President interposed with, "Come now, Bates, he's not half so bad as you think. Besides that, I must tell you, he did me a good turn long ago. When I took to the law, I was going to court one morning, with some ten or twelve miles of bad road before me, and I had no horse. The Judge overtook me in his wagon. 'Hello, Lincoln, are you not going to the court house? Come in, and I'll give you a seat.' Well, I got in, and the Judge went on reading his papers. Presently the wagon struck a stump on one side of the road; then it hopped off to the other. I looked out, and I saw the driver was jerking from side to side in his seat, so, says I, 'Judge, I think your coachman has been taking a little drop too much this morning.' 'Well, I declare, Lincoln,' said he, 'I should not much wonder if you are right, for he has nearly upset me half a dozen times since starting.' So, putting his head out of the window, he shouted, 'Why, you infernal scoundrel, you are drunk!' Upon which, pulling up his horses, and turning round with great gravity, the coachman said, 'By gorra! that's the first rightful decision you have given for the last twelvemonth!'"

> This could be connected with a controversy in December 1862 when, over objections by Bates, AL appointed to the Supreme Court his old crony Judge David Davis—but neither Bates's diaries nor his biographers mention the story.

54.   A gentleman was telling at the White House how a friend of his had been driven away from New Orleans as a Unionist, and how, on his expulsion, when he asked to see the writ by which he was expelled, the deputation which called on him told him that the government had made up their minds to do nothing illegal, and so they had issued no illegal writs, and simply meant to make him go of his own free will. "Well," said Mr. Lincoln, "that reminds me of a hotel-keeper down at St. Louis, who boasted that he never had a death in his hotel, for whenever a guest was dying in his house he carried him out to die in the street."

55.   One of the new levies of troops required the appointment of a large additional number of brigadier and major-generals. The applications and recommendations accordingly poured in in immense

numbers. They were carried to the President for examination, by the bushel-basketful. Mr. Lincoln came upon one wherein the claims of a certain worthy (not in the service at all) "for a generalship" were glowingly set forth. But the applicant didn't specify whether he wanted to be brigadier or major-general. The President observed this difficulty, and solved it by a lucid endorsement. The clerk, on receiving the paper again, found written across its back, "Major-General, I reckon. A. Lincoln."

56.   Some one was smoking in the presence of the President and complimented him on having no vices, neither drinking nor smoking. "That is a doubtful compliment," answered the President; "I recollect once being outside a stage in Illinois and a man sitting by me offered me a segar. I told him I had no vices. He said nothing, smoked for some time, and then grunted out, 'It's my experience that folks who have no vices have plagued few virtues.'"

> William Herndon says the event took place in 1850 when AL rode the stage to Washington in company with a Kentuckian, and that AL did not know whether it was meant as a joke or an insult (Herndon-Weik papers, Library of Congress, 8 January 1886, microfilm 9: 1906–1909). Herndon's version goes through a litany of offering smokes and drinks, then concludes with an action that suggests AL meant it as just another story: he is described as having "really laughed himself tired, kicked out, in fact, the bottom of the stage— tore out the crown of his hat by running his hand through it, &c &c."

57.   The President is rather vain of his height, but one day a young man called on him who was certainly three inches taller than the former; he was like the mathematical definition of the straight line — length without breadth. "Really," said Mr. Lincoln, "I must look up to you; if you ever get in a deep place you ought to be able to wade out."

58.   That reminds us of the story told of Mr. Lincoln somewhere when a crowd called him out. He came out on the balcony with his wife (who [is] somewhat below medium height,) and made the following "brief remarks": "Here I am, and here is Mrs. Lincoln. That's the long and short of it."

> This was on the occasion of a serenade, according to F. B. Carpenter in H. J. Raymond, *Life and Public Services of AL* (1865), p.

749. An odd variant appeared in the *Centennial History of Butler County, Ohio* (1905) as quoted by D. J. Ryan, "Lincoln and Ohio," *Ohio Archaeological and Historical Society*, 32 (1923), 68: "When the train stopped, Lincoln appeared on the back platform with his travelling companion, Congressman John A. Gurley of Cincinnati. The crowd had caught sight of Lincoln first, and set up a great cheering, but on the appearance of Gurley, there came uproarious laughter. Lincoln was in good humor and saw the point at once. Now, Gurley was a very short man, and he whom he was chaperoning was six feet four. Standing side by side, before alighting, Lincoln, after a good laugh, said: 'My friends, this is the long of it,' pointing to himself, then, laying his hand on Gurley's head, 'and this is the short of it.' "

59.   Dr. Hovey, of Dansville, N.Y., called at the White House and found the occupant on horseback, ready for a ride. He approached and said: "President Lincoln, I thought I would call and see you before leaving the city, and hear you tell a story." The President greeted him pleasantly, and asked where he was from. The reply was, "From Western New York." "Well, that's a good enough country without stories," replied the President and off he rode.

60.   Some moral philosopher was telling the President one day about the undercurrent of public opinion. He went on to explain it at length, and drew an illustration from the Mediterranean Sea. The current seemed very curiously to flow in both from the Black Sea and the Atlantic Ocean, but a shrewd Yankee, by means of a contrivance of floats, had discovered that at the outlet into the Atlantic only about thirty feet of the surface water flowed inward, while there was a tremendous current under that flowing out. "Well," said Mr. Lincoln, much bored, "that don't remind me of any story I ever heard of."

Entries 61–71 are from *Lincolniana, or the Humors of Uncle Abe*, a jokebook compiled in New York for the Democratic presidential campaign of 1864—"Democratic Clubs and Committees supplied on liberal terms." The compiler, "Andrew Adderup," dates his preface, "Springfield, Ill. April 1," as part of the fun, though his last joke is dated 16 May.

61.   Some one ventured to ask Uncle Abe, soon after his arrival at the White House, how he got the sobriquet of "Honest Abe."

"Oh," said he, "I suppose my case was pretty much like that of a country merchant I once read of. Some one called him a 'little rascal.' 'Thank you for the compliment,' said he, 'Why so?' asked the stigmatizer. 'Because that title distinguishes me from my fellow tradesmen, who are all *great* rascals.' " (Page 19)

> This is a simple switch from a common story appearing, for example, in the *American Jest Book* (Philadelphia, 1833), p. 96, where the "country merchant" is called "a shopkeeper," with no mention of "Uncle Abe."

62.   "I attended court many years ago at Mt. Pulaski, the first county seat of Logan County, and there was the jolliest set of rollicking young Lawyers there that you ever saw together. There was Bill F[?ickli]n, Bill H[erndo]n, L[eonard] S[wet]t, and a lot more, and they mixed law and Latin, water and whisky, with equal success. It so fell out that the whisky seemed to be possessed of the very spirit of Jonah. At any rate, S[wet]t went out to the hog-pen, and, leaning over, began to 'throw up Jonah.' The hogs evidently thought it feed time, for they rushed forward and began to squabble over the voided matter.

"'Don't fight (hic),' said S[wet]t: 'there's enough (hic) for all.' " (Page 55)

> O. B. (Bill) Ficklin himself could have supplied this ridicule of AL's close crony, because he was both a Democrat and an old companion familiar with Swett's drinking habit.

63.   A committee, just previous to the fall of Vicksburg, solicitous for the *morale* of our armies, took it upon themselves to visit the President and urge the removal of General Grant.

"What for?" asked Uncle Abe.

"Why," replied the busy-bodies, "he drinks too much whisky."

"Ah!" rejoined Uncle Abe, "can you inform me, gentlemen, where General Grant procures his whisky?"

The committee confessed they could not.

"Because," added Uncle Abe, with a merry twinkle in his eye, "if I can find out, I'll send a barrel of it to every General in the field!" (Page 61)

> As Mort R. Lewis pointed out in the *Lincoln Herald*, 60 (1958), 89, this is a switch on an old jestbook favorite, appearing, for instance, in *Joe Miller's Complete Jest Book* (1845), p. 494, where the King

of England makes the comment about General James Wolfe. The telegrapher A. B. Chandler says AL once denied telling it: "Mr. Lincoln said that he had heard the story before, and that it would have been very good if he had said it, but that he didn't. He supposed it was 'charged to him, to give it currency.' He then said the original of the story was in King George's time. Bitter complaints were made to the King against his General Wolfe in which it was charged that he was mad. The King replied angrily: 'I wish he would bite some of my other generals then' " (William H. Ward, *AL: Tributes* [1895], p. 220). I wonder if perhaps AL said rather that he had not invented it, for John Eaton records his telling it during an interview, summer 1863, in *Grant, L., and the Freedmen* (1907), p. 90: "A company of Congressmen came to me to protest that Grant ought not to be retained as a commander of American citizens. I asked what was the trouble. They said he was not fit to command such men. I asked why, and they said he sometimes drank too much and was unfit for such a position. I then began to ask them if they knew what he drank, what brand of whiskey he used, telling them most seriously that I wished they would find out. They conferred with each other and concluded they could not tell what brand he used. I urged them to ascertain and let me know, for if it made fighting generals like Grant, I should like to get some of it for distribution."

64.   [Discussing the prospect of Salmon P. Chase resigning as Secretary of the Treasury to run for President:] Old Abe replied that "it is not so easy a thing to let Chase go. I am situated very much as the boy was who held the bear by the hind legs. I will tell you how it was. There was a very vicious bear which, after being some time chased by a couple of boys, turned upon his pursuers. The boldest of the two ran up and caught the bear by the hind legs, while the other climbed up into a little tree, and complacently witnessed the conflict going on beneath, between the bear and his companion. The tussle was a sharp one, and the boy, after becoming quite exhausted, cried out in alarm, 'Bill, for God's sake come down and help me let this darned bear go!' " (Page 74)

> A. T. Rice and F. F. Browne concur that this was AL's response to the person who brought news of the butchery at Fredericksburg, 13 December 1862. But Rice gives it as a story about two farm boys, James and John, pursued by a hog—*Reminiscences of AL* (1886), p. xxvi. Browne's version is about two Illinois boys pursued by a dog—*Everyday Life of AL* (1887), p. 574. Lacking a statistical count, my impression is that various collections prefer the hog version.

65.   One night Uncle Abe came wet and cold to a cross road tavern in Indiana, and found the fire more thoroughly blockaded with Hoosiers than mother [Secretary of Navy Gideon] Welles has been able to blockade the Southern Confederacy. Abe ordered the landlord to carry his horse a peck of catfish. "He can't eat catfish," said Boniface. "Try him," said Abe, "there's nothing like trying." The crowd all rushed after the landlord to see Abe's horse eat the peck of catfish. "He won't eat them, as I told you," said the landlord on returning. "Then," coolly responded Uncle Abe, who had squatted on the best seat, "bring them to me and I'll eat them myself." (Page 75)

> This is the most remarkable of switches. For the first half of the century this story had been told about Ben Franklin who asks the landlord to feed his horse oysters—*Ben Franklin Laughing*, ed. P. M. Zall (1980), pp. 119–120. But now the setting is transferred to Indiana and the oysters miraculously transformed to catfish.

66.   "There was a darkey in my neighborhood, called Pompey, who, from a certain quickness in figuring up the prices of chickens and vegetables, got the reputation of being a mathematical genius.

"Johnson, a darkey preacher, heard of Pompey, and called to see him. 'Here ye're a great mat'm'tishum, Pompey.' 'Yes sar, you jas try.' 'Well Pompey, Ize compound a problem in mat'matics.' 'All right, sar.' 'Now, Pompey, spose dere am tree pigeons sittin' on a rail fence, and you fire a gun at 'em and shoot one, how many's left?' 'Two, ob coors,' replies Pompey after a little wool scratching. 'Ya-ya-ya,' laughs Mr. Johnson; 'I knowed you was a fool, Pompey; dere's *none* left— one's dead, and d'udder two's flown away.'" (Page 77)

> Discounting the silly attempt at dialect (e.g., misspelling "hear" for phonetic fidelity), two eyewitnesses testify to AL's having told this favorite of early American jestbooks. It appears, for instance, in the *American Jest Book* (Philadelphia, 1789), p. 43, as a compliment to a New Jersey Black whose common sense undercuts a pretentious scholar, the version AL is reported to have told Goldwin Smith by W. D. Kelley—in A. T. Rice, *Reminiscences of AL* (1886), pp. 287–288. Smith's own diary for 16 November 1864 mentions AL's "stories— the three pigeons" (*Life and Opinions*, ed. T. A. Haultain [1913], p. 290).

67.   It seems he had accompanied a young lady to one of the hospitals in the capital where the sympathizing creature, as in duty bound, became interested in a wounded soldier. To all her inquiries as

to the location of the wound, however, she could only get one reply, thus: "My good fellow where were you hit!" "At Antietam." "But where did the bullet strike you?" "At Antietam." "But where did it hit you!" "At Antietam." Becoming discouraged, she deputized Uncle Abe to prosecute the inquiry, which he did successfully. Upon his rejoining her, she was more curious than ever, when the President, taking both her hands in his said in his most impressive style, "My dear girl, the ball that hit *him*, would not have injured *you*." (Page 88)

> Echoing the concluding volume of Laurence Sterne's *Tristram Shandy* (1767), this story seems suspect from its generalized context.

68.   During the fall of 1863, Uncle Abe was riding on the Virginia side of the Potomac, between Arlington Heights and Alexandria, accompanied by Dr. N—— of New Jersey. Passing the huge earth-work fortifications, the Doctor observed: "Mr. President, I have never yet been enabled to discover the utility of constructing and maintaining those forts. What is your opinion about them?"

"Well doctor," replied Uncle Abe, "you are a medical man, and I will ask you a question in the line of your profession. Can you tell me the use of a man's nipples?" "No, I can't," said the doctor. "Well, I can tell you," said Uncle Abe— "They would be mighty handy if he happened to have a child." (Page 89)

69.   A young U.S. Officer being indicted at Chicago, for an assault on an aged gentleman, Uncle Abe began to open the case thus: "this is an indictment against a soldier for assaulting an old man." "Sir," indignantly interrupted the defendant, "I am no soldier, I am an officer!" "I beg your pardon," said Abe, grinning blandly; "then, gentlemen of the jury, this is an indictment against an *officer*, who is *no soldier*, for assaulting an old man." (Page 90)

> Another mere switch, in the jestbooks such as the New Haven collection, *Joke Upon Joke* (1818), pp. 92–93, this is commonly assigned to the Irish lawyer and politician John Philpot Curran. More recently, in *Harper's Weekly*, 4 (21 July 1860), 451, it was assigned to the Scots critic, "the celebrated Lord [Francis] Jeffrey," an attorney by profession.

70.   Yesterday a Western correspondent, in search for something definite in relation to the fighting now going on, stepped into the White House and asked the President if he had anything authentic

from General Grant. The President stated that he had not, as Grant was like the man that climbed the pole and then pulled the pole up after him.—Washington *Union*, May 16. (Page 91)

71.   An Illinois man who had known the "boy Mayor," John [B.] Hay, from boyhood, was expressing to Uncle Abe, after the massacre at Olustee [20 February 1864], some regret that he should have supposed him capable of any military position.

"About Hay," said Uncle Abe, "the fact was, I was pretty much like Jim Hawks, out in Illinois, who sold a dog to a hunting neighbor, as a first-rate coon dog. A few days after, the fellow brought him back, saying he 'wasn't worth a cuss for coons.' 'Well,' said Jim, 'I tried him for everything else, and he wasn't worth a d——n, and so I thought he *must* be good for coons.'" (Page 65)

> This is told about "a hoosier" in the *Old American Comic Almanac* (Boston, 1842), p. 4, and more recently, still with no mention of AL, in *Leslie's Illustrated Newspaper*, 8 (26 November 1859), 401, but the context lends considerable credence.

> Entries 72–79 are from *Old Abe's Jokes* issued in New York by T. R. Dawley who, calling himself "Publisher for the Millions," also issued *The President Lincoln Campaign Songster* in the same year, 1864. But that his motives were commercial rather than political is indicated by his including in some printings of *Old Abe's Jokes* a vicious attack on Mrs. Lincoln's background and personality. The remainder of the text also appeared in 1864 with a collection of war songs published by Hurst and Company of New York as *The Picket Lines*.

72.   Old Abe, once reminded of the enormous cost of the war, remarked, ah, yes! that reminds me of a wooden-legged amateur who happened to be with a Virginia skirmishing party when a shell burst near him, smashing his artificial limb to bits, and sending a piece of iron through the calf of a soldier near him. The soldier 'grinned and bore it' like a man, while the amateur was loud and emphatic in his lamentation. Being rebuked by the wounded soldier, he replied: 'Oh, yes; it's all well enough for you to bear it. Your leg didn't cost you anything, and will heal up; but I paid two hundred dollars for mine!' (Page 42)

73.   [Concluding a tediously long dialogue purporting to be an interview between the President and an ancient Black soldier:]

'Then patriotism and honor are nothing to you?'

'Nuffin whatever, sa— I regard them as among the vanities.'

'If our soldiers were like you, traitors might have broken up the government without resistance.'

'Yes, sa, dar would hab been no help for it. I wouldn't put my life in de scale 'ginst any goberment dat eber existed, for no goberment could replace de loss to me.'

'Do you think any of your company would have missed you if you had been killed?'

'Maybe not, sa— a dead white man ain't much to dese sogers, let alone a dead nigga— but I'd a missed myself and dat was de pint wid me.' (Pages 52–53)

> Not elsewhere associated with AL, this story appears in *Fun of War*, National Tribune Library no. 15, 9 January 1897, pp. 2–3, with the Black soldier being interviewed by "a newspaper correspondent."

74.   President Lincoln tells the following story of Col. W. [?Robert L. Wilson] who had been elected to the legislature, and had also been judge of the county court. His elevation, however, had made him somewhat pompous, and he became very fond of using big words. On his farm he had a very large and mischievous ox called 'Big Brindle,' which frequently broke down his neighbors' fences, and committed other depredations, much to the Colonel's annoyance.

One morning after breakfast in the presence of Mr. Lincoln who had stayed with him over night, and who was on his way to town, he called his overseer and said to him: 'Mr. Allen, I desire you to impound Big Brindle, in order that I may hear no animadversions on his eternal depredations.'

Allen bowed and walked off, sorely puzzled to know what the Colonel meant. So after Col. W. left for town, he went to his wife and asked her what Col. W. meant by telling him to impound the ox. 'Why, he meant to tell you to put him in a pen,' said she.

Allen left to perform the feat, for it was no inconsiderable one, as the animal was very wild and vicious, and after a great deal of trouble and vexation succeeded. 'Well,' said he, wiping the perspiration from his brow, and soliloquizing, 'this is impounding, is it? Now, I am dead sure that the Colonel will ask me if I impounded Big Brindle, and I'll bet I puzzle him as he did me.'

The next day the Colonel gave a dinner party, and as he was not aristocratic, Mr. Allen, the overseer, sat down with the company. After the second or third glass was discussed, the Col. turned to the overseer and said: 'Eh, Mr. Allen, did you impound Big Brindle, sir?'

Allen straightened himself, and looking around at the company said: 'Yes, I did, sir, but old Brindle transcended the impannel of the impound, and scatterlophisticated all over the equanimity of the forest.'

The company burst into an immoderate fit of laughter, while the Colonel's face reddened with discomfiture. 'What do you mean by that, sir?' said the Colonel.

'Why, I mean, Colonel,' said Allen, 'that old Brindle, being prognosticated with an idea of the cholera, ripped and tared, snorted and pawed dirt, jumped the fence, tuck to the woods, and would not be impounded no how.'

This was too much; the company roared again, in which the Colonel was forced to join, and in the midst of the laughter Allen left the table, saying to himself as he went, 'I reckon the Colonel won't ask me to impound any more oxen.' (Pages 75–77)

> Paymaster of the Army, Colonel Wilson had been AL's crony in the Illinois legislature as well as a long-term circuit and probate judge. See R. R. Wilson, *Intimate Memories of L* (1945), pp. 26–27.

75.   Some one was discussing the character of a copperhead clergyman, in the presence of Mr. Lincoln, a time-serving Washington clergyman. Says Mr. Lincoln to his visitor, 'I think you are rather hard upon Mr. Blank. He reminds me of a man in Illinois who was tried for passing a counterfeit bill. It was in evidence that before passing it he had taken it to the cashier of a bank and asked his opinion of the bill, and he received a very prompt reply that the bill was a counterfeit. His lawyer who had heard of the evidence to be brought against his client, asked him just before going into court, 'Did you take the bill to the cashier of the bank and ask him if it was good?' 'I did,' was the reply. 'Well— what was the reply of the cashier?' The rascal was in a corner, but he got out of it in this fashion: 'He said it was a pretty, tolerable, respectable sort of a bill.' (Page 102)

76.   A western correspondent writes: 'A visitor, congratulating Mr. Lincoln on the prospects of his re-election, was answered by that indefatigable story-teller with an anecdote of an Illinois farmer, who

undertook to blast his own rocks. His first effort at producing an explosion proved a failure. He explained the cause by exclaiming, 'Pshaw, this powder has been shot before.' (Page 103)

77.   When Mrs. [Clement] Vallandigham left Dayton to join her husband, just before the election, she told her friends that she expected never to return until she did so as the wife of the Governor of Ohio.

Mr. Lincoln is said to have got off the following:— 'That reminds me of a pleasant little affair that occurred out in Illinois. A gentleman was nominated for Supervisor. On leaving home on the morning of election, he said— 'Wife, to-night you shall sleep with the Supervisor of this town.'

The election passed, and the confident gentleman was defeated. The wife heard the news before her defeated spouse returned home. She immediately dressed for going out, and waited her husband's return, when she met him at the door. 'Wife, where are you going at this time of night?' he exclaimed.

'Going?' she replied, 'why, you told me this morning that I should to-night sleep with the Supervisor of this town, and as Mr. L. is elected instead of yourself, I was going to his house.' (Pages 109–110)

78.   [Informed by a visitor that rumors about Ohio preferring Salmon P. Chase for president "all amounted to nothing":] At this announcement the President seemed well pleased and rubbing his hands, he exclaimed, 'That reminds me of a story. Some years ago two Irishmen landed in this country, and taking the way out into the interior after labor, came suddenly near a pond of water, and to their great horror they heard some bull-frogs singing their usual song,— B-a-u-m!— B-a-u-m!— B-a-u-m! They listened and trembled, and feeling the necessity of bravery they clutched their shellalies and crept cautiously forward, straining their eyes in every direction to catch a glimpse of the enemy, but he was not to be found. At last a happy idea came to the most forward one and he sprang to his mate, and exclaimed, 'and sure, Jamie, it is my opinion it's nothing but a *noise*.' (Page 121)

> F. B. Carpenter, *Six Months at the White House* (1866), p. 155, says, "He once told me this story"; Benjamin Cowen, *AL, an Appreciation* (1909), p. 36, says it applied to General Fremont's presidential campaign; and Ward Lamon, *Recollections of AL* (1895), pp. 194–195, says it applied to censorship. Lamon's book was compiled by his daughter, Dorothy, who omitted a version of his

own still extant in his notes at the Huntington Library (ms. LN 2405 [6], pp. 9–10), where it concludes: "Their approach frightened the frogs to hide in the water. All was silent as death. The Irishmen lay in waiting but were greatly disappointed that the enemy did not put in an appearance. After watching for some time, and he did not show up, now thoroughly disgusted as well as disappointed in an Opportunity of a free fight, a happy thought struck one of them who pulled the sleeve of the other and said in a whisper— 'Pat it is my deliberate opinion that it was nothing but a noise— and they took it with them.' " Lamon himself published a similar version in an unidentified newspaper of 1888 (Judd Stewart scrapbook, Huntington Library, 151179, 2:132).

79.   In answer to a curiosity seeker who desired a permit to pass the lines to visit the field of Bull Run after the first battle [July 1861], Mr. Lincoln made the following reply as his answer:

A man in Cortlandt county raised a porker of such unusual size that strangers went out of their way to see it. One of them the other day met the old gentleman and inquired about the animal. 'Wall, yes,' the old fellow said; 'he'd got such a critter, mighty big un; but he guessed he would have to charge him about a shillin' for lookin' at him.' The stranger looked at the old man for a minute or so; pulled out the desired coin, handed it to him and started to go off. 'Hold on,' said the other, 'don't you want to see the hog?' 'No,' said the stranger, 'I have seen as big a hog as I want to see!'

And you will find that fact the case yourself, if you should happen to see a few *live* rebels there as well as dead ones. (Page 124)

1865

 Entries 80–82 are from Joseph H. Barrett, *Life of AL* (1865). They were not in the edition of 1860.

80.   [Lamenting that he had to respond to serenades with speeches:] These serenade speeches bother me a good deal, they are so hard to make. I feel very much like the steam doctor, who said he could get along well enough in his way of practice with almost every case, but he was always a little puzzled when it came to mending a broken leg. (Page 822)

81.   [At the Hampton Roads peace conference, 3 February 1865, meeting with British arbitrator R. M. T. Hunter:] Mr. Hunter

made a long reply, insisting that the recognition of [Jefferson] Davis' power to make a treaty was the first and indispensable step to peace, and referring to the correspondence between King Charles the First and his Parliament, as a reliable precedent of a constitutional ruler treating with rebels.

Mr. Lincoln's face then wore that indescribable expression which generally preceded his hardest hits, and he remarked: "Upon questions of history I must refer you to Mr. [W. H.] Seward, for he is posted in such things, and I don't profess to be bright. My only distinct recollection of the matter is, that Charles lost his head." (Page 826)

> Quoting the Augusta (Georgia) *Chronicle and Sentinel*, 7 June 1865. The version in Ward Lamon's notes has an additional clause: "and I have no head to spare" (Huntington Library ms. LN 2418A, p. 460).

82.   Mr. [R. M. T.] Hunter said something about the inhumanity of leaving so many poor old negroes and young children destitute by encouraging the able-bodied negroes to run away, and asked, what are they— the helpless— to do?

Mr. Lincoln said that reminded him of an old friend in Illinois, who had a crop of potatoes, and did not want to dig them. So he told a neighbor that he would turn in his hogs, and let them dig them for themselves. "But," said the neighbor, "the frost will soon be in the ground, and when the soil is hard frozen, what will they do then?" To which the worthy farmer replied, "Let 'em root!" (Page 827)

> Again quoting the Augusta *Chronicle and Sentinel*, 7 June 1865. The same story in more dramatic form is given by F. B. Carpenter in H. J. Raymond, *Life and Public Services of AL* (1865), p. 746, where it concludes with the farmer, Mr. Case, scratching his head and at length stammering: "Well, it may come pretty hard on their *snouts*, but I don't see but that it will be 'root, hog, or die!'" Alexander Stephens, who negotiated for the Confederacy at the conference, wrote in his journal for 31 May 1865 that Carpenter was confused and that the newspaper was more accurate: "Mr. Lincoln's conclusion was simply, 'Let 'em root!' the reply of the farmer. To this I said, 'That, Mr. President, must be the origin of the adage, 'Root, pig, or perish'" (*Recollections*, ed. M. L. Avary [1910], p. 137).

Entries 83–86 are from a London jestbook, *A Legacy of Fun by Abraham Lincoln* (1865), an anti-Lincoln publication

compiled from American jokebooks and newspapers, but
chiefly from English jestbooks—merely attaching his name
to old stories.

83.   A crony of Abe's— a man named [?O. H.] Payne, was appointed a general at Illinois; in reference to his election the following
is recorded, which the president tells with great *gusto:* One day a
wealthy old lady, whose plantation was in the vicinity of the camp,
came in and inquired for General Payne. When the commander made
his appearance, the old lady in warm language told him that his men
had stolen her last coop of chickens, and demanded its restoration or
its value in money. "I am sorry for you, madam," replied the general,
"but I can't help it. The fact is, madam, we are determined to squelch
out the rebellion, if it cost every d——d chicken in Tennessee." (Page 5)

84.   I knew an old preacher, out west, who, on a very cold day,
when describing hell, said "it was an awful place and that the cold was
unbearable." One of his congregation, at the close of the sermon, took
upon himself to ask the preacher why he had described hell as being
cold, when all eminent divines said it was the very reverse. "Oh, sir,"
said the preacher, "I had good reason, for if I had preached the reverse,
I should have had them running away to warm themselves." (Page 8)

> In the *Royal Court Jester* (179–), pp. 52–53, this is a dialogue
> between two Scotch clergymen.

85.   "Friend Lincoln," said a celebrated Western farmer, one
day, to the President, "thee knows almost everything. Can thee tell me
how I am to preserve my small beer in the back yard? My neighbors
are often tapping it of nights."— "Put a barrel of old Madeira by the
side of it, let the rogues but get a taste of that, and I warrant they'll
never touch your small beer any more." (Page 10)

> This is another example of switching a jest from Ben Franklin to
> AL (see 65). In place of the "celebrated Western farmer" had been
> Franklin's "celebrated Quaker lawyer of Philadelphia"—*Ben
> Franklin Laughing,* ed. P. M. Zall (1980), p. 153.

86.   A poet was in the habit of pestering the President with his
books. On one occasion he brought one to the President, who told
him to put it into rhyme. He did so, and brought it back. "Ah!" said
Abe, "it will do now; it is rhyme, formerly it was neither rhyme nor
reason." (Page 43)

Another jestbook favorite, this one traditionally belongs to Thomas More. In John Hoddesdon, *History of Sir Thomas More* (1652), pp. 138–139, he advises a friend to turn a book into verse and later says: "Now it is Rime, before it was neither Rime nor Reason."

87.   "I heard a story last night about Daniel Webster when a lad, which was new to me, and it has been running in my head all the morning. When quite young, at school, Daniel was one day guilty of a gross violation of the rules. He was detected in the act, and called up by the teacher for punishment. This was to be the old-fashioned 'feruling' of the hand. His hands happened to be very dirty. Knowing this, on his way to the teacher's desk he *spit* upon the palm of his *right* hand, wiping it off upon the side of his pantaloons. 'Give me your hand, sir,' said the teacher, very sternly. Out went the right hand, partly cleansed. The teacher looked at it a moment, and said, 'Daniel, if you will find another hand in this school-room as filthy as that, I will let you off this time!' Instantly from behind his back came the *left* hand. 'Here it is, sir,' was the ready reply. 'That will do,' said the teacher, 'for this time; you can take your seat, sir!'"

> F. B. Carpenter, "Anecdotes and Reminiscences of President Lincoln," in H. B. Raymond, *Life and Public Services of AL* (1865), p. 748. As Mort R. Lewis points out in *Lincoln Herald*, 60 (1958), 89, the story appeared in *Joe Miller's Jests* (1845), p. 414, as about a "Dr. Wall." But in *Six Months at the White House* (1866), p. 131, Carpenter adds that Mrs. Ann S. Stephens told the story to AL. AL in turn told it to L. E. Chittenden (*Recollections of President Lincoln* [1891], pp. 333–334) and to Byron Johnson, President of the Sunday School Union, while reviewing the children's annual parade (*AL and Boston Corbett* [1914], p. 17).

88.   One of the last, if not the very last story told by President Lincoln, was to one of his Cabinet who came to see him, to ask if it would be proper to permit Jake Thompson to slip through Maine in disguise and embark for Portland. . . . "By permitting him to escape the penalties of treason," persistently remarked the Secretary, "you sanction it." "Well," replied Mr. Lincoln, "let me tell you a story. There was an Irish soldier here last summer, who wanted something to drink stronger than water, and stopped at a drugshop, where he espied a soda-fountain. 'Mr. Doctor,' said he, 'give me, plase, a glass of soda-wather, an' if yes can put in a few drops of whiskey unbeknown to any one, I'll be obleeged.'"

F. B. Carpenter, Ibid., p. 757; in *Six Months at the White House* (1866), p. 283, he says AL's "last" story was rather *135*. *Harper's Monthly*, 31 (September 1865), 539, quotes the Cincinnati *Gazette's* memoirs of General Sherman's North Carolina campaign: Sherman said that when he asked the President whether to capture Jeff Davis or let him escape, the only reply he could get was this story, except then told about "an old temperance lecturer" who stops at a friend's house for lemonade but is offered something stronger. "No," replied the lecturer, "I couldn't think of it; I'm opposed to it on principle; but," he added, with a longing glance at the black bottle that stood conveniently at hand, "if you could manage to put in a drop *unbeknownst* to me, I guess it wouldn't hurt me much!" And Moncure D. Conway's *Autobiography* (1904), 1:307, tells of visiting AL in January 1862 and hearing still another variant, this time applied to hopes of emancipation: "Perhaps it may be in the way suggested by a thirsty soul in Maine who found he could only get liquor from a druggist; as his robust appearance forbade the plea of sickness, he called for soda, and whispered, 'Couldn't you put a drop of the creeter intu it unbeknownst to yourself?' "

Entries 89–113 are from copies of correspondence and interviews with AL's old friends conducted by William H. Herndon in 1865–1866. The originals are now in the Library of Congress, but the copies made in 1866 by John G. Springer under Herndon's direction are in the Huntington Library—ms. LN 2408, 3 volumes. References after each entry are to volume and page number of the copies, which have been collated with the originals.

89.   [Letter from J. R. Herndon, 25 June 1865:] There is one anecdote that I must tell you, that took place when he was a boy; he told me himself. He said that he used to be very fond of Coon hunting and his father used to oppose this hunting, but he would slip out of a night after the old man had gone to bed, and take a hunt, but they had a small feist Dog that would detect them when they would return; so one night he took the feist along, they caught a coon and skinned him and then stretched it over the little dog and sewed him up and turned him loose and put the other dogs on the track, and they ran him home and caught him in the yard, and the old man jumped up and hissed the dogs on the feist, thinking it was a coon, and they killed the feist; they couldn't come up to his relief. The next morning when the old man went to examine the coon, it was the little dog; they were

called up and were both threshed, but the little dog never told on them any more when they went a coon hunting. (1:534)

90.   [Letter from J. R. Herndon, 3 July 1865:] You say the Little Dog story is too good to be kept out, and you want some more of his Indiana storys. . . . As to his Indiana storys; he has told me many of them; there is one that he told me, about an old Baptist Preacher,— the meeting house was way off in the woods from any other house, and was only used once a month; this preacher was dressed in coarse linen pants, and shirt of the same material; the pants were made after the old fashion, with big bag legs and but one button to the waist- bands, and two flap buttons, no suspenders; and the shirt had crimp sleeves and one button on the collar. He raised up in the Pulpit and took his Text, thus: I am the Christ whom I shall represent to-day; about this time one of these blue Lizards or scorpions ran up his legs; the old man began to slap away on his legs, but missed the Lizard, and kept getting higher up, he unbuttoned his pants at one snatch, and kicked off his pants, but the thing kept on up his back; the next motion was for the collar button of his shirt, and off it went. In the house was an old Lady, who took a good look at him, and said, well, if you repre- sent Christ, I am done believing in the Bible. This anecdote he told somewhere in his speech, in reply to some of the opposite candidates, who had represented themselves something extra. (1:520–521)

> When William Herndon and Jesse Weik published this in *Herndon's Lincoln* (1889), 1:80n, its rough edges appeared polished; e.g., "Continuing the sermon, the preacher slyly loosened the central button which graced the waistband of his pantaloons, and with a kick off came that easy-fitting garment."

91.   [The same letter goes on:] He was once while living in Salem, called on by one Pete Lukins, to prove his character and standing as to the validity of his oath. The Attorney said, please state what you know as to the character of Mr. Lukins as for truth and veracity. Well, said Mr. Lincoln, he is called lying Pete Lukins. But, said the Lawyer, would you believe him on oath. He turned round and said, ask Esquire Green— he has taken his testimony under oath many times. Green was asked the question and answered, I never believe anything he says unless somebody else swears the same thing. (1:521)

92.   [The same letter continues:] There was a [man] that use to come to Salem and get tight and stay until dark; he was afraid of

Ghosts and someone had to go home with him; well, Lincoln persuaded a fellow to take a sheet and go in the road and perform Ghost. He then sent an other Ghost and the man and Lincoln started home. The Ghost made his appearance and the man became much frightened, but the second Ghost made his appearance and frightened the first Ghost half to death, that broke the fellow from staying until dark any more. (1:522)

93.   [Letter from J. W. Wartman, 21 July 1865, reporting a story from John W. Lamar:] Old Mr. Lamar (squire's father) was one day going to election— and I (squire L——) was on the horse behind him. We fell in company with an old man named James Larkin— this man Larkin was a great brag, always relating some miraculous story or other. While riding along we overtook Abe Lincoln going to the polls on foot. Old man Larkin commenced telling Lincoln about the great speed and "bottom" of the mare he was riding.

Why, said Larkin, "Yesterday I run her *five* miles in *four* minutes, and she never drew a *long* breath." I guess, quietly replied Lincoln, She drew a great many *short ones*. (1:173)

> When Ida Tarbell, later in the century, interviewed John Lamar, he told her this version (*Early Life of AL*, ed. Paul Angle [1974], pp. 85–86). But in the Herndon-Weik papers, Library of Congress microfilm 9:1464–1465, a letter from Lamar to Herndon, 18 May 1867, says it happened at the election: "he steped up before Abe in the croud and comenced talking to abe and comenced braging on his horse and sed abe I have got the best horse in the county have you   yes I run him five miles this morning in 4 minats and he never fetched a long breath   I persume sir he fetched a good maney short ones sed abe   Larkins semed to think that abe did not appesiate his talk very well and was about to go abord of abe—Lincoln looked as if he did not cear and told some kind of a joke that fit Larkins case and put the croud in a uproar of laftar and Larkin dride up"

94.   [Herndon's notes on interview with Nat Grigsby, 16 September 1865:] As we were going down to Thompsons, G[rigsby] told me this story— which I had heard before. A man by the name of Charles Harper was going to mill— had an extremely long wheat bag on the horse and was met by sister Gordon— who said to Bro. Harper— Bro. H. your bag is too long— No said Bro. Harper— it is only too long in the summer. They were Bro. and Sister in the church— Mrs. Gordon told her husband of the vulgar— Gordon made a fuss— had a

church trial— Lincoln got the secret— wrote a witty piece of Poetry on the scene and conversations— The Poetry of Abe was good— witty &c as said by all who read it. (1:95)

95.   [Interview with James C. Richardson, September 1865:] Two other Grigsby boys— men rather— got married on the same night at the same house— though they did not marry sisters— they had an infair at old man Grigsby's and all the neighbors, excepting the Lincoln family were invited— Josiah Crawford the book man helped to get up the infair; he had a long, huge, blue nose. Abe Lincoln undoubtedly felt miffed— insulted— pride wounded &c. Lincoln I know felt wronged about the book transaction [in which Crawford overcharged him for damaging a borrowed copy of Weems's *Life of Washington*]. After the infair was ended the two women were put to bed. The candles were blown out upstairs— the gentlemen— the two husbands were invited and shown to bed. Chas. Grigsby got into bed with, *by an accident* as it were, with Reuben Grigsby's wife and Reuben got into bed with Charles' wife, by accident as it were. Lincoln, I say, was mortified and he declared that he would have revenge. Lincoln was by nature witty and here was his chance. So he got up a witty *poem*— called the Book of Chronicles, in which the infair— the mistake in partners— Crawford and his blue nose, came in each for its share— and this poem is remembered here in Indiana in scraps better than the Bible— better than Watts' Hymns. This was in 1829— and the first production that I know of that made us feel that Abe was truly and realy *some*. This called the attention of the People to Abe intellectually. Abe dropped the Poem in the road carelessly— lost it as it were— it was found by one of the Grigsby's boys satirised who had the good manly sense to read it— keep it— preserve it for years— if it is *not in existence now*. (1:127–128)

> Sixty pages later appear "The Chronicles" as recited from memory by Elizabeth Crawford, transcribed by her son, 4 January 1866 (1:186–189). His transcription is reprinted in Emanuel Hertz, *The Hidden Lincoln* (1938), pp. 285–287.

1866

96.   [Letter from Joseph Gillespie, 31 January 1866:] He could convey his ideas on any subject through the form of a simple story or homely illustration with better effect than any man I ever knew. To illustrate—: I was talking with him once about State Sovereignty— He

said the advocates of that theory always reminded him of the fellow who contended that the proper place for the big kettle was inside of the little one. (2:36)

97.   [Letter from Abner Y. Ellis, 1 February 1866:] In early times the boys in and about old Sangamon Town got up a free chicken fight, or free to all to enter his rooster by paying 25 cents entrance fee.

Well, Bap [McNabb] had a very splendid Red Rooster and he with others was entered. Well, the eventful day arrived, and Bap with his little beauty was there in all his splendor. The [crowd] arrives: and into the ring they toss their chickens, Bap's with the rest, but no sooner had the little beauty discovered what was to be done, he dropped his tail and run. Bap, being very much disappointed picked him up and went home, loosing his quarter and dishonored chicken. And as soon as he got home he tossed his pet down in the yard on his own dung-hill— The little fellow then stood up and flirted out his beautiful feathers and crowed, as brave as a lion. Bap viewed closely and remarked: Yes you dam little cuss! you are great on a parade, but you are not worth a dam in a fight. It is said that Mr. L. remarked to a friend soon after McClellan's fizzle before Richmond, that Little McClellan reminded him of Bap McNabb's rooster. (1:419–420)

> W. H. Herndon and Jesse Weik, *AL: The True Story* (1889), 1:117–118, gives AL a more active role by having the men choose him umpire.

98.   [The same letter continues:] Do you remember his Ground Squirrel Story? For fear you may not, I will try and tell it, as best I can.

Well an American an Irishman and a Dutchman were together and the American proposed that one of them should ask a question, each for the other to answer it and if they failed to answer it, they were to stand treat, and it was agreed to. Well, asked the American, how is it the little ground squirrel digs his hole in the ground without leaving any dirt at its mouth?

I can tell that, shure, it is because the squirrel begins his digging at the bottom. All right! said the American.

Ah! said the Dutchman, but how does the little fellow get down there. Oh! said Paddy, that is a question of your own asking, and for you only to answer.

Well! let's have the Lager, said the good natured Dutchman. (1:420)

99.   [The same letter goes on:] I am fearful that my selection of stories are not good and will be rather tiresome, so I will close with:

Daddy can Hold me.
Yes, Daddy can hold me.

Two brave young men were going to fight, and were both stripping for the conflict, and both equally eager by all outward appearances to get together, but their friends interfered and were holding the most noisy one back; when he discovered his antagonist coming towards him, he said to his friends, Why don't some of you hold the other man! Daddy can hold me! Yes, Daddy, hold me, Daddy! For you know my temper! (1:421)

> Harper's Monthly, 29 (November 1864), 820, gives this as "a California story" about a lawyer and a farmer arguing the merits of wine and whiskey with bowie knives until the lawyer shouts: "Hold us, boys! hold us! Two of you hold him; one can hold me!"

100.   [The letter from Ellis continues:] I suppose you have heard about the young democrat that was willing to swear that he ought to have a vote, but he wanted to explain.

He said he was honestly 21, but he had been cheated out of one year by his mother's having a miscarriage the first time, and he blamed the black Republicans [i.e., anti-slavery wing of the party] with it: they had made his father drunk and he frightened his mother. (1:421)

101.   [Ellis continues:] Josh Beasley and Sam Meeks had been at Logger-heads for a long time, but one day they met in a lane.

And Beasley spoke to Meeks and M. indignantly replied: Don't speak to me, Sam Beasley, for I consider myself entirely beneath your notice. (1:423)

102.   [The same letter goes on:] Old Mrs. Pattingill, a selfpossessed old lady in the Back woods in Indiana, went to town for the first time, and stopped at a Tavern for supper. The Land-Lady politely asked her which she would have, Tea or Coffee. Her reply was, Store Tea and Boughton Sugar in it if you please Mam. (1:423)

103.   [Our selection from this letter concludes:] There was once an old toper in Salem (I have forgotten his name), complaining to

Lincoln and Jack Armstrong that he had outlived all of his friends, but, said he, I have one yet, that is in this old jug, pulling out a quart jug and taking a horn at the same time. Jack said to him, look here old fellow, if you don't quit drinking, you will not live to see Christmas. I bet you, said he, 50 bushels of corn I will live to see Christmas. It is a bet, said Jack. And Lincoln was the witness. The old chap won the corn, and went and gathered it in Armstrong's cornfield. This was in the fall of 1833, the bet was made. (1:423–424)

> Ellis was supposed to be supplying Herndon with stories AL used to tell, but it is unclear whether these were AL's or his own, and thus I have omitted such riddles as: "Bob once sold John Burnap. He asked John how it was that the Sailors knew that there was a man in the moon. John said No— he could not tell. But how did they? Well, said Bob, they had been to *sea*" (1:421).

104.   [Letter from Charles F. Hart, 3 May 1866, about his father's visit to the White House in February 1863:] My father then remarked there were too many who wanted to be officers who are not suited to it, and Mr. Lincoln replied, "Yes, it is so. That reminds me of a story I heard in a small town in Illinois where I once lived. Every man in town owned a fast horse, each one considering his own the fastest, so to decide the matter there was to be a trial of all the horses to take place at the same time. One old man living in the town known as "Uncle" was selected as umpire; when it was over and each one anxious for his decision, the old man putting his hands behind his back said "I have come to one conclusion, that where there are so many fast horses in our little town, none of them are any great shakes." (2:295)

105.   [Interview with Caleb Carman, 12 October 1866:] I saw Abe at a show one night at Sangamon town— up stairs at my uncle's— Jacob Carman; the Showman cooked eggs in Abe's hat— Abe, when the man called for the hat, said— "Mr., the reason I didn't give you my hat before was out of respect to your Eggs— not care for my hat." (1:358)

106.   [Letter from John B. Weber, 5 November 1866, recounting a long anecdote about how AL as a young surveyor stayed overnight at the farm of a transplanted Pennsylvania and told stories around the fireplace:] He then said, when I was a little boy, I lived in the State of Kentucky where drunkenness was very common on election days; at an election, said he, in a village near where I lived, on a day when the weather was inclement and the roads exceedingly muddy, a toper

named Bill got brutally drunk and staggered down a narrow alley where he layed himself down in the mud, and remained there until the dusk of the evening, at which time he recovered from his stupor; finding himself very muddy— immediately started for a pump (a public watering place on the street) to wash himself. On his way to the pump another drunken man was leaning over a horse post; this, Bill mistook for the pump and at once took hold of the arm of the man for the handle, the use of which set the occupant of the post to throwing up; Bill believing all was right put both hands under and gave himself a thorough washing. He then made his way to the grocery for something to drink. On entering the door one of his comrades exclaimed in a tone of surprise, Why Bill, what in the world is the matter? Bill said in reply, I g-d you ought to have seen me before I was washed. (2:168–169)

> Weber's elaborate development of the context in contrived "literary" style makes this suspect. The story, an old one, appeared in the London jestbook, *Royal Court Jester* (179?), p. 52, among other exploits of a celebrated city drunk.

107.   [Letter from J. H. Wickizer, 25 November 1866:] The following shows his ready wit:

In 1858, in the Court at Bloomington, Illinois, Mr. Lincoln was engaged in a case of no very great importance, but the Attorney on the other side, Mr. S., a young lawyer of fine abilities (now a Judge) was always very sensitive about being beaten, and in this case manifested unusual zeal and interest. The case lasted till late at night, when it was finally submitted to the jury— Mr. S. spent a sleepless night in anxiety, and early next morning, learned to his great chagrin, he had lost the case. Mr. Lincoln met him at the Courthouse and asked him what had become of his case— with lugubrious countenance and melancholy tone Mr. S. said "It's gone to h——l."— "O well," said Mr. L., "then you'll see it again." (2:447)

> *Harper's Weekly* for 14 November 1857 (1:734) had told how the London wit Douglas Jerrold heard about an auctioneer whose business was going to the devil: "Oh, then, he'll get it again," said the wit.

108.   [Letter from J. H. Littlefield, 11 December 1866, about AL's reaction to planning a military expedition down the Yazoo River:] There was a man in Illinois a good many years since that was troubled with an old sow and her pigs—again and again the old man & his sons drove her out and repeatedly found her in the lot. One day

he & his boys searched about & found that she got into the lot through a certain hollow log that had been placed in the fence; they took out this log & built up the fence by placing the log a little differently than before, & the next day, what was the astonishment of the Old Lady to find that she & her *litter* came out of the log *outside* of the field instead of *inside*. "It is just so with the Yazoo River expedition," said Mr. L. "It comes out of the same side of the log."

> Not in the Huntington Library copies but from the Herndon-Weik papers, Library of Congress, microfilm 8: 1284, to retain chronological order. This story seems connected to one in *Leslie's Illustrated Newspaper*, 2 (15 November 1856), 355, that does not mention AL but is about a notable crooked tree: "I afterwards saw that tree cut down and made into rails for a hog pasture. The hogs would crawl through twenty times a day, and so crooked were them rails, that every time the hogs got out they found themselves back in the pasture again!"

109.   [Interview with J. T. Speed, no date:] I feel, said Lincoln— jokingly— like a little neighbor boy of mine in Indiana— his father was a hunter— he was tender and chicken hearted; his father one night caught an old coon and her young— killed the old one and all the young except one—   tied a little rope around the neck of it, and told the boy to watch it while he, the father, went and got a chain—   the boy was afraid his father would treat it cruelly—   Lincoln went over to see the boy— the boy was apparently crying— was tender— never would throw at a bird— said to Abe— "I wish this Coon would get away—, but if I let him go, dad will whip me—, I do wish it would run off—." So I feel by these leading rebels— Davis, Lee &c. I wish they could get away— yet if I let 'em loose— dad— the People would whip me— and yet I do wish they would run away out of the land &c. (2:64)

> F. B. Carpenter, *Six Months at the White House* (1866), p. 284, gives it as a story about a Springfield boy who bought the coon with his own money and, as the novelty wore off, wished it would run away so he could tell his folks "that he got away from me." A similar version is given by AL's bodyguard, William B. Crook, in *Harper's Monthly*, 115 (1907), 524, describing events the day after AL returned from visiting Richmond in April 1865.

110.   [Interview with C. C. Brown, no date:] Lincoln told stories— one of which was Washingtons picture in a necessary— privy in England— make an Englishman S-h-t. (2:160)

This must allude to the story reported by Abner Y. Ellis in a statement to Herndon— Herndon-Weik papers, Library of Congress, microfilm 14:1637: "I once heard Mr. Lincoln tell an anecdote on Col[onel] Ethan Allen of Revolutionary notoriety which I have never heard from any one besides him and for your amusement I will try and tell it as well as I can

"It appears that shortly after we had pease with England Mr. Allen had occasion to visit England, and while their the English took Great pleasure in teasing him, and trying to make fun of the Americans and General Washington in particular And one day they got a picture of General Washington, and hung it up the Back House where Mr Allen could see it

"And they finally asked Mr A. if he saw that picture of his friend in the Back House

"Mr Allen said No. but said he thought that it was a verry appropriate [place] for an Englishman to keep it Why they asked, for said Mr Allen their is Nothing that will make an Englishman SHIT so quick as the Sight of Genl Washington And after that they let Mr Allen [and] Washington alone."

111.   [The same interview continues:] In the morning after my marriage Lincoln met me and said— "Brown why is a woman like a barrel— C. C. B. could not answer. Well, said Lincoln— You have to raise the hoops before you put the head in." (2:160)

112.   [Note from J. T. Stuart about Billy Fagan, no date:] In the year 1838-9, town of Springfield, there lived a man by the name of Uncle Billy Fagan; he was a [blank] man— a gentleman and a wit. A young lawyer had just come from K[entuck]y a Mr ———

After having been here a few days the gentleman dressed up in his rich broad cloth and walked up town to the grocery— the usual and [blank] place of business of most [blank] to see the new world he was about settle and leaning up against a post looking on [blank] Uncle Billy saw him— and edged his way up to him and after shrewdly eyeing— penetrating the young lawyer— He accosted the young lawyer these— "You are a stranger in these parts, I guess"— and the lawyer said in reply— "Yes, Sir, I am a stranger." Uncle Billy eyed the lawyer again from head to foot, keenly and shrewdly and thus again addressed the lawyer— "Stranger, where are you from" and to which the stranger replied— "From Kentucky—" "Kentucky— eh! Kentucky— eh!" responded Uncle Billy— The old gentleman eyed the young lawyer again and again— from head to foot— paused awhile— threw his keen grey eye up to the strangers face and interrogated the lawyer again, thus— "What might your business be stranger—" "My profession is that of a lawyer, Sir," responded the Attorney. Uncle Billy now more particularly scanned and scrutinized the lawyer— thought— cocked his eye up— put his finger on the side of his nose as if in meditation &c.— reflected— and thus again said— "Stranger, may I tell you what I think of you?" The lawyer rose up in a dignified way, expecting to get a compliment from the old gentleman whom the lawyer had detected as more than an ordinary loafer. Said— "Yes, sir— I should like to have your opinion—" Uncle Billy then put his finger on the soft part of his nose close to his cheek as if in study and meditation, said— "Stranger, I think you are— are— a damned slim chance." (2:196–197)

> The second edition of Ward Lamon's *Recollections* (1911), p. 296, says that AL told this story with Stuart himself as the young lawyer.

113.   [Interview with J. H. Matheny, no date:] Says that about 1837-8-9— a parcel of young men in this city formed a kind of Political Society— association or what not— Lincoln once or twice wrote short Poems for the book. None of the Poems are recollected in full. One verse of one, on seduction by Lincoln runs thus:

> Whatever Spiteful fools may say—
> Each jealous, ranting yelper—
> No woman ever *played* the *whore*
> Unless she had a man to help her. (2:211)

 Entries 114–119 are from an anthology by Frank Moore, *Anecdotes, Poetry and Incidents of the War* (1866).

114.   Judge [Joseph G.] Baldwin, of California, an old and highly respectable and sedate gentleman, called on General [Henry W.] Halleck, and, presuming upon a familiar acquaintance in California a few years since, solicited a pass outside of the lines to see a brother in Virginia, not thinking that he would meet with a refusal, as both his brother and himself were good Union men. "We have been deceived too often," said General Halleck, "and I regret I can't grant it." Judge B. then went to Stanton, and was very briefly disposed of with the same result. Finally he obtained an interview with Mr. Lincoln, and stated his case. "Have you applied to General Halleck?" inquired the

President. "And met with a flat refusal," said Judge B. "Then you must see Stanton," continued the President. "I have, and with the same result," was the reply. "Well, then," said the President with a smile of good humor, "I can do nothing, for you must know *that I have very little influence with this Administration!*" (Pages 177–178)

115.   "Mr. President," said a friend to him, "there isn't much left of [Confederate General J. B.] Hood's army [defeated December 1864], is there?"

"Well, no, [Joseph] Medill; I think Hood's army is about in the fix of Bill Sykes's dog, down in Sangamon county. Did you ever hear it?"

Of course, the answer was, "Never."

"Well, Bill Sykes had a long, *yaller* dog, that was forever getting into the neighbors' meat-houses and chicken-coops. They had tried to kill it a hundred times, but the dog was always too smart for them. Finally, one of them got a bladder of a coon, and filled it up with powder, tying the neck around a piece of punk. When he saw the dog coming he fired the punk, split open a hot biscuit and put the bladder in, then buttered all nicely and threw it out. The dog swallowed it at a gulp. Pretty soon there was an explosion. The head of the dog lit on the porch, the fore-legs caught astraddle the fence, the hind-legs fell in the ditch, and the rest of the dog lay around loose. Pretty soon Bill Sykes came along, and the neighbor said: 'Bill, I guess there ain't much of that dog of your'n left.' 'Well, no,' said Bill; 'I see plenty of pieces, but I guess that dog, *as a dog*, ain't of much more account.' Just so, Medill, there may be fragments of Hood's army around, but I guess that dog, *as a dog*, ain't of much more account." (Page 194)

> A correspondent in *Scribner's*, 15 (March 1878), 886, says AL on the same occasion told this as about Slocum and his dog, Bill; while F. F. Browne, *Every-day Life of AL* (1887), pp. 616–617, says he told it on another occasion about Bill Sykes's yellow dog done in by "mischievous small boys."

116.   A lieutenant, whom debts compelled to leave his fatherland and service, succeeded in being admitted to the late President Lincoln, and, by reason of his commendable and winning deportment and intelligent appearance, was promised a lieutenant's commission in a cavalry regiment. He was so enraptured with his success, that he deemed it a duty to inform the President that he belonged to one of the oldest noble houses in Germany. "O, never mind that," said Mr.

Lincoln; "you will not find that to be an obstacle to your advancement."
(Pages 269–270)

117.   A gentleman called on the President, and solicited a pass for Richmond. "Well," said the President, "I would be very happy to oblige you, if my passes were respected; but the fact is, sir, I have, within the last two years, given passes to two hundred and fifty thousand men to go to Richmond, and not one has got there yet." (Page 435)

118.   During a conversation on the approaching election, in 1864, a gentleman remarked to President Lincoln that nothing could defeat him but Grant's capture of Richmond, to be followed by his nomination at Chicago and acceptance. "Well," said the President, "I feel very much like the man who said he didn't want to die particularly, but if he had got to die, that was precisely the disease he would like to die of." (Page 447)

119.   A Western farmer sought the President day after day until he procured the much desired audience. He had a plan for the successful prosecution of the war, to which Mr. Lincoln listened as patiently as he could. When he was through, he asked the opinion of the President upon his plan. "Well," said Mr. Lincoln, "I'll answer by telling you a story. You have heard of Mr. Blank, of Chicago? He was an immense loafer in his way— in fact, never did anything in his life. One day he got crazy over a great rise in the price of wheat, upon which many wheat speculators gained large fortunes. Blank started off one morning to one of the most successful of the wheat speculators, and with much enthusiasm laid before him a plan by which he (the said Blank) was certain of becoming independently rich. When he had finished, he asked the opinion of his hearer upon his plan of operations. The reply came as follows: 'My advice is that you stick to your business.' 'But,' asked Blank, 'What is my business?' 'I don't know, I am sure, what it is,' says the merchant; 'but whatever it is, I advise you to stick to it.'" (Page 510)

 Entries 120–135 are from F. B. Carpenter, *Six Months at the White House with Abraham Lincoln* (1866), based on his own observation except for 127–135 which he obtained from others.

120.   As the different members of the Cabinet came in, the President introduced me, adding in several instances,— "He has an idea of painting a picture of us all together." This, of course, started conversation on the topic of art. Presently a reference was made by some one to [Thomas D.] Jones, the sculptor, whose bust of Mr. Lincoln was in the crimson parlor below. The President, I think, was writing at this instant. Looking up, he said, "Jones tells a good story of General [Winfield] Scott, of whom he once made a bust. Having a fine subject to start with, he succeeded in giving great satisfaction. At the closing sitting he attempted to define and elaborate the lines and markings of the face. The General sat patiently; but when he came to see the result, his countenance indicated decided displeasure. 'Why, Jones, what have you been doing?' he asked. 'Oh,' rejoined the sculptor, 'not much, I confess, General; I have been working out the details of the face a little more, this morning.' 'Details?' exclaimed the General, warmly; '——— the details! Why, my man, you are spoiling the bust!' " (Pages 34–35)

121.   Something was said soon after we started [on a walk] about the penalty which attached to high positions in a democratic govern- ment— the tribute those filling them were compelled to pay to the public. "Great men," said Mr. Lincoln, "have various estimates. When Daniel Webster made his tour through the West years ago, he visited Springfield among other places, where great preparations had been made to receive him. As the procession was going through the town, a barefooted little darkey boy pulled the sleeve of a man named T., and asked,— 'What the folks were all doing down the street?' 'Why, Jack,' was the reply, 'the biggest man in the world is coming.' Now, there lived in Springfield a man by the name of G.,— a very corpulent man. Jack darted off down the street, but presently returned, with a very dis- appointed air. 'Well, did you see him?' inquired T. 'Yees,' returned Jack; 'but laws— he ain't half as big as old G.' " (Pages 36–37)

122.   It was, perhaps, in connection with the newspaper attacks, that he told, during the sitting [2 March 1864], this story.— "A traveller on the frontier found himself out of his reckoning one night in a most inhospitable region. A terrific thunder-storm came up, to add to his trouble. He floundered along until his horse at length gave out. The lightning afforded him the only clew to his way, but the peals of thunder were frightful. One bolt, which seemed to crash the earth

beneath him, brought him to his knees. By no means a praying man, his petition was short and to the point,— 'O Lord, if it is all the same to you, give us a little more light and a little less noise!' " (Page 49)

123.   [Related to Carpenter by a member of a bankers' group:] A member of the delegation referred to the severity of the tax laid by Congress upon the State Banks. "Now," said Mr. Lincoln, "that reminds me of a circumstance that took place in a neighborhood where I lived when I was a boy. In the spring of the year the farmers were very fond of the dish which they called greens, though the fashionable name for it nowadays is spinach, I believe. One day after dinner, a large family were taken very ill. The doctor was called in, who attributed it to the greens, of which all had freely partaken. Living in the family was a half-witted boy named Jake. On a subsequent occasion, when greens had been gathered for dinner, the head of the house said: 'Now, boys, before running any further risk in this thing, we will first try them on Jake. If he stands it, we are all right.' And just so, I suppose," said Mr. Lincoln, "Congress thought of the State Banks!" (Pages 53–54)

> Ward Lamon, "Administration of Lincoln" (1886), p. 443, says AL told this story in joking about a dream of being assassinated: "As long as this imaginary assassin continues to exercise his amusement on others I can stand it; and I really think I am in more danger of dying from eating spinach or greens than I am from being killed by an assassin."

124.   Shortly after this event [Simon Cameron's resigning as Secretary of War, 11 January 1862] some gentlemen called upon the President, and expressing much satisfaction at the change, intimated that in their judgment the interests of the country required an entire reconstruction of the Cabinet. Mr. Lincoln heard them through, and then shaking his head dubiously, replied, with his peculiar smile: "Gentlemen, when I was a young man I used to know very well one Joe Wilson, who built himself a log-cabin not far from where I lived. Joe was very fond of eggs and chickens, and he took a good deal of pains in fitting up a poultry shed. Having at length got together a choice lot of young fowls,— of which he was very proud,— he began to be much annoyed by the depredations of those little black and white spotted animals, which it is not necessary to name. One night Joe was awakened by an unusual cackling and fluttering among his chickens. Getting up, he crept out to see what was going on. It was a

bright moonlight night, and he soon caught sight of half a dozen of the little pests, which with their dam were running in and out of the shadow of the shed. Very wrathy, Joe put a double charge into his old musket, and thought he would 'clean' out the whole tribe at one shot. Somehow he only killed *one*, and the balance scampered off across the field. In telling the story, Joe would always pause here, and hold his nose. 'Why didn't you follow them up, and kill the rest?' inquired the neighbors. 'Blast it,' said Joe, 'why, it was eleven weeks before I got over killin' *one*. If you want any more skirmishing in that line you can just do it yourselves!' " (Pages 138–139)

> In A. T. Rice, *Reminiscences of AL by Distinguished Men of His Time* (1886), p. 236, Titian J. Coffey recalled the circumstance but gives a slightly different version of the story, concluding: " 'I took aim, blazed away, killed one, and he raised such a fearful smell that I concluded it was best to let the other six go.' "

125.   Mr. Lincoln was always ready to join in a laugh at the expense of his person, concerning which he was very indifferent. Many of his friends will recognize the following story,— the incident having actually occurred,— which he used to tell with great glee:—

"In the days when I used to be 'on the circuit,' I was once accosted in the cars by a stranger, who said, 'Excuse me, sir, but I have an article in my possession which belongs to you.' 'How is that?' I asked, considerably astonished. The stranger took a jack-knife from his pocket. 'This knife,' said he, 'was placed in my hands some years ago, with the injunction that I was to keep it until I found a man *uglier* than myself. I have carried it from that time to this. Allow me *now* to say, sir, that I think *you* are fairly entitled to the property.' " (Pages 148–149)

> *L's Third Secretary: Memoirs of William O. Stoddard*, ed. W. O. Stoddard, Jr., (1955), pp. 74–75, has a slightly different version recollected by the White House doorkeeper, Edward Moran, concluding: "When Joe Simpkins give it to me, he said if ever I was to meet a man homelier than I be, I was to give it to him. Mister, this here's your knife." In the London jestbook, *Wit and Wisdom* (1826), pp. 89–90, the same story is given as "a fact" about Mr. Lawson, master-painter at the New York dockyard, given a knife by a sailor who says, "I belong to the Ugly Club of London"— whose members are obligated to pass on the knife to any person uglier than themselves. Later, in *Harper's Monthly* "Editor's Drawer" for September 1858 (17:565), the story is told about

himself by "Judge Jones of Indiana, celebrated alike for his want of beauty and his superior shrewdness as a criminal lawyer." And in the "Editor's Drawer" for July 1852 (5:271) we learn: "They have a practice at the West of giving to the ugliest man . . . a jack-knife, which he carries until he meets with a man uglier than himself, when the new customer 'takes the knife' with all its honors."

126.   [After Carpenter tells him the story of a Black who prefaced his prayers by reminding the Lord he was a good window washer:] After a hearty laugh at what he called this "direct way of putting the case," he said: "The story that suggests to me, has no resemblance to it save in the 'washing windows' part. A lady in Philadelphia had a pet poodle dog, which mysteriously disappeared. Rewards were offered for him, and a great ado made without effect. Some weeks passed, and all hope of the favorite's return had been given up, when a servant brought him in one day, in the filthiest condition imaginable. The lady was overjoyed to see her pet again, but horrified at his appearance. 'Where *did* you find him?' she exclaimed. 'Oh,' replied the man, very unconcernedly, 'a negro down the street had him tied to the end of a pole, *swabbing* windows.' " (Page 159)

127.   [A delegation from New York urged him to launch naval attacks against Southern ports to divert rebel troops from Washington.] Mr. Lincoln said the project reminded him of the case of a girl in New Salem, who was greatly troubled with a "singing" in her head. Various remedies were suggested by the neighbors, but nothing tried afforded any relief. At last a man came along,— "a common-sense sort of man," said he, inclining his head towards the gentlemen complimentarily,— "who was asked to prescribe for the difficulty. After due inquiry and examination, he said the cure was very simple. 'What is it?' was the anxious question. 'Make a plaster of *psalm-tunes,* and apply to her feet, and draw the "singing" *down,*' was the rejoinder." (Page 239)

128.   [Telling James A. Garfield about consulting with Admiral L. M. Goldsborough on the feasibility of landing north of Norfolk and learning that the Navy had not tried to find a landing site:] "Now," said I, "Admiral, that reminds me of a chap out West who had studied law, but had never tried a case. Being sued, and not having confidence in his ability to manage his own case, he employed a fellow-lawyer to manage it for him. He had only a confused idea of the meaning of law

terms, but was anxious to make a display of learning, and on the trial constantly made suggestions to his lawyer, who paid no attention to him. At last, fearing that his lawyer was not handling the opposing counsel very well, he lost all patience, and springing to his feet cried out, 'Why don't you go at him with a *capias*, or a *surre-butter*, or something, and not stand there like a confounded old *nudum-pactum?*' " (Page 241)

129.   An allusion to a question of law in the course of conversation suggesting the subject, Mr. Lincoln said: "The strongest example of 'rigid government' and 'close construction' I ever knew, was that of Judge ———. It was once said of him that he would *hang* a man for blowing his nose in the street, but that he would *quash* the indictment if it failed to specify which *hand* he blew it with!" (Page 254)

> In Joseph G. Baldwin, *Flush Times of Alabama and Mississippi* (1853), p. 24, the lawyer Sar Kasm is so described: "He might approve of a law making it death for a man to blow his nose in the street, but would be for rebelling if it allowed the indictment to dispense with stating in which hand he held it."

130.   One of Mr. Lincoln's "illustrations" in my hearing, on one occasion, was of a man who, in driving the hoops of a hogshead to "head" it up, was much annoyed by the constant falling in of the top. At length the bright idea struck him of putting his little boy inside to "hold it up." This he did; it never occurring to him till the job was done, how he was to get his child out. "This," said he, "is a fair sample of the way some people always do business." (Page 256)

> In *Harper's Weekly*, 5 (1 June 1861), 339, the story, not attributed to AL, concludes: "After completing the work much to his satisfaction, he was astonished to find his boy inside the cask, and without a possibility of getting out, except through the bung-hole."

131.   In a time of despondency, some visitors were telling the President of the "breakers" so often seen ahead— "this time surely coming." "That," said he, "suggests the story of the school-boy, who never could pronounce the names 'Shadrach,' 'Meshach,' and 'Abednego.' He had been repeatedly whipped for it without effect. Sometime afterwards he saw the names in the regular lesson for the day. Putting his finger upon the place, he turned to his next neighbor, an older boy, and whispered, 'Here come those "tormented Hebrews" again.' " (Pages 256–257)

The more common version, as told to Senator J. B. Henderson, Missouri, has AL tell the story when he sees through the window three senators coming to the White House—as in Isaac N. Phillips, *AL by Some Men Who Knew Him*, ed. Paul Angle (1969), pp. 51–52, or A. D. White, *Autobiography* (1907), 2:127, quoting Adlai Stevenson. Senator Henderson's version concludes: "Look! there come them three d——d fellers again."

132.   [When General J. W. Phelps took Ship Island, near New Orleans, in the spring of 1862 and issued a proclamation freeing slaves, a friend asked AL why he seemed indifferent to that act.] "Well," said Mr. Lincoln, "I feel about that a good deal as a man whom I will call 'Jones,' whom I once knew, did about his wife. He was one of your meek men, and had the reputation of being badly henpecked. At last, one day his wife was seen switching him out of the house. A day or two afterward a friend met him in the street, and said: 'Jones, I have always stood up for you, as you know; but I am not going to do it any longer. Any man who will stand quietly and take a switching from his wife, deserves to be horsewhipped.' 'Jones' looked up with a wink, patting his friend on the back. 'Now *don't*,' said he: 'why, it didn't *hurt* me any; and you've no idea what a *power* of *good* it did Sarah Ann!'" (Pages 273–274)

133.   [To an insistent delegation of clergy seeking to revise the way military chaplains were being chosen:] "Without any disrespect, gentlemen, I will tell you a 'little story.' Once, in Springfield, I was going off on a short journey, and reached the depot a little ahead of time. Leaning against the fence just outside the depot was a little darkey boy, whom I knew, named 'Dick,' busily digging with his toe in a mud-puddle. As I came up, I said, ' "Dick," what are you about?' 'Making a "*church*," ' said he. 'A church?' said I; 'what do you mean?' 'Why, yes,' said 'Dick,' pointing with his toe, 'don't you see? there is the shape of it; there's the "steps" and "front door"— here the "pews," where the folks set— and there's the "pulpit." ' 'Yes, I see,' said I, 'but why don't you make a "minister?" ' 'Laws,' answered 'Dick,' with a grin, 'I hain't got *mud* enough!'" (Page 277)

134.   One of the last stories I heard from Mr. Lincoln was concerning John Tyler, for whom it was to be expected, as an old Henry Clay Whig, he would entertain no great respect. "A year or two after Tyler's accession to the Presidency," said he, "contemplating an excursion in some direction, his son went to order a special train of cars.

It so happened that the railroad superintendent was a very strong Whig. On 'Bob's' making known his errand, that official bluntly informed him that his road did not run any special trains for the President. 'What!' said 'Bob,' 'did you not furnish a special train for the funeral of General Harrison?' 'Yes,' said the superintendent, stroking his whiskers; 'and if you will only bring your father here in that shape, you shall have the best train on the road.' " (Page 278)

135.   The last story told by Mr. Lincoln was drawn out by a circumstance which occurred just before the interview with Messrs. [Schuyler] Colfax and [George] Ashmun, on the evening of his assassination.

Marshal [Ward] Lamon of Washington had called upon him with an application for the pardon of a soldier. After a brief hearing the President took the application, and when about to write his name upon the back of it, he looked up and said: "Lamon, have you ever heard how the Patagonians eat oysters? They open them and throw the shells out of the window until the pile gets higher than the house, and then they move;" adding: "I feel to-day like commencing a new pile of pardons, and I may as well begin it just here." (Pages 284–285)

136.   [From "The Editor's Drawer," *Harper's Monthly*, February 1866:] Since the assassination of the late much-lamented President, "Old Abe's jokes" have naturally been but little in vogue. . . . This that I'm going to tell was related to me by Albert B. Chandler, who was and is a cipher operator in the office of Major [Thomas] Eckert, now Assistant-Secretary of War:

"The President was sitting by my table," said Albert, "one evening, as was his custom almost every evening, reading the dispatches of the afternoon. There was nothing in any of the dispatches of much importance. All was still without, save the peculiar nasal, whining cry of newsboys' song— 'Philadelphia In-*qui*-ry!' The President laid down the last slip and his spectacles simultaneously, and caught up the newsboys' cry, repeating, 'Philadelphia In-*qui*-ry!' in their very accent and key. After singing about three verses of the laconic song, he said: 'Boys, did I ever tell you the joke the Chicago newsboys came on me?' And Albert and [David] Bates and Charley Tinker, the only audience of the President, as with one voice, said 'No,' and intimated that they would like to know it. 'Well,' said Mr. Lincoln, 'soon after I was nominated for President at Chicago, I went up one day, and one

of the first really distinguished men who waited on me was a picture-
man, who politely asked me to favor him with a sitting for my picture.
Now at that time there were less photographs of my phiz than at
present, and I went straightway with the artist, who detained me but
a moment, and took one of the most really life-like pictures I have
ever seen of myself, from the fact that he gave me no *fixing* nor *positions*.
But this stiff, ungovernable hair of mine was all sticking every way,
very much as it is now, I suppose; and so the operation of his camera
was but "holding the mirror up to nature." I departed, and did not
think of pictures again until that evening I was gratified and flattered
at the cry of newsboys who had gone to vending the pictures: " 'Ere's
yer last picter of Old Abe! He'll look better when he gets his *hair*
combed!" ' "

> Volume 32, page 405. The Chicago photographer is unknown,
> but I would guess that the photograph is Number 111 in Frederick
> Hill Meserve, *The Photographs of AL* (1944). "The mirror up to
> nature," of course, is from *Hamlet* III.ii.22. Albert Chandler re-
> peated a substantially similar story in the "Lincoln Number" of
> *The Independent*, 4 April 1895, rptd. *AL: Tributes from His Asso-
> ciates*, ed. by W. H. Ward (1895), pp. 218-219.

137.   [From "The Editor's Drawer," *Harper's Monthly*, March
1866:] During Mr. Lincoln's practice of his profession of the law, long
before he was thought of for President, he was attending the Circuit
Court which met at Bloomington, Illinois. The Prosecuting Attorney,
a lawyer by the name of [Ward] Lamon, was a man of great physical
strength, and took particular pleasure in athletic sports, and was so
fond of wrestling that his power and experience rendered him a formidable and generally successful opponent. One pleasant day in the
fall Lamon was wrestling near the court-house with some one who had
challenged him to a trial, and in the scuffle made a large rent in the
rear of his unmentionables. Before he had time to make any change
he was called into court to take up a case. The evidence was finished,
and Lamon got up to address the jury, and having on a somewhat
short coat his misfortune was rather apparent. One of the lawyers, for
a joke, started a subscription paper, which was passed from one
member of the bar to another as they sat by a long table fronting the
bench, to buy a pair of pantaloons for Lamon, "he being," the paper
said, "a poor but worthy young man." Several put down their names
with some ludicrous subscription, and finally the paper was laid by
some one in front of Mr. Lincoln, on a plea that he was engaged in

writing at the time. He quietly glanced over the paper, and immediately took up his pen and wrote after his name, "I can contribute nothing *to the end in view.*"

> Volume 32, p. 535. Lamon's own version says this took place about 1849, "in the early days of our acquaintance" (*Recollections of AL*, ed. Dorothy Lamon [1895], p. 16).

138.   [A correspondent recounting for "The Editor's Drawer," *Harper's Monthly*, September 1866, how AL replied to a request that an unpleasant colonel be transferred:] "This reminds me of a little story. It was in the Mexican war— at the battle of Monterey, I believe— that a little Irish captain from Sangamon County was ordered by his Colonel to a position, so and so, with his Company. After hearing the order, the little Captain straightened up full height, and said: 'Colonel, will yez be so kind as to tell that to my min yoursel'; for, by jabers, Colonel, I'm not on spakin' terms wid my Company!' "

> Volume 33, pp. 536–537. The story flourished long before the Mexican War; it appeared in the New York jestbook, *American Magazine of Wit* (1808), pp. 186–187.

1867

Entries 139–142 are from a 63-page pamphlet, *Lincoln's Anecdotes*, published in New York by the American News Company and claiming to embrace "all the authentic anecdotes and stories."

139.   Here is a little story told by General [C. B.] Fisk that Mr. Lincoln relished very much, and often repeated. The General had begun his military life as a colonel; and, when he raised his regiment in Wisconsin, he proposed to his men that he should do all the swearing of the regiment. They assented; and for months no instance was known of the violation of the promise. The Colonel had a teamster named John Todd, who, as the roads were not always the best, had some difficulty in commanding his temper and his tongue. John happened to be driving a mule-team through a series of mud-pools a little worse than usual, when, unable to restrain himself any longer, he burst forth in a volley of energetic oaths. The Colonel took notice of the offense, and brought John to an account. "John," said he, "didn't you promise to let me do all the swearing of the regiment?" "Yes, I did, Colonel," he replied, "but the fact was the swearing had to be done then, or not at all, and you weren't there to do it." (Page 30)

140.   [AL is said to have told how Edward Moran, the White House doorkeeper] went with [Millard] Fillmore to look at a carriage which the necessities of some Southern magnate had thrown upon the market.

"Well, Edward," said the President [Fillmore], "and how will it do for the President of the United States to buy a second-hand carriage?"

"And sure, yer Excellency, and ye're only a second-hand President, ye know!" (Page 41)

> In *Harper's Monthly*, 5 (October 1852), 710, the story, not connected with AL, is told about ex-President John Tyler and his Hibernian coachman.

141.   [When General R. C. Schenck had trouble recruiting Blacks in Maryland because he could not distinguish free from runaway recruits, he appealed to AL for instructions and was told to use his "best judgment":] "You see, Schenck," continued Mr. Lincoln, "we are like an old acquaintance of mine who settled on a piece of '*galled*' prairie. It was a terrible rough place to clear up; but after a while he got a few things growing— here and there a patch of corn, a few hills of beans, and so on. One day a stranger stopped to look at his place, and wanted to know how he managed to cultivate so rough a spot. 'Well,' was the reply, 'some of it *is* pretty rough. The smaller stumps I can generally root out or burn out; but now and then there is an old settler that bothers me, and there is no other way but to plough around it.' "Now, Schenck," Mr. Lincoln concluded, "at such a time as this, troublesome cases are constantly coming up, and the only way to get along at all is to plough around them." (Pages 48–49)

> Smith D. Fry, *Lincoln and Lee* (1922), p. 110, quotes Senator James Harlan telling a more dramatic version AL gave in reply to a query about the "Mormon question." Harlan's version concludes the dialogue between farmer and wife: "Mother, I've got that big black-gum log question off of my mind at last. It's all settled. It won't worry us any more."
>
> "Lan's sake, Josiah," exclaimed the old deaconess, "how on airth have you got it done for?"
>
> " 'Tain't done for, Cynthy," he replied. "It's jest settled, once and fer all. We must do jest what we been a'doin' all the time; and that's the only thing to do. We've jest got to plow around the derned old thing."
>
> An unusual variant by William McNeely in Osborne H. Oldroyd,

Lincoln Memorial (1882), p. 396, has AL riddling the audience during the Douglas debates: "He said: There were large poplar trees in Kentucky, and he knew a man who had a very large one, and nothing near to pile upon it, so as to burn it, and it was so large that it could not be hauled away; and he then asked if any one could tell what they did about it? No one answering, he told them: 'They went around it.' 'Just so,' said Mr. Lincoln, 'Mr. Douglas will have to do with his Kansas-Nebraska bill, just go around it.' "

142.   The day after the issue of the Emancipation Proclamation Senator [B. F.] Wade called upon the President to congratulate him. He was met by Mr. Lincoln, asking if he remembered the fable illustration of "the attempt to wash the blackamoor *white*," and the result— the death of the *black*. "And," continued Mr. Lincoln, "I fear in this case that between the North and the South the chances are that the poor *negro* will get *scrubbed* to *death*." (Page 50)

> In *Aesop's Fables*, tr. Thomas James (1848), pp. 183–184, the blackamoor "all but died from the cold he caught."

143.   [In a newspaper article, F. B. Carpenter telling how Hugh McCulloch, then Comptroller of Currency, brought a deputation of bankers to visit:] Mr. Lincoln was writing at his desk by the window of his office as the party entered. Mr. McCulloch went to him, and, leaning over the desk, said: "Mr. President, I wish to introduce to you a number of financial gentlemen who have come to Washington to see about the new loan. As bankers, they are obliged to hold our national securities, and I can therefore vouch for their loyalty; for you know how the good book says, 'Where the *treasure* is, there will the *heart* be also!' "

Mr. Lincoln, without looking up, instantly replied, "There is another version of that, Mr. McCulloch. The same book says 'Where the *carcass* is, there will the *eagles* be gathered together.' "

> Unidentified clipping in Huntington Library scrapbook number 15, p. 60. Allusions elsewhere in the article put the date shortly after 28 September 1867. A similar story in a letter by the Rev. A. H. Goodpasture to William Herndon, 31 March 1869 (Herndon-Weik papers, Library of Congress microfilm 9: 1520–1521), speaks of AL's visit to Petersburg in 1846: "There was quite a croud with Mr. Lincoln, all in good glee, and as I was passing them, I thought I would say something, and remarked that Where

the great ones are there will the people be. Mr. Lincoln replyed
Ho! *Parson,* a little more Scriptural; Where the carces is there will
the eagles be gathered together!"

1868

144.   [In "The Editor's Drawer," *Harper's Monthly* (March 1868),
a petitioner recalls asking AL to handle his case personally rather than
have a nameless, impatient Secretary handle it:] "Perhaps," said Mr.
Lincoln, "there is that difference between the Secretary and myself;
and it recalls a story told to me by [Lorenzo] Sweat, of Maine: A man
in his neighborhood had a small bull-terrier that could whip all the
dogs of the neighborhood. The owner of a large dog which the terrier
had whipped asked the owner of the terrier how it happened that the
terrier whipped every dog he encountered? 'That,' said the owner of
the terrier, 'is no mystery to me; your dog and other dogs get half
through a fight before they are ready; now, *my dog is always mad!*' "

Volume 36, pp. 537.

145.   On another occasion the same gentleman solicited Mr.
Lincoln to release a number of men, women, and children who had
been arrested by order of General [David] Hunter. After listening to
the statement the President said, "Did you ever read a book called
'Flush Times in Alabama?' " "No, Sir," was the reply. "Well, you ought
to for there is a case in it which just fits this: An old Judge had a
propensity for fining offenders, no matter what the offense. On one
occasion the regular term of court was not long enough to close all the
cases and enable the Judge to order fines, so he held an adjourned
term for that purpose, and while intently occupied in that agreeable
duty the stove-pipe fell; whereupon the Judge, enraged at the inter-
ruption, without stopping to learn the cause, called out, 'Sheriff, arrest
every one in the room! Mr. Clerk, enter a fine against every one of
them!' Then, looking through his spectacles and seeing the crowd, his
Honor said, 'Stop, Mr. Clerk; enter a fine against every one in the
room, women and children alone excepted.' "

Ibid., pp. 537–538. In Joseph G. Baldwin, *Flush Times of Alabama
and Mississippi* (1853), p. 168, the judge says: "Clerk, consider the
whole court house fined— women and children half price."

1876

146.   [Referring to the Trent affair of 1861:] To those who represented to him the danger which would be incurred in allowing the

public to become exasperated, and the impossibility for America to support at once a civil war and a foreign war [with Great Britain], he replied with one of those anecdotes he excelled in telling. "My father," he said, "had a neighbor from whom he was only separated by a fence. On each side of that fence there were two savage dogs, who kept running backward and forward along the barrier all day, barking and snapping at each other. One day they came to a large opening recently made in the fence. Perhaps you think they took advantage of this to devour each other? Not at all; scarcely had they seen the gap, when they both ran back, each on his own side, with their tails between their legs. These two dogs are fair representatives of America and England."

[Louis d'Orleans,] Comte de Paris, *History of the Civil War in America* (1876), 1:470–471.

147.   [During summer 1862 a delegation complained about the conduct of the war in the West:] He rose from his chair and said, "Judge List, this reminds me of an anecdote which I heard a son of yours tell in Burlington in Iowa. He was trying to enforce upon his hearers the truth of the old adage that three moves is worse than a fire. As an illustration he gave an account of a family who started from Western Pennsylvania, pretty well off in this world's goods when they started. But they moved and moved, having less and less every time they moved, till after a while they could carry every thing in one wagon. He said that the chickens of the family got so used to being moved, that whenever they saw the wagon sheets brought out they laid themselves on their backs and crossed their legs, ready to be tied. Now, gentlemen, if I were to listen to every committee that comes in at that door, I had just as well cross my hands and let you tie me."

Joshua Fry Speed, *Reminiscences of AL* (1884), p. 30, from a lecture in 1876 or 1877.

148.   [Replying to W. C. Reeves, of Virginia, who advised surrendering the forts and property in the Southern States:] Mr. Lincoln asked him if he remembered the fable of the Lion and the Woodsman's Daughter. Mr. Reeves said that he did not. Aesop, said the President, reports that a lion was very much in love with a woodsman's daughter. The fair maid, afraid to say no, referred him to her father. The lion applied for the girl. The father replied, your teeth are too long. The lion went to a dentist and had them extracted. Returning, he asked for his bride. No, said the woodsman, your claws are too long. Going

back to the dentist, he had them drawn. Then, returning to claim his bride, the woodsman, seeing that he was disarmed, beat out his brains. "May it not be so," said Mr. Lincoln, "with me, if I give up all that is asked."

> Ibid., pp. 31–32. In Thomas James, tr., *Aesop's Fables* (1848), pp. 63–64, the woodsman merely drives "the unreasonable suitor from his door."

1878

Entries 149–155 are from Noah Brooks, "Personal Reminiscences of Lincoln," *Scribner's Monthly Magazine* for February and March 1878, volume 15. Correspondent for the Sacramento *Union*, Brooks had known AL since 1856 and in Washington became one of his closest friends.

149.   He told, with evident enjoyment, a story of Orpheus C. Kerr's, in which a dying sailor was represented as asking the attendants in a hospital that his aged grandmother might be brought to him. The point in the story was that a messenger was sent to the navy department to implore Secretary Welles to personate the grandmother for this occasion only, and that he declined with regret, giving as his excuse that he was very busy examining a model of Noah's ark, with a view to its introduction into the United States Navy. Having told this anecdote, Lincoln turned to me and said, "I hope Mr. Welles will never hear that I told this story on him." Somewhat nettled by his manner, I said, good-humoredly, "It will not be your fault, Mr. President, if he does not hear of it, for I have heard you tell it at least a dozen times." (Page 564)

> In R. H. Newell, *Orpheus C. Kerr Papers*, 1st ser. (1866), p. 285, a member of "the Pennsylvania Mud-larks" suffering a cold in the head is visited by a surgeon who wants to amputate his left leg; it is then that the patient asks to send for his grandmother. Kerr visits the Secretary, "but the latter was so busy examining a model of Noah's Ark that he could not be seen." AL must have expanded the story from this hint.

150.   Lincoln particularly liked a joke at the expense of the dignity of some high civil or military official. One day, not long before his second inauguration, he asked me if I had heard about Stanton's meeting a picket on Broad River, South Carolina, and then told this

story: "Gen. [J. G.] Foster, then at Port Royal, escorted the secretary up the river, taking a quartermaster's tug. Reaching the outer lines on the river, a picket roared from the bank, 'Who have you got on board that tug?' The severe and dignified answer was, 'The secretary of war and Major-General Foster.' Instantly the picket roared back, 'We've got major-generals enough up here— why don't you bring us up some hard-tack?' " (Page 564)

151.   He used to say that the grim grotesqueness and extravagance of American humor were its most striking characteristics. There was a story of a soldier in the army of the Potomac, carried to the rear of battle with both legs shot off, who, seeing a pie-woman hovering about, asked, "Say, old lady, are them pies sewed or pegged?" (Page 564)

152.   And there was another one of a soldier at the battle of Chancellorsville, whose regiment, waiting to be called into the fight, was taking coffee. The hero of the story put to his lips a crockery mug which he had carried, with infinite care, through several campaigns. A stray bullet, just missing the coffee-drinker's head, dashed the mug into fragments and left only its handle on his finger. Turning his head in that direction, the soldier angrily growled, "Johnny, you can't do that again!" (Page 564)

> This seems a switch of the old jestbook favorite about a soldier in a similar spot, with the punchline: "Zounds! the drink's all spilt" (P. M. Zall, *Nest of Ninnies* [1970], pp. 173–174). But it may also be combined with the story reported by Frank Moorè, *Anecdotes, Poetry & Incidents of the War* (1866), p. 48, concerning the soldier "about to bite a cartridge, when a musket-ball struck the cartridge from his fingers" who "cooly facing the direction from which the shot came . . . took out another cartridge, and exclaimed: 'You can't do that again, old fellow.' "

153.   [On the day of his reelection,] Lincoln was as bright and cheery as the beautiful November day. He had a new story of Tad's wit and humor; for the lad was very clever. Tad had burst into his father's office, early in the day, with the information that the detachment of Pennsylvania troops, quartered on the White House grounds, on the Potomac front, "were voting for Lincoln and Johnson." The excited lad insisted on his father's going to the window to see this spectacle. Seeing a pet turkey which had been spared from the cook's knife, at Christmas, in answer to Tad's tearful petition, Lincoln said,

"What business had the turkey stalking about the polls in that way? Does he vote?"

"No," was the quick reply of the boy, "he's not of age." (Page 677)

154.   He never forgot a good story, and his apt application of those which lay in his mind gave them peculiar crispness and freshness. Here is a case in point: In 1863, a certain captain of volunteers was on trial in Washington for a misuse of the funds of his company. The accused officer made only a feeble defense and seemed to treat the matter with indifference. After a while, however, a new charge— that of disloyalty to the government— came into the case. The accused was at once excited to a high degree of indignation and made a very vigorous defense. He appeared to think lightly of being convicted of embezzling, but to be called a traitor was more than he could bear. At the breakfast table, one morning, the President, who had been reading an account of this case in the newspaper, began to laugh and said, "This fellow reminds me of a juror in a case of hen stealing which I tried in Illinois, many years ago. [Note by Brooks: The writer is not certain, now, whether Mr. Lincoln told this story out of his own experience, or at second hand. The application, of course, was his own.] The accused man was summarily convicted. After adjournment of court, as I was riding to the next town, one of the jurors in the case came cantering up behind me and complimented me on the vigor with which I had pressed the prosecution of the unfortunate hen-thief. Then he added, 'Why, when I was young, and my back was strong, and the country was new, I didn't mind taking off a sheep now and then. But stealing hens! Oh, Jerusalem!' Now, this captain has evidently been stealing sheep, and that is as much as he can bear." (Pages 679–680)

155.   [A correspondent's recollection of AL's speech at Dixon, Illinois about 1848 includes this story "in answer to one of the arguments made by the Democratic speaker who had addressed the Dixon people the day before":] A young gentleman in Tennessee was once traveling a country road, mounted on a fine black racing horse of great value. His casual companion was a shrewd old fellow, who was known in those parts as a Yankee, and rode a rack-o'-bones of a horse, apparently hardly able to stand on his feet. The Yankee bantered the Southerner for a horse trade, which of course the Southerner indignantly declined. The Yankee however insisted that his was a very

remarkable horse, of what was known as the setter breed, which sets
for big game as a dog sets for small game, and that as animals of this
breed are very scarce, his horse was accordingly valuable. The Yankee
soon had an opportunity to demonstrate the truth of his statement,
as his horse had the peculiarity of dropping on all-fours when touched
in a certain spot by the spur or heel of the rider. The Yankee seeing
a deer on a knoll not far away, touched his raw-bones in the tender
spot, and, sure enough, down he went on all-fours, assuring the
Southerner that there was game ahead. The would-be horse-trader
told the Southerner that there must be game nearby, for his horse
never "set" in that way except when on the scent of game. Immediately
after, the deer made its appearance to the Southerner, who succeeded
in bringing him down, and so much pleased was he with the wonderful
instinct of the horse that he immediately swapped with the Yankee,
on even terms. Soon after they came to a stream which the Yankee,
mounted on the Southerner's fine horse, crossed in good style; then
standing on the opposite bank, he looked back after his companion.
The "setter horse" had sunk, his head being hardly above water; his
rider was dismounted and nearly drowned. Reaching the bank and
blowing the water from his mouth, he exclaimed: "Here, you infernal
Yankee! what kind of a horse is this to drop on his knees in the middle
of a stream?" "Hush! hush!" replied the Yankee, "keep perfectly quiet.
That's a setter horse; he sets for fish as well as for deer, and I tell you
there's game there!" (Pages 884–885)

156.   [Egbert Viele, military governor of Norfolk during 1862–
1863, recollecting a conversation with AL and Secretary of War
Stanton after the latter received a wire asking for urgent instructions
and, though he did not understand the request, replied, "All right; go
ahead"—then told AL what he had done:] "I suppose you meant,"
said Mr. Lincoln, "that it was all right if it was good for him, and all
wrong if it was not. That reminds me," said he, "of a story about a
horse that was sold at the cross-roads near where I once lived. The
horse was supposed to be fast, and quite a number of people were
present at the time appointed for the sale. A small boy was employed
to ride the horse backward and forward to exhibit his points. One of
the would-be buyers followed the boy down the road and asked him
confidentially if the horse had a splint. 'Well, mister,' said the boy, 'if
it's good for him he has got it, but if it isn't good for him he hasn't.' "

"A Trip with Lincoln, Chase, and Stanton," *Scribner's Monthly,*
16 (October 1878), 814.

1881

157.   [A British official, visiting in late summer 1864:] After a pleasant interview, the Governor alluding to the approaching presidential election, said, jokingly, but with a grain of sarcasm, "I understand, Mr. President, everybody votes in this country. If we remain until November can we vote?"

"You remind me," replied the President, "of a countryman of yours, a green emigrant from Ireland. Pat arrived in New York on election day, and was, perhaps, as eager as Your Excellency, to vote, and to vote early and late and often. So, upon his landing at Castle Garden, he hastened to the nearest voting place, and, as he approached, the judge, who received the ballots, inquired, 'who do you want to vote for? on which side are you?' Poor Pat was embarrassed, he did not know who were the candidates. He stopped, scratched his head, then, with the readiness of his countrymen, he said:

'I am fornent the Government, anyhow. Tell me, if your Honor plases, which is the rebellion side, and I'll tell you how I want to vote. In Ould Ireland, I was always on the rebellion side, and, by Saint Patrick, I'll stick to that same in America.' "

> Isaac N. Arnold, *Abraham Lincoln: a Paper read before the Royal Historical Society* (1881), p. 190. This old jestbook favorite appears in the *American Jest Book* (1833), p. 14, about an Irish immigrant to Delaware who swore that he always voted against the government, "and that he was proud to say that all his generation had done the same, since the time of the flood."

158.   [The *Daily Illinois State Register*, 29 April 1881, reprints from the Reading (Pa.) *News* a story about what happened when a committee from the Y.M.C.A. protested the appointment of the Rev. James Shrigley as a hospital chaplain during the war:] After Mr. Shrigley's name had been mentioned the President said: "Oh, yes, I have sent it to the Senate. His testimonials are highly satisfactory, and the appointment will, no doubt, be confirmed at an early day."

The young men replied: "But, sir, we have come not to ask the appointment, but to solicit you to withdraw the nomination, on the ground that Mr. Shrigley is not evangelical in his sentiments." "Ah!" said the President, "that alters the case. On what point of doctrine is the gentleman unsound?" "He does not believe in endless punishment," was the reply. "Yes," added another of the committee, "he believes that even the rebels themselves will finally be saved, and it will never do to have a man with such views a hospital Chaplain."

The President hesitated to reply for a moment, and then responded with an emphasis they will long remember: "If that be so, gentlemen, and there be any way under heaven whereby the rebels can be saved, then for God's sake let the man be appointed!"

He was appointed.

> WIlliam E. Barton, *The Soul of Abraham Lincoln* (1920), pp. 356–357. Shrigley's own report closely paralleling this one is in Osborn H. Oldroyd, *Lincoln Memorial: Album Immortelles* (1882), pp. 336-337.

1882

Entries 159–162 are from Osborne H. Oldroyd, *Lincoln Memorial: Album Immortelles* (1882) which intermixed extracts from AL's writings with eulogies and reminiscences.

159. [George W. Minier, recollecting how AL once spoke on the tariff:] "A revenue we must have. In order to keep house, we must have breakfast, dinner and supper; and this tariff business seems to be necessary to bring them. But yet, there is something obscure about it. It reminds me of the fellow that came into a grocery down here in Menard County, at Salem, where I once lived, and called for a picayune's worth of crackers; so the clerk laid them out on the counter. After sitting awhile, he said to the clerk, 'I don't want these crackers, take them, and give me a glass of cider.' So the clerk put the crackers back into the box, and handed the fellow the cider. After drinking, he started for the door. 'Here, Bill,' called out the clerk, 'pay me for your cider.' 'Why,' said Bill, 'I gave you the crackers for it.' 'Well, then, pay me for the crackers.' 'But I hain't had any;' responded Bill. 'That's so,' said the clerk. 'Well, clear out! It seems to me that I've lost a picayune somehow, but I can't make it out exactly.' So," said Lincoln, after the laugh had subsided, "it is with the tariff; somebody gets the picayune, but I don't exactly understand how." (Pages 189–190)

> John J. McGilvra says AL told the same story in a different context during 1863-64 (rpt. Ivan Doig, "The Genial White House Host and Raconteur," *Illinois State Historical Journal*, 62 [1969], 311). Common in mid-seventeenth century England (*Merry Passages and Jeasts*, ed. H. F. Lippincott [1974], p. 83), it had been in Seba Smith, "My First Visit to Portland" (1843), rpt. W. S. Burton, *Cyclopaedia of Wit and Humor* (1858), 1:231-232. *Harper's Monthly*, 5 (August 1852), 419, told it about a Dutch justice of the peace

who kept a tavern in the Mohawk Valley, but Minier's version is closer to Seba Smith's.

160.   [James E. Murdoch recalling an incident told to him "by one who stood at the President's side at the time" it occurred:] One day, a detachment of troops was marching along the avenue singing the soul-stirring strain of "John Brown." They were walled in on either side by throngs of citizens and strangers, whose voices mingled in the roll of the mighty war-song. In the midst of this exciting scene, a man had clambered into a small tree, on the side-walk, where he clung, unmindful of the jeers of the passing crowd, called forth by the strange antics he was unconsciously exhibiting in his efforts to overcome the swaying motion of the slight stem which bent beneath his weight. Mr. Lincoln's attention was attracted for a moment, and he paused in the serious conversation in which he was deeply interested and in an abstracted manner, yet with a droll cast of the eye, and a nod of the head in the direction of the man, he repeated, in his dry and peculiar utterance, the old-fashioned couplet [from the *New England Primer*]:

> "And Zaccheous he, did climb a tree,
> His Lord and Master, for to see—" (Pages 349–350)

161.   [Congressman Glenni Scofield telling how he had sought a pardon for a private convicted of knocking down his captain, but AL declined to interfere, suggesting that Congress could handle it:] I inquired what Congress could do in the matter, and quick as thought he said: "Pass a law that a private shall have a right to knock down his captain." But after the wit came the pardon. (Page 369)

162.   [Alexander Rice recalling how he petitioned him to pardon a country boy sentenced for robbing his Boston employer:] The President put on his spectacles and stretched himself at length upon his arm-chair while he deliberately read the document, and then he turned to me and asked if I met a man going down the stairs as I came up. I said that I did. "Yes," said the President; "he was the last person in this room before you came, and his errand was to get a man pardoned out of the penitentiary; and now you have come to get a boy out of jail!" Then, with one of those bursts of humor which were both contagious and irresistible, he said: "I'll tell you what it is, we must abolish those courts, or they will be the death of us. I thought it bad enough that they put so many men in the penitentiaries for me to get out; but

if they have now begun on the boys and the jails, and have roped you into the delivery, let's after them! And they deserve the worst fate," he soon continued, "because, according to the evidence that comes to me, they pick out the very best men and send them to the penitentiary; and this present petition shows they are playing the same game on the good boys, and sending them all to jail." (Pages 383–384)

> Since no federal violation was involved, AL would have had no power to pardon the boy, and thus the occasion is most unlikely.

1883

163.   [Discussing a politician from Maryland:] "Maryland must, I think, be like New Hampshire, a good State to move from." And then he told a story of a witness in a neighboring county, who, on being asked his age, replied, "Sixty." Being satisfied that he was much older, the judge repeated the question, and on receiving the same answer, admonished the witness, saying that the court knew him to be much older than sixty. "Oh," said the witness, "you're thinking about that fifteen year that I lived down on the eastern shore of Maryland; that was so much lost time and don't count."

> *Autobiography of Thurlow Weed*, ed. H. A. Weed (1883), p. 607.

164.   [After Weed quips that his appetite for sausage depends on whether pork was cheaper than dogs:] "That," said Mr. Lincoln, "reminds me of what occurred down at Joliet, where a popular grocer supplied all the villagers with sausages. One Saturday evening, when his grocery was filled with customers, for whom he and his boys were busily engaged in weighing sausages, a neighbor, with whom he had had a violent quarrel that day, came into the grocery, made his way up to the counter, holding two enormous dead cats by the tail, which he deliberately threw on the counter, saying, "This makes seven to-day. I'll call round on Monday and get my money for them."

> Ibid., p. 612.

1886

Entries 165–174 are from Allen Thorndike Rice, *Reminiscences of AL by Distinguished Men of His Time* (1886), compiled during 1885 by the distinguished editor of the *North American Review*.

165.   [F. D. Grant submits a number of anecdotes U. S. Grant had omitted from his autobiography:] Just after receiving my commission as lieutenant-general [9 March 1864], the President called me aside to speak to me privately. After a brief reference to the military situation, he said he thought he could illustrate what he wanted to say by a story, which he related as follows: "At one time there was a great war among the animals, and one side had great difficulty in getting a commander who had sufficient confidence in himself. Finally, they found a monkey, by the name of Jocko, who said that he thought he could command their army if his tail could be made a little longer. So they got more tail and spliced it on to his caudal appendage. He looked at it admiringly, and then thought he ought to have a little more still. This was added, and again he called for more. The splicing process was repeated many times, until they had coiled Jocko's tail around the room, filling all the space. Still he called for more tail, and, there being no other place to coil it, they began wrapping it around his shoulders. He continued his call for more, and they kept on winding the additional tail about him until its weight broke him down." (Pages 1–2)

> The story is in R. H. Newell's collection of his serious verse—"A Fable for Strategists" in Orpheus C. Kerr, *The Palace Beautiful & Other Poems* (1865), pp. 130–140. Gideon Welles's diary for 17 June 1863 (1:333) says AL spoke of this poem as describing McClellan calling for more troops. In the present instance Grant realized what AL meant and reassured him that he would not call for more troops. In retelling the story, AL omits the role played by Jupiter in humoring the monkey and, in the end, rescuing him.

166.   Upon one occasion, when the President was at my [U. S. Grant's] head-quarters at City Point [22 June 1864], I took him to see the work that had been done on the Dutch Gap Canal. After taking him around and showing him all the points of interest, explaining how, in blowing up one portion of the work that was being excavated, the explosion had thrown the material back into, and filled up, a part already completed, he turned to me and said: "Grant, do you know what this reminds me of? Out in Springfield, Illinois, there was a black-smith named ———. One day, when he did not have much to do, he took a piece of soft iron that had been in his shop for some time, and for which he had no special use, and, starting up his fire, began to heat it. When he got it hot he carried it to the anvil and began to hammer it, rather thinking he would weld it into an agricultural implement. He

pounded away for some time until he got it fashioned into some shape, when he discovered that the iron would not hold out to complete the implement he had in mind. He then put it back into the forge, heated it up again, and recommenced hammering, with an ill-defined notion that he would make a claw hammer, but after a time he came to the conclusion that there was more iron than was needed to form a hammer. Again he heated it, and thought he would make an axe. After hammering and welding it into shape, knocking the oxydized iron off in flakes, he concluded there was not enough of the iron left to make an axe that would be of any use. He was now getting tired and a little disgusted at the result of his various essays. So he filled his forge full of coal, and, after placing the iron in the center of the heap, took the bellows and worked up a tremendous blast, bringing the iron to a white heat. Then with his tongs he lifted it from the bed of coals, and thrusting it into a tub of water near by, exclaimed with an oath, 'Well, if I can't make anything else of you, I will make a fizzle, anyhow.' " (Pages 2–4)

167.   [Lawrence Weldon, a friend from circuit-riding days, recalls his saying:] "Do you remember a story that Bob [Lewis] used to tell us about his going to Missouri to look up some Mormon lands that belong to his father?" I said: "Mr. President, I have forgotten the details of that story, and I wish you would tell it." He then said that when Robert became of age he found among the papers of his father's a number of warrants and patents for lands in North-east Missouri, and he concluded the best thing he could do was to go to Missouri and investigate the condition of things. It being before the days of the railroads, he started on horseback with a pair of old-fashioned saddle-bags. When he arrived where he supposed his land was situated, he stopped, hitched his horse, and went into a cabin standing close by the roadside. He found the proprietor, a lean, lanky, leathery-looking man, engaged in the pioneer business of making bullets preparatory to a hunt. Mr. Lewis observed, on entering, a rifle suspended on a couple of buck horns above the fire. He said to the man: "I am looking up some lands that I think belong to my father," and inquired of the man in what section he lived. Without having ascertained the section, Mr. Lewis proceeded to exhibit his title papers in evidence, and having established a good title as he thought, said to the man: "Now, that is my title, what is yours?" The pioneer, who had by this time become somewhat interested in the proceeding, pointed his long finger toward the rifle, and said: "Young man, do you see that gun?" Mr. Lewis

frankly admitted that he did. "Well," said he, "that is my title, and if you don't get out of here pretty damned quick you will feel the force of it." Mr. Lewis hurriedly put his title papers in his saddle-bags, mounted his pony, and galloped down the road, and, as Bob says, the old pioneer snapped his gun twice at him before he could turn the corner. Lewis said that he had never been back to disturb that man's title since. "Now," said Mr. Lincoln, "the military authorities have the same title against the civil authorities that closed out Bob's Mormon title in Missouri." (Pages 211–213)

168.   [Benjamin Perley Poore, Washington correspondent for Boston newspapers and clerk of Senate printing records:] I remember his narrating his first experience in drilling his company. He was marching with a front of over twenty men across a field, when he desired to pass through a gateway into the next inclosure.

"I could not for the life of me," said he, "remember the proper word of command for getting my company endwise so that it could get through the gate, so as we came near the gate I shouted: 'This company is dismissed for two minutes, when it will fall in again on the other side of the gate!'" (Pages 218–219)

> This is suspect because the same story, not connected with AL, was popular in the spring of 1860. In Leslie's Illustrated News-paper, 9 (26 May 1860), 412, it was about "a country captain"; in Harper's Weekly, 4 (28 July 1860), 478, it was about "a Volunteer Rifle captain."

169.   [Titian J. Coffey, assistant attorney general in 1863, recalling the response when he told the President that U.S. marshals preferred to tap a legal defense fund rather than seek aid from district attorneys:] "Yes," said he, "they will now all be after the money and be content with nothing else. They are like the man in Illinois, whose cabin was burned down, and according to the kindly custom of early days in the West, his neighbors all contributed something to start him again. In his case they had been so liberal that he soon found himself better off than before the fire, and he got proud. One day, a neighbor brought him a bag of oats, but the fellow refused it with scorn. 'No,' said he, 'I'm not taking oats now. I take nothing but money.'" (Page 239)

170.   [Coffey continues:] A friend of mine was one of a delegation who called on Mr. Lincoln to ask the appointment of a gentleman

as Commissioner to the Sandwich Islands. They presented their case as earnestly as possible, and, besides his fitness for the place, they urged that he was in bad health, and a residence in that balmy climate would be of great benefit to him. The President closed the interview with this discouraging remark:

"Gentlemen, I am sorry to say that there are eight other applicants for that place, and they are all sicker than your man." (Pages 239–240)

171.   [Cassius M. Clay, Kentucky anti-slavery editor and AL's ambassador to Russia, recalls:] I was one day with Lincoln, when a report came that one of our unionists was caught in Virginia by the rebels and condemned to death, the choice being left him to be hung or shot. I saw a trace of humor pass over his sad face when he said he was reminded of a camp-meeting of colored Methodists in his earlier days. There was a brother who responded often to the preacher with "Amen," "Bless the Lord," etc. The preacher drew a strong line, sweeping the sinners on both sides into the devil's net: "All those who thus sin are in the downward *path* to ruin, and all those who so act, including about the whole human race, are on the sure *road* to hell." The unctuous brother, bewildered, cried out: "Bless the Lord, this nigger takes to the woods!" (Pages 305–306)

> Gideon Welles's diary, 2 February 1864 (1:519–520), says AL told this in more dramatic fashion when Secretary Seward faced the problem of winning Spain's friendship while supporting a Black revolt in San Domingo. Welles's rough draft is in *The Collector*, 66 (February 1953), 1–2.

172.   [James B. Fry recalls how, as provost marshal-general, he was assigned to go with him to Gettysburg:] At the appointed time I went to the White House, where I found the President's carriage at the door to take him to the station; but he was not ready. When he appeared it was rather late, and I remarked that he had no time to lose in going to the train. "Well," said he, "I feel about that as the convict in one of our Illinois towns felt when he was going to the gallows. As he passed along the road in custody of the sheriff, the people, eager to see the execution, kept crowding and pushing past him. At last he called out: 'Boys, you needn't be in such a hurry to get ahead, *there won't be any fun till I get there.*'" (Page 403)

> In the London jestbook, *Court Jester*, of about 1790, pp. 122–123, that story is told about a thief going to the gallows who says:

"There will be no sport till I come"; and the same joke appears in Hans C. Andersen's tale, "The Tinder Box" (tr. 1846) [*Classic Fairy Tales*, ed. I. and P. Opie (1974), p. 214].

173.   [David R. Locke, who wrote as Petroleum V. Nasby, recalling a conversation about 1858:] In this interview the name came up of a recently deceased politician of Illinois, whose undeniable merit was blemished by an overweening vanity. His funeral was very largely attended: "If General ——— had known how big a funeral he would have had," said Mr. Lincoln, "he would have died years ago." (Page 442)

174.   [E. W. Andrews, the assistant adjutant-general, had to accompany AL to Gettysburg in place of a general suffering boils:] After cordially greeting us and directing us to make ourselves comfortable, the President, with quizzical expression, turned to Montgomery Blair (then Postmaster-General), and said:

"Blair, did you ever know that fright has sometimes proved a sure cure for boils?"

"No, Mr. President. How is that?"

"I'll tell you. Not long ago, when Colonel ———, with his cavalry, was at the front, and the Rebs were making things rather lively for us, the colonel was ordered out on a *reconnaissance*. He was troubled at the time with a big boil where it made horseback riding decidedly uncomfortable. He hadn't gone more than two or three miles when he declared he couldn't stand it any longer, and dismounted and ordered the troops forward without him. He had just settled down to enjoy his relief from change of position when he was startled by the rapid reports of pistols and the helter-skelter approach of his troops in full retreat before a yelling rebel force. He forgot everything but the yells, sprang into his saddle, and made capital time over fences and ditches till safe within the lines. The pain from his boil was gone, and the boil too, and the colonel swore that there was no cure for boils so sure as fright from rebel yells, and that the secession had rendered to loyalty *one* valuable service at any rate." (Page 509)

     Entries 175–178 are from the typescript of Ward Hill Lamon's *Administration of Lincoln* (1886) now in the Huntington Library, LN2418, along with Lamon's notes for the book. Oddly, the manuscript corrections and the notes suggest that his anecdotes were drawn from printed sources rather than his memory, although he had been AL's law

partner and through the war served as his bodyguard. Of some twenty anecdotes, only these four seem Lamon's alone.

175.   [In conversation, Lamon says:] "Some of our friends are opposed to an accommodation because the South began the trouble and was entirely responsible for the consequences, be they what they may." "This," said [AL], "reminds me of a story told out in Illinois where I lived. There was a vicious bull in a pasture and a neighbor passing through the field, the animal took after him. He ran to a tree and got there in time to save himself and being able to run around the tree faster than the bull he managed to seize him by the tail. His bull-ship seeing himself at a disadvantage, pawed the earth and scattered gravel for awhile; then broke into a full run, bellowing at every jump. The man holding on to his tail cussing him, and asking the question— 'D——n you, who commenced this fuss?' Now, our plain duty is to settle the fuss we have before us, without reference to who commenced it." (Pages 127–128)

176.   Some time in the early part of the war a clergyman said in his presence that he "hoped the Lord was on our side." "I am not at all concerned about that," replied Mr. Lincoln. "For I know that the Lord is always on the side of the right, but it is my constant anxiety and prayer that I and this nation should be on the Lord's side." (Page 444)

177.   [A lady had come from Alexandria demanding that a church that had been converted to a hospital be reconverted.] After-wards in speaking of this incident Mr. Lincoln said that the lady as a representative of her class in Alexandria reminded him of the story of the young man who had an aged father and mother owning con-siderable property. The young man being an only son and believing that the old people had lived out their usefullness assassinated them both. He was accused, tried and convicted of the murder. When the judge came to pass sentence upon him and called upon him to give any reason he might have why the sentence of death should not be passed upon him, he with great promptness replied he hoped the court would be lenient upon him because he was a poor orphan. (Page 457)

178.   [Conferring with two other generals about G. B. McClellan's inertia:] He said he desired an expression of their opinion about the

matter for it was his opinion if some thing was not done and that soon, the bottom would fall out of the whole thing and he intended if General McClellan did not want to use the army to propose to borrow it from him, provided he could see how it could be made to do something, for "If McClellan can't fish, he ought to cut bait at a time like this." (Page 464)

179.   [Article in newspaper, "Evening Star," undated, telling how, about three months before his death, he asked the inventor of a breech-loading gun what he thought the Army would do with it, then added:] "Well, I guess it will be with you as it was with the Irishman and his sheep's head." Then Mr. Lincoln told a story which ran thus: An Irishman had a sheep's head and was dressing it for dinner. At a moment when he was not looking a fellow slipped around the corner and captured the prize, and the Irishman seeing him disappear with his sheep's head cried out: "Nivir moind, it will do ye no good; I have the recate for cooking it."

> Huntington Library scrapbook number 15, p. 164. The story must have been the one, unconnected with AL, in *Harper's Weekly*, 4 (7 July 1860), 419: "A man having bought a sheep's head, had been to a friend for a direction to dress it. As he was returning, repeating the method, and holding the purchase under his arm, a dog snatched it and ran away. 'Now, my dear boy,' said the man, 'what a fool you make of yourself! What use will it be to you, as you don't know how it is to be dressed?' "

180.   In 1862–63, the Rev. Dr. [Samuel B.] McPheeters, a prominent Presbyterian, was preaching at St. Louis. Major-General [Samuel R.] Curtis commanded in that military department. One Sunday Dr. McPheeters uttered some sentiments that were deemed disloyal. The next Sunday Dr. McPheeters found the doors of his church closed by order of General Curtis. There was immediate trouble, not alone in St. Louis, but in Washington. A committee composed of both factions went to see the President. . . . The President listened patiently, and then spoke about as follows:

"I can best illustrate my position in regard to your St. Louis quarrel by telling a story. A man in Illinois had a large watermelon patch, on which he hoped to make money enough to carry him over the year. A big hog broke through the log fence nearly every night, and the melons were gradually disappearing. At length the farmer told his son John to get out the guns, and they would promptly dispose of the disturber of their melon patch. They followed the tracks to the neighboring creek, where they disappeared. They discovered them on the opposite bank, and waded through. They kept on the trail a couple of hundred yards, when the tracks again went into the creek, but promptly turned up on the other side. Once more the hunters buffeted the mud and water, and again struck the lead and pushed on a few furlongs, when the tracks made another dive into the creek. Out of breath and patience, the farmer said, 'John you cross over and go up on that side of the creek, and I'll keep up on this side, for I believe the old fellow is on both sides.' Gentlemen," concluded Mr. Lincoln, "that is just where I stand in regard to your controversies in St. Louis. I am on both sides. I can't allow my Generals to run the churches, and I can't allow your ministers to preach rebellion."

> Henry B. Stanton, *Random Recollections*, 2d ed. (1886), pp. 114–115.

1887

Entries 181–185 are from Francis F. Browne, *Every-Day Life of AL* (1887).

181.   [In summing up a case argued against an eloquent young attorney, he pointedly ignored his opponent's argument and told the jury this story:] In early days there lived in this vicinity, over on the Sangamon river, an old Indian of the Kickapoo tribe, by the name of Johnnie Kongapod, who had been taken in charge by some good missionaries, converted to Christianity, and educated to such extent that he could read and write. He took a great fancy to poetry, and became somewhat of a poet himself. His desire was that after his death there should be placed at the head of his grave an epitaph, which he prepared himself, in rhyme, in the following words:

> "Here lies poor Johnnie Kongapod;
> Have mercy on him, gracious God,
> As he would do if he were God
> And you were Johnnie Kongapod." (Page 164)

182.   He and a certain Judge once got to bantering one another about trading horses; and it was agreed that the next morning at nine o'clock they should make a trade, the horse to be unseen up to that hour,— and no backing out, under a forfeit of twenty-five dollars. At

the hour appointed, the Judge came up, leading the sorriest looking specimen of a nag ever seen in those parts. In a few minutes Mr. Lincoln was seen approaching with a *wooden saw-horse* upon his shoulders. Great were the shouts and the laughter of the crowd; and these increased, when Mr. Lincoln, surveying the Judge's animal, set down his saw-horse, and exclaimed: "Well, Judge, this is the first time I ever *got the worst of it* in a horse-trade!" (Page 232)

183.   [As he was leaving Decatur where, on 10 May 1860, he was named the Illinois choice for the presidential nomination, he was asked by an old man, a Democrat:] "So you're Abe Lincoln?" "That's my name, sir," answered Mr. Lincoln. "They say you're a self-made man," said the Democrat. "Well, yes," said Mr. Lincoln, "what there is of me is self-made." "Well, all I've got to say," observed the old man after a careful survey of the statesman before him, "is, that it was a d——n bad job." (Page 329)

> In *Putnam's Magazine* for March 1903 (5:672–673), James Grant Wilson says the dialogue took place 12 February 1865.

184.   Mr. Lincoln once confessed that the Trent affair, occurring, as it did, at a very critical period of the war, had given him great uneasiness. When asked whether it was not a great trial to surrender the two captured Commissioners [Mason and Slidell], he said: "Yes, that was a pretty bitter pill to swallow, but I contented myself with believing that England's triumph in the matter would be short-lived, and that after ending our war successfully we should be so powerful that we could call England to account for all the embarrassments she had inflicted upon us. I felt a good deal like the sick man in Illinois who was told he probably hadn't many days longer to live, and he ought to make peace with any enemies he might have. He said the man he hated worst of all was a fellow named Brown, in the next village, and he guessed he had better commence on him first. So Brown was sent for, and when he came the sick man began to say, in a voice as meek as Moses', that he wanted to die at peace with all his fellow-creatures, and hoped he and Brown could now shake hands and bury all their enmity. The scene was becoming altogether too pathetic for Brown, who had to get out his handkerchief and wipe the gathering tears from his eyes. It wasn't long before he melted and gave his hand to his neighbor, and they had a regular lovefeast. After a parting that would have softened the heart of a grindstone, Brown had about reached the room door, when the sick man rose up on his

elbow and said, 'But, see here, Brown, if I *should* happen to get well, mind *that old grudge stands!*' So I thought if this nation should happen to get well, we might want that old grudge against England to stand." (Pages 459–460)

185.　　[Entering Richmond, 4 April 1865, the presidential party lands in the captain's gig instead of a more appropriate vessel:] Mr. Lincoln was cheerful, and had his "little story" ready for the occasion. "Admiral [David Porter], this brings to my mind a fellow who once came to me to ask for an appointment as minister abroad. Finding he could not get that, he came down to some more modest position. Finally he asked to be made a tide-waiter. When he saw he could not get that, he asked me for *an old pair of trousers.* It is sometimes well to be *humble.*" (Page 690)

186.　　[In the New York *Tribune*, 23 January 1887, Augustus Brandegee recalls how as a young Connecticut congressman he sought a political favor for a friend:] I was put forward to state the case, and urged it with all the arguments I could muster. Mr. Lincoln listened with a half serious, half comic expression, asked some pointed questions which showed that he took in the full inwardness of the situation, and when I had concluded, said: "You remind me of a young lawyer in Sangamon County who had hung out his shingle for a long time without having a client. At last he got one, but feeling very anxious not to lose his first case, he thought he would go down and state it to the justice who was to try it and ascertain in advance what he thought of it. So he went down one Sunday evening and stated it for all it was worth, and concluded by asking the justice how he would probably decide it. 'As you state the case,' replied the justice, 'I should be obliged to decide against you. But you had better bring the case. Probably the other side will make so much worse a showing that I shall have to decide the case in your favor.'"

> Clipping in Judd Stewart scrapbook, Huntington Library accession number 151179, 5 vols., 2:47. Emanuel Hertz, *Lincoln Talks* (1939), pp. 250–251, has a more dramatic version concluding: "'What, Squire! You don't say so?' 'Yes, I couldn't help it, as you state it, but then I don't know but the other side might help you out so I could stand by you'"— from the Norwalk (Conn.) *Gazette* undated.

187.　　[In a syndicated newspaper article, Ward Lamon relates how the public printer John D. Defrees objected to the phrase "sugar coated" in a presidential message to Congress:] "This reminds me," continued Mr. Lincoln, "of a story told about J. Fenimore Cooper, the distinguished novelist," and he proceeded, in a style of inimitable drollery, to relate the following: "While in London, some time during the reign of George IV., and while General Jackson was President of the United States, Mr. Cooper was frequently subjected to annoyance and humiliation by the ribald jests and vulgar criticisms employed by the nobility, especially in referring to what they were pleased to call 'the coarse provincialisms habitual with the American people.' Mr. Cooper was peculiarly sensitive to this kind of criticism. He was as ready to defend the people of his nationality against charges of impropriety in their speech as he was to maintain the dignity, honor, virtue and intelligence of his abused countrymen. He had suffered the taunts and jeers of *milords* until their insolence became unbearable.

"On one occasion, when Mr. Cooper was present, a young sprig of nobility was relating his experience in America. He spoke with lordly unction of the shocking want of culture, which he had observed, 'ye knaw,' among our people. He said that while in the United States, just after the election of General Jackson, he was a visitor at the Hermitage, where the President introduced him to Mrs. Jackson. That lady was suffering with a severe cold which caused her to cough incessantly. Milord tendered his sympathy, bewailed her misfortune and expressed, in the most approved style of gallantry, his hope for her speedy recovery, when she replied: 'The General *kicked the kiver* off me last night, and that's what's the matter. It won't last long.' This caused a laugh all round; in fact, it brought down the house.

"Mr. Cooper saw his opportunity. 'Gentlemen,' said he, 'there is a difference, I grant, between our republican simplicity and the forms of politeness that prevail in this kingdom. It is one of the rights inherent in our republicanism to kick the blankets off the conjugal bed. Mother Jackson may have been unfortunate in choosing a word not pleasing to your cultured ears; but you will observe, gentlemen, that it was *her own husband* who kicked the "kiver" off her. I have noticed, and you will see by reading the libel for a divorce filed by his Majesty, *your* King, against his wife, Queen Caroline, that he charges, in language not at all courtly, that the "kiver" was kicked off *his* royal wife *by some other fellow*.'

"No, John," said Mr. Lincoln, "*sugar-coated* is the proper 'kiver,' and I don't propose to have it kicked out of my message."

Clipping in Judd Stewart scrapbook, Huntington Library accession number 151179, 2:128. In his message to the special session of Congress, 4 July 1861, AL accused the South of sugarcoating rebellion by asserting states' rights as Constitutional doctrine (W, 4:433). I have not found the Cooper story elsewhere. His own book about visiting London, February-May 1828, praises the Englishman's simplicity of speech for calling "a spade a spade" in contrast to American "elegance"! (*Gleanings in Europe*, 2 vols., ed. R. E. Spiller [1930], 2:386)

188.   [While General George B. McClellan was entertaining AL, a telegram arrived describing a fierce battle but reporting minimum casualties out of proportion to its fierceness.] The President quietly listened to my reading of the telegram, and then said it reminded him of a notorious liar, who attained such a reputation as an exaggerator that he finally instructed his servant to stop him, when his tongue was running too rapidly, by pulling his coat or touching his feet. One day the master was relating wonders he had seen in Europe, and described a building which was about a mile long and a half-mile high. Just then the servant's heel came down on the narrator's toes, and he stopped abruptly. One of the listeners asked how broad this remarkable building might be; the narrator modestly replied, "About a foot!"

> George B. McClellan, *McClellan's Own Story* (1887), p. 162. In the *Family Joe Miller* (1848), p. 91, it is a friend rather than servant who interrupts; and when the company laughs, the liar says: "Zounds, if you had not trod upon my toe, I should have made it as broad as it was long."

Entries 189–201 are from the Herndon-Weik manuscripts at the Library of Congress, materials collected about 1887 for Herndon's biography of AL, written in collaboration with Jesse Weik—who subsequently collected material into the 1920s. References are to microfilm copies, with reel numbers followed by frame numbers.

189.   [Abner Y. Ellis recalling that AL's reading consisted of newspapers:] He was very fond of short storys one & two columns long, like Cousin Sally Dillard— Becky Wilson's Courtship— The down Easter & the Bull— How a bashful Young Man became a Married Man with 5 little bashful Boys, & How he and his read headed Wife became Millerites and before they wer to ascend they agreed to make a clean breast of it to each other   The old man insisted that the Wife should own up first as she had promised in her Marriage Vow to first obay her husband   Well Dear said she our little Sammy is not

your child   Well said the husband whoes is he   Oh Dear said she; he is the one eyed shoe makers ` he came to see me once when you was away and in an evil hour I gave way. Well said the husband is the rest mine   No said she they belong to the Neighbourhood

       Well said the old man I am ready to leave; *Gabarial blow your horn.*

       I have thought that Mr. L. had something to do with its getting up   he used to tell it with embellishments. I suppose you have heard him telling it. he said he never saw a Millerite but what he thought of the story. [14: 1633]

190.   [In a letter, 23 June 1887, about AL's patronage, H. C. Whitney recalls an episode:] I was in the Indian service for a few days before August [1861] and I merely said to Lincoln one day—"Everything is drifting into the war & I guess you will have to put me in the Army." He says "I'm making Generals now & in a few days I will be making Quartermasters & I'll then fix you." [10: 2154]

191.   [In his next letter, 27 August 1887, Whitney recalls life on the circuit:] He was at Urbana once prosecuting a man named A. G. Carle in Urbana for seduction & one S. H. Busey an adverse witness tried to create the impression that he was a great ladies man. Lincoln went for him in his speech thus, "There's Busey— he pretends to be a great heart smasher— does wonderful things with the girls— but I'll venture that he never entered his flesh but once & that is when he fell down & stuck his finger in his ———" right out in open Court. Things were free & easy in Urbana & Danville. [10: 2184]

192.   [Replying to Weik's request for more anecdotes, Whitney writes, 17 September 1887:] All that I ever heard him say about John A. Logan was to tell an anecdote thus: "When John was in the Legislature a Committee was raised to meet some one or body to discuss the subject of Dram Shop license; some member proposed to pass a Resolution to the effect that the Committee had no right to adopt or propose any ultra temperance policy &c; but John squelched it by saying Oh! that is needless; the noses of this Committee are an emphatic declaration of their anti temperance principles." [12: 386]

193.   [Whitney continues:] The first story I ever heard Lincoln tell was in Court. Court stopped to hear— "its like the lazy preacher who used to read very long sermons: when asked how so lazy a man

used to write such long sermons, one of his deacons said; 'Oh! he gets to writing & is too lazy to stop.' " [12:386]

> An embellished version is in Anthony Gross, *Lincoln's Own Stories* (1912), pp. 37–38: the scene is the courtroom of Judge David Davis who asks his opinion of a lengthy document submitted by a "somewhat indolent lawyer." An analogue, sometimes confused with this, is a jestbook favorite—here from *The Humorist's Own Book* (1834), p. 213—"It was well answered by Archbishop Tillotson, when King William III complained of the shortness of his sermon, 'Sire,' said the archbishop, 'could I have bestowed more time upon it, it would not have been so long.' "

194.   [Herndon tells Weik about a group of Democrats called Locofocos who claimed to be the true descendants of the Founding Fathers but who, said AL, were frauds—as in this story:] Once an old farmer in the Country heard a devil of a racket in his hen house— heard it often before, so he thought to get up and see what was the matter and kill this thing, if it was some wild animal. He got up— lit his candle and went gun in hand— to see and fight it out. On going into the hen house he looked around on the floor & in the roosts and at last found his enemy, a pole cat crouched in the corner with two or three dead chickens. The farmer seized the pole cat and dragged him out and all who know the nature of such a cat know what followed— a devil of a stink. The pole cat demurred as well as he could in his own language saying that he was no such brute as charged, but an innocent animal and a friend of the farmer just come to take care of his chickens. The farmer to this replied— "You look like a pole cat— just the size of a pole cat— act like one," snuffing up his nose "and smell like one and you are one by God, and I'll kill you, innocent & as friendly to me as you say you are." "These locofocos," said Lincoln "claim to be true democrats, but they are only locofocos— they look like locofocos— just the size of locofocos— act like locofocos— and" turning up his nose and backing away a little on the Stand as if the smell was about to smother him "are locofocos by God." [11: 2876]

> Apparently Weik was puzzled, for in a later message Herndon advised him to look up "locofoco" in the *American Cyclopedia* [11: 2918].

195.   [Herndon supplies an eyewitness report from Mrs. Norman Vannattin about how she and a younger (13-year-old) sister were bringing cows in from the prairie about 1855; the sister was skipping

backwards on the sidewalk when she tripped up:] As she was running with her head toward Lincoln, he going east and she going west— her foot caught in the pavement somehow & was about to receive a terrible fall, when Lincoln stretched out his long arms and caught her and saved her from a hard fall on the bricks. Lincoln looked down into the girl's face while he held her in his arms with one of his kind, tender, and sympathetic looks and instantly thereby assured the girl that she was safe in his great arms. The little girl looked up and smiled and thanked Lincoln for what he did. Lincoln put the girl on her feet, saying to her— "Now my little daughter you can say that you have been in Abraham's bosom." The girl laughed most heartily at Lincoln's offhand hit. [11: 2879–2880]

> When Weik published the story in the *Outlook* for 13 February 1909, p. 348, he romanticized it (e.g., "lifting her tenderly"), gave the girl a name (Mary Tuft) and an anxious mother.

196.   [Herndon sends Weik two stories:]

No. 1 A Story of Lincoln or a Story which he loved to tell.

Lincoln was a diffident man— rather shy & not self-possessed in society— especially in a promiscuous crowd of ladies & gentlemen and at a party; he admired audacity— a quick-witted man— one self-possessed & not having much cheek— Well there was a party once, not far from here, which was composed of ladies and gentlemen— a fine table was set & the people were greatly enjoying themselves. Among the crowd was one of those men who had audacity— was quick-witted— cheeky & self possessed— never off his guard on any occasion. After the men & women had enjoyed themselves by dancing— promenading— flirting &c they were told that the supper was set. The man of audacity— quick witted— self possessed & equal to all occasions was put at the head of the table to carve the turkeys— chickens & pigs. The men and women surrounded the table & the audacious man being chosen carver whetted his great carving knife with the steel and got down to business & commenced carving the turkey, but he expended too much force & let a fart— a loud fart so that all the people heard it distinctly. As a matter of course it shocked all terribly. A deep silence reigned. However the audacious man was cool & entirely self possessed; he was curiously & keenly watched by those who knew him well, they suspecting that he would recover in the end and acquit himself with glory. The man with a kind of sublime audacity, pulled off his coat, rolled up his sleeves— put his coat deliberately on a chair— spat on his hands— took his position at the head of the table— picked up the carving knife & whetted it again, never cracking a smile nor moving a muscle of his face. It now became a wonder in the minds of all the men & women how the fellow was to get out of his dilemma; he squared himself and said loudly & distinctly— "Now by God I'll see if I can't cut up this turkey without farting." [11: 2887–2888]

> Herndon adds that AL said: "I worshipped the fellow." Then he adds also: "As a matter of course no such thing ever happened and yet it is a good story to show the power of audacity" and that he heard AL tell the story "often and often."

197.   No. 2 One of Lincoln's Stories

There was a lady down in Egypt who had a good husband & some little ones upon whom the lady fondly, like a mother, doted— in fact almost worshipped. She saw nothing but manliness— beauty & smartness in one of her boys about 12 or 14 years of age. Every time any gentleman or ladies called in to see the lady she would call up the boy— pat him on the head with a kind of fond mother's blessings: she would praise him & eulogize him to the skies— would make the boy say smart things and do great things, in her eyes. As the story goes she, the mother thought that her boy was a pink of perfection & would be president of the United States & the very type of a moral, good & loving boy. The father of the boy was less foolish & more thoughtful than the mother. The boy one day got sleepy & so he thought he would retire & go to sleep in the trundle bed which rolled under the larger bed & out again as circumstances required. The boy crawled into bed & at the same time a large she cat— a pet— one of the house, went to bed with him. Soon after the boy went to bed some ladies & gentlemen called in to see the family. As was the custom & habit of the mother lady, she commenced eulogizing her fine, pretty & moral boy & at last to clinch the argument and to have the boy exhibit himself in proof of what she said she cried out— "Tommy— come out here, the ladies & gentlemen wish to see you." Tommy kept still— said nothing though he heard his mother's call. The mother said again putting in her surliest tone— "*Tommy— Tommy*, come come out here the ladies & gentlemen very much want to see you." Tommy grunted & rolled over, somewhat vexed at the calls and said sharply—

"Mother— *damn* it— let me alone till I f——k this damned old she cat and get her with kitten."

There was fainting about this time, caused by the shock. When the husband came home in the Evening this good wife & mother told her husband all that was said and done. The husband said to his wife— "I warned you that that boy would make you blush & your heart ache sometime—" [11: 2888–2889]

> Herndon adds a note: "Lincoln told this story in 62–3 to Judge Weldon & others who told it to me & I at the time wrote it out and put it in a small book which I loaned to [Ward] Lamon, but can't get it back."

198.   [Herndon sends Weik an elaborate, six-page "Law Story" AL told about a case in Coles County around 1850 when he was assigned by the court to defend a hog stealer who was clearly guilty yet refused to confide in AL, only assuring him they would win the case— as they did. Curious, AL takes him aside after the verdict and demands to know how he could be so certain:] Mr. Lincoln still insisted on knowing the facts and said— "Come let us have no fooling now"— Spoke Lincoln. The man at last said— "Well Lincoln my good fellow I'll tell you. I did steal the hogs and more of 'em than I was indicted for— many more and sold 'em to my neighbors, the jury: They knew that if I was convicted that they would have to pay for the hogs that I sold 'em, as they belonged to Mr ——— and Mr ——— and the jury knew it from the evidence. Now Lincoln do you see where the joke comes in? I knew that I would be cleared— didn't I tell you so. ["] Lincoln was astonished at the fellow & his story: he used to tell the story on circuit with great gusto and to the delight of his brother attys of the bar [11:2898.]

> Herndon adds a note: Lincoln would laugh over the story most heartily, saying— "That case beat me, badly— more than any I ever had."

199.   [In a long letter, Herndon explains his ideas about biography to Weik, then inserts this story:] Again, while we are in this line of moral rhetoric let me tell you of an other story which Lincoln used to tell about his wife. As you are aware it was hard for Mrs Lincoln to keep a girl and she could, as a general rule, only get those who could hardly get any place— generally unchaste girls. One night some one got a ladder and put it up on the north end of Lincoln's "two

story" house where there was a window which being raised let the fellow into the girl's room. Mrs Lincoln heard things rattle up stairs at a great rate. She went and got a neighbor man, a Mr ——— to go up stairs and keep the men off the girl. This, was just what the man wanted & prayed for: he went— found the ladder and was by Mrs Lincoln shown the room, and in it he went. Mrs. Lincoln seemed too terribly scared and I guess was so. Mr. Lincoln had been down to the Supreme Court rooms and was coming home at about 12 o'c. Mrs. Lincoln was up and when she heard Lincoln coming she ran out into the street with her night close only on and hastily said "Mr Lincoln— *Mr Lincoln* there has been a man here up stairs with our girl and I had to get a neighbor man to go into the girl's room and keep the man away." The fact of Mrs Lincoln getting a man & such a man as F—— was to keep off an other man from the girl— just the very opportunity which Mr ——— wanted was so utterly ridiculous to Mr Lincoln that he actually rolled on the pavement, bursting with laughter. Mr. Lincoln saw that his wife did not catch on, but seemed to be much offended at Lincoln, who to pacify his wife said— "Mary— *Mary hush*— won't there soon be a man in bed with you to keep the man off—" Mrs. Lincoln now began to see the ridiculousness of what she had done and said to Mr. Lincoln in one of her sweetest smiles— "Now Mr Lincoln please don't tell this on me— come won't you promise me never to tell it?["] "Well," said Lincoln full of laughter yet— "I reckon I won't, Mary." [11:2935-2936]

> Herndon goes on to say that AL did tell the story at the court-house next morning "amid roars of rib bursting laughter." The allusion to AL's "two story" house refers to a common story in which he returns from a long absence to find Mrs. Lincoln has built an added story to the house. Pretending to be mystified, he asks a neighbor where the Lincoln house is (14: 1366-1367).

200.   [Charles Friend from Kentucky writes to Herndon, 20 August 1889, telling how Dr. J. H. Rodman was sent to the White House as representative of LaRue County to present AL a gold-headed cane then being engraved:] Lincoln sayed how will I know who gave it to me, Dr says the names of the Donars will be ingraved on it "to the President A Lincoln," Abe sayed what a fool, I am like the Irishman that went to the Post Office & when the Post Master asked his name sayed faith, an't my name on the lether" of Course my name will be on the cane. [10: 2537]

The jest about the Irishman appeared in *Harper's Weekly*, 9 (18 February 1865), 99, where it concluded: "Sure you will find it on the back of the letter!"

201.   [Friend goes on to describe the visit:] President asked Dr Rodman about the Cessnas Brownfields Friends Ashcrofts Kirkpatricks & at last sayed where is my old friend and playmate Austin Golliher, Sayed Abe "I would rather see Golliher than any man living, he played me a drty trick once and I want to pay him up, One Sunday Golliher and another boy and my self wer out in the woods on knob Creek playing and hunting around for young squirrels when I climbed up a tree and left Austin and the other boy on the grown   shortly Golliher shut his eyes like he was a sleep I noticed his hat sat straight with the reverse side up I thought I would shit in his hat   Golliher was watching and when I let the load drop he swaped hats and my hat caught the whole charge," At this recital the President laughed heartily. [10: 2535]

1889

202.   [A telegrapher recalls the evening of 27 August 1861:] I told the President that General McClellan was on his way from Arlington to Fort Cochrane, that our pickets still held Ball's and Bailey's Cross Roads and that no firing had been heard since sunset. The President then inquired if any firing had been heard *before* sunset, and upon my replying there had been none reported, laughingly said, "That puts me in mind of a party who, in speaking of a freak of nature, described it as a child who was black from the hips down, and, upon being asked the color from the hips up, replied *black*, as a matter of course."

> William B. Wilson, *Glimpse of the United States Military Corps and of AL* ("read before the United Service Club of Philadelphia, January 16, 1889"), page 20. The allusion was probably to an old April Fool's joke as described in *Book of Anecdotes and Joker's Knapsack* (1871), p. 221: As husband and wife finish breakfast on All Fool's Day, "By the by," said the lady, "how came you to tell me such a story about one side of that child's face being white?"
> "No, no," said he, as he put on his hat, "you were mistaken. I said one side was black. You did not ask me about the other side; that was black, too. First of April, my dear, first of April, you know."

203.   [William Herndon recalling AL's love of good stories:] Returning from off the circuit once he said to Mr. Herndon: "Billy, I

heard a good story while I was up in the country. Judge [David] D[avis] was complimenting the landlord on the excellence of his beef. 'I am surprised,' he said, 'that you have such good beef. You must have to kill a whole critter when you want any.' 'Yes,' said the landlord, 'we never kill less than a whole critter.' "

> W. H. Herndon and J. W. Weik, *Herndon's Lincoln*, 3 vols. (1889), 2:317.

1892

Entries 204–207 are from Henry Clay Whitney, *Life on the Circuit with Lincoln* (1892).

204.   Lincoln was much amused at this story, which he used to tell: In 1858 he had an appointment in Cumberland county, and after he had spoken, a Dr. Hamburgher (a bitter Democrat) impudently jumped up and said he would reply. So Lincoln took a seat on the outer edge of the plank seats and listened.

Hamburgher presently got violent and insulting, when a little, insignificant looking, lame man limped up to Lincoln and said: "Don't mind *him*; I know *him*; I live here; I'll take care of *him*; watch me"; and two or three times he circulated around to Lincoln and repeated the admonition. When Hamburgher concluded, the little lame man was on the platform and at once commenced a reply, and had proceeded but a short time when Hamburgher roared out: "That's a lie." "Never mind," retorted the lame man, patronizingly, "I'll take that from YOU— in fact, I'll take anything from you, except your *pills*." This cut the doctor to the raw. "You scoundrel," exclaimed he, "you know I've quit practicing medicine." The little lame man instantly dropped down on his sound knee, and, raising his hands in mock worship, exclaimed: "Then, thank God! the country is safe." (Page 179)

> The nucleus of the story is an old favorite best known in *Joe Miller's Jests* (1739), p. 63, where the painter Sir Godfrey Kneller is warned by neighbor Dr. Ratcliffe to do anything he wants to with the garden gate except paint it. Sir Godfrey says he would take anything from the doctor but his physic. More recently it had appeared in *Harper's Monthly*, 25 (June 1862), 132.

205.   I never heard him narrate but one story in a speech, which was this: "A man on foot, with his clothes in a bundle, coming to a running stream which he must ford, made elaborate preparations by

stripping off his garments, adding them to his bundle, and, tying all to the top of a stick, which enabled him to raise the bundle high above his head to keep them dry during the crossing. He then fearlessly waded in and carefully made his way across the rippling stream, and found it in no place up to his ankles." (Pages 179–180)

> In an undated clipping from the New York *Mail & Express* (Judd Stewart scrapbook Huntington Library accession 151179, 2:4–5), a correspondent offers a pertinent recollection: Riding the circuit, AL guided the party of lawyers and judges through back roads of Logan County. As they approached Salt Creek, he warned the road might be flooded and advised stripping and carrying their clothes in a bundle atop their heads. And so they did: "all stark naked on horseback, riding single file through an open country, under a hot, summer sun, and, as it developed, there was not enough water under their horses' feet to house a frog. . . . Judge [David] Davis used to say, with a grim smile, 'I always had a suspicion that Mr. Lincoln knew there wasn't water enough in that creek bottom to float a chip.' "

206.   There was a small merchant in Chicago, whom (to suppress his real name) I will call Blower, and who sold out his store and embraced the trade, or profession, of politics. Lincoln had great contempt for him, although he gave him an office; but he said to me one day: "That Blower can compress the most words in the fewest ideas of any man I ever knew." (Page 182)

207.   [A New Jersey congressman] called on the President with two of his constituents, in order to see Lincoln, as they would a show. "Mr. President," said he, "this is Mr. X. and Mr. Y., and they are among the weightiest men in Southern New Jersey." After they had gone Lincoln said: "I wonder that end of the state didn't tip up when they got off of it." (Page 182)

208.   [During the summer and fall, 1863, Salmon P. Chase was rumored to be seeking the presidential nomination; AL facetiously suggested to Alexander McClure that he "decline" Chase—i.e., declare that he had withdrawn his name from consideration:] I was surprised of course at the novel suggestion, and said to him, "Why Mr. Lincoln, how could that be done?" He answered, "Well, I don't know exactly how it might be done, but that reminds me of a story of two Democratic candidates for Senator in Egypt, Illinois, in its early political

times. That section of Illinois was almost solidly Democratic, as you know, and nobody but Democrats were candidates for office. Two Democratic candidates for Senator met each other in joint debate from day to day, and gradually became more and more exasperated at each other, until their discussions were simply disgraceful wrangles, and they both became ashamed of them. They finally agreed that either should say anything he pleased about the other and it should not be resented as an offense, and from that time on the campaign progressed without any special display of ill temper. On election night the two candidates, who lived in the same town, were receiving their returns together, and the contest was uncomfortably close. A distant precinct, in which one of the candidates confidently expected a large majority, was finally reported with a majority against him. The disappointed candidate expressed great surprise, to which the other candidate answered that he should not be surprised, as he had taken the liberty of declining him in that district the evening before the election. He reminded the defeated candidate that he had agreed that either was free to say anything about the other without offense, and added that under that authority he had gone up into that district and taken the liberty of saying that his opponent had retired from the contest, and therefore the vote of the district was changed, and the declined candidate was thus defeated. I think," added Lincoln, with one of his heartiest laughs, "I had better decline Chase."

> Alexander K. McClure, *Lincoln and Men of War-Times* (1892), pp. 135–136.

1895

209.   He remarked that he had been warned against this appointment [of E. M. Stanton as Secretary of War], and had been told that it never would do; that "Stanton would run away with the whole concern, and that he would find he could do nothing with such a man unless he let him have his own way." The President then told a story of a minister out in Illinois who was in the habit of going off on such high flights at camp meetings that they had to put bricks in his pockets to keep him down. "I may have to do that with Stanton; but if I do, bricks in his pocket will be better than bricks in his hat. I'll risk him for a while without either."

> H. L. Dawes, "Recollections of Stanton under Lincoln," *Atlantic Monthly*, 73 (February 1894), 163.

Entries 210–213 are from the Lincoln number of *The Independent*, 4 April 1895, reprinted in William H. Ward, ed., *Abraham Lincoln: Tributes from His Associates* (1895).

210.   [Grace Greenwood (Sara Jane Lippincott) describing him as a storyteller:] As was characteristic of him, he evidently was most amused by one wherein the joke was against himself. As I recall it, the story ran that a certain honest old farmer, visiting the capital for the first time, was taken by the member from his "deestrick" to some large gathering or entertainment, at which he was told he could see the President. Unfortunately, Mr. Lincoln did not appear; and the Congressman, being a bit of a wag and not liking to have his constituent disappointed, pointed out Mr. R., of Minnesota, a gentleman of a particularly round and rubicund countenance; the worthy farmer, greatly astonished, exclaimed: "Is that Old Abe? Well, I du declare! He's a better-lookin' man than I expected to see; but it does seem as if his troubles had driven him to drink." (Pages 112–113)

> In her *Records of Five Years* (1867), Lippincott had said: "I really think that Mr. Lincoln's propensity for story-telling has been exaggerated by his enemies. I had once the honor of conversing with him, or rather of hearing him converse, for several minutes, and in all that time he only told *four* little stories" (p. 159).

211.   [Albert C. Chandler recalls AL's visits to the telegraph office during wartime:] It had so happened for several days that Major [Thomas] Eckert had been out whenever the President came into the office. Coming in one day and finding the Major counting money at his desk, Mr. Lincoln remarked that he believed the Major never came to the office any more except when he had money to count. The Major declared that his being out when the President happened to come in was simply a coincidence, and this reminded him, the Major, of a story: "A certain tailor in Mansfield, Ohio, was very stylish in dress and airy in manner. Passing a shopkeeper's door one day the shopkeeper puffed himself up, and gave a long blow expressive of the inflation of the conceited tailor, who indignantly turned and said: 'I'll learn you not to blow when I'm passing,' to which the shopkeeper instantly replied: 'And I'll teach you not to pass while I'm blowing.'" The President said that was very good— very like a story which he had heard of a man who was driving through the country in an open buggy, and was caught at night in a pouring shower of rain. He was hurrying forward toward shelter as fast as possible; passing a farmhouse, a man,

apparently struggling with the effects of bad whisky, thrust his head out of the window and shouted loudly, "Hullo! hullo!" the traveller stopped and asked what was wanted. "Nothing of you," was the reply. "Well, what in the d—— do you shout hullo for when people are passing?" angrily asked the traveller. "Well, what in the d—— are you passing for when people are shouting hullo?" replied the inebriate. (Page 219)

> An analogue of the major's joke was in *Shakespeare's Jests* (1767), p. 57; AL tops it with another old favorite, as in *Merry Fellow's Companion* (Philadelphia, 1789), p. 60, and more recently *Harper's Weekly*, 1 (23 May 1857), 334: "'Boy,' said an ill-tempered old fellow to a noisy lad, 'What are you *hollerin'* for when I am going by?' 'Humph,' returned the boy, 'what are you going by for when I am *hollerin'*?'"

212.   He then mentioned a bright saying which he had recently heard during the riots in New York [13 July 1863] in which the Irish figured most conspicuously: "It is said that General Kilpatrick is going to New York to quell the riot; but his name has nothing to do with it." (Page 220)

> Unfortunately for the pun, it was not General Judson Kilpatrick but General John Dix who headed the federal troops.

213.   [Chandler continues:] On one occasion we had received news of a series of raids into rebel territory. . . . No State seemed free from our incursions. The President said it put him in mind of a weary traveller in one of the Western States, who, after journeying all day, came at night to a small log cabin. He went in and asked the occupants if he could be accommodated with food and lodging. He was told they could provide him with a place to sleep, but that there was not a "bite of victuals" in the house. The traveller gladly accepted the pallet of straw, and soon fell asleep; but was awakened in a short time by whispers which disclosed that there was a cake baking in the ashes, and the woman and her husband were congratulating themselves on the way in which they had kept their food and deceived the hungry traveller. Feeling angry that they should have told him they had nothing to eat when it was not true, and that they were now "chuckling" over it, he determined to spoil their game. He began to move restlessly, and finally got up and complained of feeling very badly. The woman asked him what was the matter. He told her he was much distressed in mind and could not sleep, and went on to say that his father when

he died had left him a large farm, but that he had no sooner taken possession than mortgages began to appear, and, taking the fire poker, he said: "My farm was situated like this," illustrating by drawing the poker through the ashes, so as to entirely surround the ash cake with the lines. "First one man got so much of it off on this side; then another brought in a mortgage and took off another piece there; then another there, and another there, and there and there," drawing the poker through the ashes each time to explain locations, "until," said he, "there was nothing of the farm left to me at all, which I presume is the case with your cake." "And I reckon," said Mr. Lincoln, "that the prospect is now very good for soon having the Rebellion as completely cut up as that ash cake was." (Pages 220–221)

 Entries 214–217 are from Ward Hill Lamon, *Recollections of AL, 1847-1865*, ed. Dorothy Lamon (1895).

214.   He knew a fellow once who had saved up fifteen hundred dollars, and had placed it in a private banking establishment. The bank soon failed, and he afterward received ten per cent of his investment. He then took his one hundred and fifty dollars and deposited it in a savings bank, where he was sure it would be safe. In a short time this bank also failed, and he received at the final settlement ten per cent on the amount deposited. When the fifteen dollars was paid over to him, he held it in his hand and looked at it thoughtfully; then he said, "Now, darn you, I have got you reduced to a portable shape, so I'll put you in my pocket." (Page 37)

215.   [Accused of embezzling $40, an officer seeking a pardon claims it was only $30, and AL replies:] "That reminds me of a man in Indiana, who was in a battle of words with a neighbor. One charged that the other's daughter had three illegitimate children. 'Now,' said the man whose family was so outrageously scandalized, 'that's a lie, and I can prove it, for she only has two.' " (Page 83)

216.   [Anthony J. Bleeker presenting letters of recommendation is asked by AL to read them aloud:] Before Mr. Bleeker had got half through with the documents, the President cried out, "Oh, stop! you are like the man who killed the dog." Not feeling particularly flattered by the comparison, Mr. Bleeker inquired, "In what respect?" Mr. Lincoln replied, "He had a vicious animal which he determined to dispatch, and accordingly knocked out his brains with a club. He

continued striking the dog until a friend stayed his hand, exclaiming, 'You needn't strike him any more, the dog is dead; you killed him at the first blow.' 'Oh, yes,' said he, 'I know that; but I believe in punishment after death.' So, I see, you do." (Pages 137–138)

217.   [Quoting General J. B. Fry about complaints respecting the draft sent by a Northern governor:] They did not disturb Mr. Lincoln in the least. In fact, they rather amused him. After reading all the papers, he said in a cheerful and reassuring tone: "Never mind, those dispatches don't mean anything. Just go right ahead [drafting from his state]. The governor is like the boy I saw once at the launching of a ship. When everything was ready, they picked out a boy and sent him under the ship to knock away the trigger and let her go. At the critical moment everything depended on the boy. He had to do the job well by a direct, vigorous blow, and then lie flat and keep still while the ship slid over him. The boy did everything right; but he yelled as if he were being murdered, from the time he got under the keel until he got out. I thought the skin was all scraped off his back; but he wasn't hurt at all. The master of the yard told me that this boy was always chosen for that job, that he did his work well, that he never had been hurt, but that he always squealed in that way. That's just the way with Governor ———. . . . He only wants to make you understand how hard his task is, and that he is on hand performing it." (Pages 139–140)

1896

Entries 218–220 are from Clifton M. Nichols, *Life of AL* (1896).

218.   In speaking of certain odd doings in the army, Old Abe said that reminded him of another story, as follows:

On one occasion when a certain general's purse was getting low, he remarked that he would be obliged to draw on his banker for some money.

"How much do you want, father?" said the boy.

"I think I shall send for a couple of hundred," replied the general.

"Why, father," said his son, very quietly, "I can let you have that amount."

"You can let me have it!" exclaimed the general, in surprise; "where did you get so much money?"

"I won it at playing draw-poker with your staff, sir!" replied the youth.

It is needless to say that the earliest morning train bore the "gay young gambolier" toward his home. (Page 290)

219.   Mr. Lincoln being found fault with for making another "call" [for conscription], said that if the country required it, he would continue to do so until the matter stood as described by a western provost marshal, who says:

"I listened a short time since to a butternut-clad individual, who succeeded in making good his escape, expatiate most eloquently on the rigidness with which the conscription was enforced south of the Tennessee river. His response to a question propounded by a citizen ran somewhat in this wise:

" 'Do they conscript close over the river?'

" 'Stranger, I should think they did! *They take every man who hasn't been dead more than two days!*'

"If this is correct, the Confederacy has at least a ghost of a chance left." (Page 294)

220.   And of another, a Methodist minister in Kansas, living on a small salary, who was greatly troubled to get his quarterly instalment. He at last told the non-paying trustees that he must have his money, as he was suffering for the necessaries of life.

"Money!" replied the trustees, "you preach for money? We thought you preached for the good of souls!"

"Souls!" responded the reverend, "I can't eat souls; and if I could, it would take a thousand such as yours to make a meal!" (Page 294)

221.   During one of his visits to Chicago he was the guest of a friend, Mr. E——, whose residence was in the fashionable part of the city. It was in the summer of 1858 and about the time of the campaign with Douglas. He was sitting with his host and family on the front veranda facing a small park one evening when he noticed among the children a little fellow who was fat and exceptionally short of stature. "That boy," he observed roguishly, "reminds me of a man named [Enoch] Moore in Springfield, who suffered the loss of both feet in a railroad accident and whose legs are now so short that when he walks in the snow the seat of his trousers wipes up his footprints."

A newspaper article by Jesse Weik, "The Real Lincoln," syndicated by the American Press Association, 1896, in the Huntington
Library's Stewart scrapbook, accession 151179, 2:31. D. H. Bates,
Lincoln in the Telegraph Office (1907), pp. 206–207, says that he
used a similar comparison in connection with a telegrapher's
signature: "That reminds me of a short-legged man in a big overcoat, the tail of which was so long that it wiped out his footprints
in the snow."

222.　　　Another letter was from a Catholic priest asking him to
suspend the sentence of a man ordered put to death. "If I don't suspend
it tonight," he observed, "the man will surely be suspended tomorrow."

　　　Ibid., 2:32.

1897

223.　　　[In the Chicago *Times-Herald* a correspondent reports an
interview with Philip Clark, pioneer of Sangamon County, about AL:]
"In one of his early races for Congress I heard him debate with Peter
Cartwright, who was the terror of every local orator, as his opponent.
He asked Cartwright if General Jackson did right in the removal— I
believe it was— of the bank deposits. Cartwright evaded the question
and gave a very indefinite answer. Lincoln remarked that Cartwright
reminded him of a hunter he once knew who recognized the fact that
in summer the deer were red and in winter gray, and at one season
therefore a deer might resemble a calf. The hunter had brought down
one at long range when it was hard to see the difference, and boasting
of his own markmanship had said: 'I shot at it so as to hit it if it was a
deer and miss it if a calf.' This convulsed the audience, and carried
them with Lincoln."

　　　Ibid., 2:54. The article is undated, but Clark had died 18 February
　　　1897 and this was in the nature of an obituary. The story itself,
　　　unconnected with AL, was in *Harper's Monthly*, 6 (January 1853),
　　　278, about two Western hunters called Hoffman and Cowan.

224.　　　[Another unidentifiable news article reports an incident:]
During the late civil war an officer who enjoyed close personal relations
with President Lincoln called at the white house, and in the course of
a private interview complained bitterly of certain criticisms passed on
his conduct in a campaign by the secretary of war. And while repeating
such criticism gave way to great passion. Lincoln patiently heard him

to the end, then said: "You seem very angry. Did you ever hear what made Finnigan mad? I'll tell you. Finnigan came home late from the club one night sober, but in such a temper that he knocked over a lot of furniture. Mrs. Finnigan was aroused, and sitting up in bed, asked, 'What's the matter, Finnigan?' 'I'm mad, mad as a hornet.' 'What's made you so?' 'Flaherty down yonder; he called me a liar.' 'But, man, why didn't you make him prove it?' 'That's why I'm so mad; he did!' "

Ibid., 2:13–14.

 Entries 225–227 are from Horace Porter, *Campaigning with Grant* (1897).

225.   [Discussing the use of Black troops at the front:] "I think, general, we can say of the black boys what a country fellow who was an old-time abolitionist in Illinois said when he went to a theater in Chicago and saw [Edwin] Forrest playing *Othello* [?in 1848]. He was not very well up in Shakspere, and didn't know that the tragedian was a white man who had blacked up for the purpose. After the play was over the folks who had invited him to go to the show wanted to know what he thought of the actors, and he said: 'Waal, layin' aside all sectional prejudices and any partiality I may have for the race, derned ef I don't think the nigger held his own with any on 'em.' " The Western dialect employed in this story was perfect. (Page 219)

226.   [Speaking of a new powder being prepared for 15-inch guns:] "Well, it's rather larger than the powder we used to buy in my shooting days. It reminds me of what occurred once in a country meeting-house in Sangamon County. You see, there were very few newspapers then, and the country storekeepers had to resort to some other means of advertising their wares. If, for instance, the preacher happened to be late in coming to a prayer-meeting of an evening, the shopkeepers would often put in the time while the people were waiting by notifying them of any new arrival of an attractive line of goods. One evening a man rose up and said: 'Brethren, let me take occasion to say, while we're a-waitin', that I have jest received a new inv'ice of sportin' powder. The grains are so small you kin sca'cely see 'em with the naked eye, and polished up so fine you kin stand up and comb yer ha'r in front of one o' them grains jest like it was a lookin'-glass. Hope you'll come down to my store at the cross-roads and examine that powder for yourselves.' When he had got about this far a rival powder-merchant in the meeting, who had been boiling over

with indignation at the amount of advertising the opposition powder was getting, jumped up and cried out: 'Brethren, I hope you'll not believe a single word Brother Jones has been sayin' about that powder. I've been down thar and seen it for myself, and I pledge you my word that the grains is bigger than the lumps in a coal-pile; and any one of you, brethren, ef you was in your future state, could put a bar'l o' that powder on your shoulder and march squar' through the sulphurious flames surroundin' you without the least danger of an explosion.' "
(Pages 221–222)

227.   "Well, there is a good deal of terror in cold steel. I had a chance to test it once myself. When I was a young man, I was walking along a back street in Louisville one night about twelve o'clock, when a very tough-looking citizen sprang out of an alleyway, reached up to the back of his neck, pulled out a bowie-knife that seemed to my stimulated imagination about three feet long, and planted himself square across my path. For two or three minutes he flourished his weapon in front of my face, appearing to try to see just how near he could come to cutting my nose off without quite doing it. He could see in the moonlight that I was taking a good deal of interest in the pro-ceeding, and finally he yelled out, as he steadied the knife close to my throat: 'Stranger, kin you lend me five dollars on that?' I never reached in my pocket and got out money so fast in all my life. I handed him a bank-note, and said, 'There's ten, neighbor; now put up your scythe.' "
(Pages 424–425)

> If this was indeed AL's it was hardly autobiography. The same story is in Louis Gaylord Clark, "Knicknacks from an Editor's Table" (1853) in W. S. Burton, *Cyclopaedia of American Wit & Humor* (1858), 1:359–360, where it concludes with the stranger using the money to gamble successfully and redeem the knife.

228.   [In a report by the *Washington Post* (undated) of Senator John Palmer's recollecting AL's stories:] A certain Judge Krum, a lawyer, had been complaining of the treatment he had received from local judges. He swore he meant to carry his case to the supreme court and humiliate the upstart judge who had decided against him. Mr. Lincoln spoke in his quiet, dry way:
"That makes me think of a story. There was a certain man who dreamed that a treasure was buried, and that to find it he had but to dig in a certain spot. His labors were to be crowned with success only on condition that he keep silent while he was digging. He began

to dig. A terrific battle was waged near him. A naval encounter was fought near by. Innumerable tried to engage him in conversation. Still he kept silent. A great giant passed, walking very rapidly. The digger did not even turn his head. After a while a dwarf came prancing along, walking as if he were nine feet high.

" 'Say,' he said to the digger, 'did a giant pass here?'

"The digger did not answer. The dwarf repeated his inquiry. No answer.

" 'Can't you answer a civil question?' asked the dwarf. No answer.

" 'O, well,' said the dwarf, 'I'll just walk along and overtake him.'

"Then the digger broke the silence.

" 'The h——l you will!' he said."

Huntington Library Stewart scrapbook, 151179, 2:126. The senator served from 4 March 1891 to 3 March 1897.

1898

229.   [The *Detroit Free Press*, 9 January 1898, interviews 88-year-old Richard W. Thompson who recalls AL's opinion of one claim:] I will say of your case that it suggests to me a story I once heard about Sam Brown, lawyer, in Illinois. This fellow could not make a living for himself and family by practicing law, so he decided to enter the merchandising business. In pursuance of this purpose he ordered a large bill of goods from an eastern firm. The firm at once wired its western correspondent in regard to Sam Brown's credit. The correspondent replied that Sam was worth over $100,000 and gave the following itemized statements of his possessions:

"He has a beautiful wife, with black hair and lustrous eyes; I should say she is worth $50,000. He has two children, one a little girl, who is the image of her mother, and the other a bright and amiable boy. The girl is worth at least $25,000 and if the boy were mine you could not buy him for $50,000. Besides these objects of value, Mr. Brown has an old table worth 25 cents, an inkstand worth 10 cents and a pocket-knife worth 5 cents. But, over and above all I have named, Sam has, in the corner of his office, a great big rat hole that is worth looking into."

Huntington Library Stewart scrapbook, 151179, 2:29–30. In the more common concise version, the story is about "Jim Price," and

AL himself makes the report of his assets—as in Emanuel Hertz, *Lincoln Talks* (1939), p. 312.

1899

230.   [The New York Sunday *Tribune*, 21 May 1899, reporting a story told at a recent reception by General Daniel E. Sickles who, while AL visited his camp, noticed his melancholy and suggested a means to cheering him:] "I at last proposed to the women that they should draw up in line and kiss him. They entered heartily into the joke, but no one seemed equal to the task of being first. Whereupon I turned to Princess Salm-Salm [wife of one officer] and declared that as she was the youngest, the sprightliest and the most courageous of the company it should devolve upon her to set the example and head the march.

"'But, General,' objected the Princess, 'he is so very tall, I will never be able to get up to him.' 'Ah,' replied I, 'if you will but intimate ever so slightly your intention, I am sure Lincoln will do all in his power to overcome the difficulty.'

"It is needless to say," continued the General, "that the idea succeeded. . . . That night the President mentioned the kissing episode to Mrs. Lincoln. 'Who were they?' asked Mrs. Lincoln. 'The Princess Salm-Salm and other charming women,' replied the President. 'Ah,' said she, who from this moment was a stanch enemy of the Princess, 'what could you expect? These women are all circus riders.' . . .

"Soon after this event in the camp I dined with President and Mrs. Lincoln, and was greatly discomfited by the frigid demeanor of my hostess that she maintained against every attempt the President made to restore peace between us, for Mrs. Lincoln was not yet able to forgive me for my sin against her in being instrumental in bringing about the camp kissing.

"Finally, almost in despair, Lincoln turned to me, and in his quiet way remarked, 'I am told, General, that you are an extremely religious man.'

"'I am entirely undeserving of the credit,' I replied.

"'I believe,' continued Mr. Lincoln, 'that you are not only a great Psalmist, but a Salm-Salmist.'"

Section 3:2. Emanuel Hertz, *Lincoln Talks* (1939), p. 658, gives a romantic version, complete with little Tad witnessing the kiss and telling his momma.

1901

Entries 231–246 are from the comprehensive collection, *"Abe" Lincoln's Yarns and Stories*. Although the title page of this oft-reprinted book advertises an introduction and anecdotes by Colonel Alexander K. McClure, Pennsylvania newspaper publisher who had known AL well, I suspect he contributed little other than the introduction.

231.   This callow politician delighted in interrupting public speakers, and at last Lincoln determined to squelch him. One night while addressing a large meeting at Springfield, the fellow became so offensive that "Abe" dropped the threads of his speech and turned his attention to the tormentor. . . .

"This noisy friend reminds me of a certain steamboat that used to run on the Illinois river. It was an energetic boat, was always busy. When they built it, however, they made one serious mistake, this error being in the relative sizes of the boiler and the whistle. The latter was usually busy, too, and people were aware that it was in existence.

"This particular boiler to which I have reference was a six-foot one, and did all that was required of it in the way of pushing the boat along; but as the builders of the vessel had made the whistle a six-foot one, the consequence was that every time the whistle blew the boat had to stop." (Page 30)

> Emanuel Hertz, *Lincoln Talks* (1939), p. 44, attributes this report to Senator Daniel W. Voorhees, without source reference.

232.   [Quoting from "Personal Recollections of Lincoln" by Judge H. W. Beckwith, of Danville, Illinois, as a good example of AL's skill in "condensing the law and the facts of an issue in a story":] "A man, by vile words, first provoked and then made a bodily attack upon another. The latter, in defending himself, gave the other much the worst of the encounter. The agressor, to get even, had the one who thrashed him tried in our Circuit Court on a charge of an assault and battery. Mr. Lincoln defended, and told the jury that his client was in the fix of a man who, in going along the highway with a pitchfork on his shoulder, was attacked by a fierce dog that ran out at him from a farmer's dooryard. In parrying off the brute with the fork, its prongs stuck into the brute and killed him.

" 'What made you kill my dog?' said the farmer.

" 'What made him try to bite me?'

" 'But why did you not go at him with the other end of the pitchfork?'

" 'Why did he not come after me with his other end?' "

(Page 43)

This is a simple switch from *Joe Miller's Jests* (1739), p. 59; more recently in *Harper's Weekly*, 2 (19 June 1858), 398.

233.   [Speaking of braggart Union officers:] "These fellows remind me of the fellow who owned a dog which, so he said, just hungered and thirsted to combat and eat up wolves. It was a difficult matter, so the owner declared, to keep that dog from devoting the entire twenty-four hours of each day to the destruction of his enemies. He just 'hankered' to get at them.

"One day a party of this dog-owner's friends thought to have some sport. These friends heartily disliked wolves, and were anxious to see the dog eat up a few thousand. So they organized a hunting party and invited the dog-owner and the dog to go with them. They desired to be personally present when the wolf-killing was in progress.

"It was noticed that the dog-owner was not over-enthusiastic in the matter; he pleaded a 'business engagement,' but as he was the most notorious and torpid of the town loafers, and wouldn't have recognized a 'business engagement' had he met it face to face, his excuse was treated with contempt. Therefore he had to go.

"The dog, however, was glad enough to go, and so the party started out. Wolves were in plenty, and soon a pack was discovered, but when the 'wolf-hound' saw the ferocious animals he lost heart, and, putting his tail between his legs, endeavored to slink away. At last— after many trials— he was enticed into the small growth of underbrush where the wolves had secreted themselves, and yelps of terror betrayed the fact that the battle was on.

"Away flew the wolves, the dog among them, the hunting party following on horseback. The wolves seemed frightened, and the dog was restored to public favor. It really looked as if he had the savage creatures on the run, as he was fighting heroically when last sighted.

"Wolves and dog soon disappeared, and it was not until the party arrived at a distant farmhouse that news of the combatants was gleaned.

" 'Have you seen anything of a wolf-dog and a pack of wolves around here?' was the question anxiously put to the male occupant of the house, who stood idly leaning upon the gate.

" 'Yep,' was the short answer.

" 'How were they going?'

" 'Purty fast.'

" 'What was their position when you saw them?'

" 'Well,' replied the farmer, in a most exasperatingly deliberate way, 'the dog was a leetle bit ahead.' " (Pages 62–63)

234.   "That reminds me of a fellow out in Illinois, who had better luck in getting prairie chickens than any one in the neighborhood. He had a rusty old gun no other man dared to handle; he never seemed to exert himself, being listless and indifferent when out after game, but he always brought home all the chickens he could carry, while some of the others, with their finely trained dogs and latest improved fowling-pieces, came home alone.

" 'How is it, Jake?' inquired one sportsman, who, although a good shot, and knew something about hunting, was often unfortunate, 'that you never come home without a lot of birds?'

"Jake grinned, half closed his eyes, and replied: 'Oh, I don't know that there's anything queer about it. I jes' go ahead an' git 'em.'

" 'Yes, I know you do; but how do you do it?'

" 'You'll tell.'

" 'Honest, Jake, I won't say a word. Hope to drop dead this minute.'

" 'Never say nothing, if I tell you?'

" 'Cross my heart three times.'

"This reassured Jake, who put his mouth close to the ear of his eager questioner, and said, in a whisper: 'All you got to do is jes' to hide in a fence corner an' make a noise like a turnip. That'll bring the chickens every time.' " (Page 64)

235.   Mr. Lincoln enjoyed the description of how this Congressman led the race from Bull's Run, and laughed at it heartily. "I never knew but one fellow who could run like that," he said, "and he was a young man out in Illinois. He had been sparking a girl, much against the wishes of her father. In fact, the old man took such a dislike to him that he threatened to shoot him if he ever caught him around his premises again.

"One evening the young man learned that the girl's father had gone to the city, and he ventured out to the house. He was sitting in the parlor, with his arm around Betsy's waist, when he suddenly spied the old man coming around the corner of the house with a shotgun. Leaping through a window into the garden, he started down a path at the top of his speed. He was a long-legged fellow, and could run like greased lightning. Just then a jack-rabbit jumped up in the path in front of him. In about two leaps he overtook the rabbit. Giving it a kick that sent it high in the air, he exclaimed: 'Git out of the road, gosh dern you, and let somebody run that knows how.'" (Pages 123–124)

236.   "A fellow who lived out of town, on the bank of a large marsh, conceived a big idea in the money-making line. He took it to a prominent merchant, and began to develop his plans and specifications. 'There are at least ten million frogs in that marsh near me, an' I'll just arrest a couple of carloads of them and hand them over to you. You can send them to the big cities and make lots of money for both of us. Frogs' legs are great delicacies in the big towns, an' not very plentiful. It won't take me mor'n two or three days to pick 'em. They make so much noise my family can't sleep, and by this deal I'll get rid of a nuisance and gather in some cash.'

"The merchant agreed to the proposition, promised the fellow he would pay him well for the two carloads. Two days passed, then three, and finally two weeks were gone before the fellow showed up again, carrying a small basket. He looked weary and 'done up,' and he wasn't talkative a bit. He threw the basket on the counter with the remark, 'There's your frogs.'

"'You haven't two carloads in that basket, have you?' inquired the merchant.

"'No,' was the reply, 'and there ain't no two carloads in all this blasted world.'

"'I thought you said there were at least ten millions of 'em in that marsh near you, according to the noise they made,' observed the merchant. 'Your people couldn't sleep because of 'em.'

"'Well,' said the fellow, 'accordin' to the noise they made, there was, I thought, a hundred million of 'em, but when I had waded and swum that there marsh day and night fer two blessed weeks, I couldn't harvest but six. There's two or three left yet, an' the marsh is as noisy as it uster be. We haven't catched up on any of our lost sleep yet. Now, you can have these here six, an' I won't charge you a cent fer 'em.'

"You can see by this little yarn," remarked the President, "that these boisterous people [deluging him with advice] make too much noise in proportion to their numbers." (Pages 203–204)

237.   Mr. Roland Diller, who was one of Mr. Lincoln's neighbors in Springfield, tells the following:

"I was called to the door one day by the cries of children in the street, and there was Mr. Lincoln, striding by with two of his boys, both of whom were wailing aloud. 'Why, Mr. Lincoln, what's the matter with the boys?' I asked.

" 'Just what's the matter with the whole world,' Lincoln replied. 'I've got three walnuts, and each wants two.' " (Page 211)

238.   One of Mr. Lincoln's warm friends was Dr. Robert Boal, of Lacon, Illinois. Telling of a visit he paid to the White House soon after Mr. Lincoln's inauguration, he said: "I . . . remember one story he told to me on this occasion.

"Tom Corwin, of Ohio, had been down to Alexandria, Va., that day and had come back and told Lincoln a story which pleased him so much that he broke out in a hearty laugh and said: 'I must tell you Tom Corwin's latest. Tom met an old man at Alexandria who knew George Washington, and he told Tom that George Washington often swore. Now, Corwin's father had always held the father of our country up as a faultless person and told his son to follow in his footsteps.

" ' "Well," said Corwin, "when I heard that George Washington was addicted to the vices and infirmities of man, I felt so relieved that I just shouted for joy." ' " (Page 235)

239.   [General George B. McClellan] reminds me of the story of a man out in Illinois who, in company with a number of friends, visited the State penitentiary. They wandered all through the institution and saw everything, but just about the time to depart this particular man became separated from his friends and couldn't find his way out.

He roamed up and down one corridor after another, becoming more desperate all the time, when, at last, he came across a convict who was looking out from between the bars of his cell door. Here was salvation at last. Hurrying up to the prisoner he hastily asked: "Say! how do you get out of this place?" (Page 344)

240.   On one occasion when Mr. Lincoln was going to attend a
political convention one of his rivals, a liveryman, provided him with
a slow horse, hoping that he would not reach his destination in time.
Mr. Lincoln got there, however, and when he returned with the horse
he said: "You keep this horse for funerals, don't you?" "Oh, no,"
replied the liveryman. "Well, I'm glad of that, for if you did you'd
never get a corpse to the grave in time for the resurrection." (Pages
315–316)

> A. J. Conant, "A Portrait Painter's Reminiscence of Lincoln,"
> *McClure's*, 32 (March 1909), 516, claimed he told AL this one,
> which the President said was "one of the best stories I ever heard."
> As Mort Lewis points out in "Lincoln's Humor," *Lincoln: a Con-
> temporary Portrait*, ed. A. Nevins and I. Stone (1962), pp. 174–175,
> this version is stripped of lifelike details such as are found in
> Helen Nicolay, *Personal Traits of AL* (1912), pp. 26–28; e.g., when
> ordering the horse, AL mentions "that he was anxious to get
> there early and do a little log-rolling before the meeting opened,"
> and his concluding remarks are: "I know it is true. I know by his
> gait how much time you have spent training him to go before a
> hearse. But it is all labor lost, my friend. He will never do. He is
> altogether too slow. He couldn't get a corpse to the cemetery in
> time for the resurrection!"

241.   [During Cabinet discussion of a ticklish international
problem, he reminisces about peddling wares along the way as the
family moved from Indiana to Illinois in 1829:] "Just before we left
Indiana and crossed into Illinois," continued Mr. Lincoln solemnly,
speaking in a grave tone of voice, "we came across a small farm-house
full of nothing but children. These ranged in years from seventeen
years to seventeen months, and all were in tears. The mother of the
family was red-headed and red-faced, and the whip she held in her
right hand led to the inference that she had been chastising her brood.
The father of the family, a meek-looking, mild-mannered, tow-headed
chap, was standing in the front door-way, awaiting— to all appearances— his turn to feel the thong.

          "I thought there wasn't much use in asking the head of
that house if she wanted any 'notions.' She was too busy. It was evident
an insurrection had been in progress, but it was pretty well quelled
when I got there. The mother had about suppressed it with an iron
hand, but she was not running any risks. She kept a keen and wary
eye upon all the children, not forgetting an occasional glance at the
'old man' in the doorway.

"She saw me as I came up, and from her look I thought she was of the opinion that I intended to interfere. Advancing to the doorway, and roughly pushing her husband aside, she demanded my business.

" 'Nothing, madame,' I answered as gently as possible; 'I merely dropped in as I came along to see how things were going.'

" 'Well, you needn't wait,' was the reply in an irritated way, 'there's trouble here, an' lots of it, too, but I kin manage my own affairs without the help of outsiders. This is jest a family row, but I'll teach these brats their places ef I hev to lick the hide off ev'ry one of them. I don't do much talkin', but I run this house, an' I don't want no one sneakin' 'round tryin' to find out how I do it, either.'

"That's the case here with us," the President said in conclusion. "We must let the other nations know that we propose to settle our family row in our own way, and 'teach these brats their places' (the seceding States) if we have to 'lick the hide off' of each and every one of them. And, like the old woman, we don't want any 'sneakin' 'round' by other countries who would like to find out how we are to do it, either." (Pages 342–343)

> The occasion of this story could have been France's proposal in November 1862 for an international conference of France, Russia and Great Britain to mediate the war—which Russia and Great Britain rejected.

242.   [Responding to repeated demands that General U. S. Grant be removed:] "Out in my State of Illinois there was a man nominated for sheriff of the county. He was a good man for the office, brave, determined and honest, but not much of an orator. In fact, he couldn't talk at all; he couldn't make a speech to save his life.

"His friends knew he was a man who would preserve the peace of the county and perform the duties devolving upon him all right, but the people of the county didn't know it. They wanted him to come out boldly on the platform at political meetings and state his convictions and principles; they had been used to speeches from candidates, and were somewhat suspicious of a man who was afraid to open his mouth.

"At last the candidate consented to make a speech, and his friends were delighted. The candidate was on hand, and, when he was called upon, advanced to the front and faced the crowd. There was a glitter in his eye that wasn't pleasing, and the way he walked out to the front of the stand showed that he knew just what he wanted to say.

" 'Feller Citizens,' was his beginning, the words spoken quietly, 'I'm not a speakin' man; I ain't no orator, an' I never stood up before a lot of people in my life before; I'm not goin' to make no speech, 'xcept to say that I can lick any man in the crowd!' " (Page 348)

243.   [Responding to a delegation of officers protesting the promotion of a particularly unpopular general:] "You remind me," said the President . . . "of a visit a certain Governor paid to the Penitentiary of his State. It had been announced that the Governor would hear the story of every inmate of the institution, and was prepared to rectify, either by commutation or pardon, any wrongs that had been done to any prisoner.

"One by one the convicts appeared before His Excellency, and each one maintained that he was an innocent man, who had been sent to prison because the police didn't like him, or his friends and relatives wanted his property, or he was too popular, etc., etc. The last prisoner to appear was an individual who was not all prepossessing. His face was against him; his eyes were shifty; he didn't have the appearance of an honest man, and he didn't act like one.

" 'Well,' asked the Governor, impatiently, 'I suppose you're innocent like the rest of these fellows?'

" 'No, Governor,' was the unexpected answer; 'I was guilty of the crime they charged against me, and I got just what I deserved.'

"When he had recovered from his astonishment, the Governor, looking the fellow squarely in the face, remarked with emphasis: 'I'll have to pardon you, because I don't want to leave so bad a man as you are in the company of such innocent sufferers as I have discovered your fellow-convicts to be. You might corrupt them and teach them wicked tricks. As soon as I get back to the capital, I'll have the papers made out.'

"You gentlemen," continued the President, "ought to be glad that so bad a man, as you represent this officer to be, is to get his promotion, for then you won't be forced to associate with him and suffer the contamination of his presence and influence. I will do all I can to have the Senate confirm him." (Pages 351–352)

Mort Lewis, "Lincoln's Humor," *Lincoln: a Contemporary Portrait*, ed. A. Nevins and I. Stone (1962), p. 181, found this in *Joe Miller's Complete Jest-Book* (1845) about the Duke of Ossuna, Viceroy of Naples, freeing a galley slave: "Here, take away this rascal, lest he should corrupt all these honest men."

244.   [Noting that only one member of the Cabinet supported his wishing to avoid conflict with England:] "I am reminded," the President said after the various arguments had been put forward by the members of the Cabinet, "of a fellow out in my State of Illinois who happened to stray into a church while a revival meeting was in progress. To be truthful, this individual was not entirely sober, and with that instinct which seems to impel all men in his condition to assume a prominent part in proceedings, he walked up the aisle to the very front pew.

         "All noticed him, but he did not care; for awhile he joined audibly in the singing, said 'Amen' at the close of the prayers, but, drowsiness overcoming him, he went to sleep. Before the meeting closed, the pastor asked the usual question— 'Who are on the Lord's side?'— and the congregation arose en masse. When he asked, 'Who are on the side of the Devil?' the sleeper was about waking up. He heard a portion of the interrogatory, and, seeing the minister on his feet, arose.

         " 'I don't exactly understand the question,' he said, 'but I'll stand by you, parson, to the last. But it seems to me,' he added, 'that we're in a hopeless minority.' " (Pages 352–353)

> David H. Bates, *Lincoln in the Telegraph Office* (1907), pp. 98–99, describes the emergency meeting when two Confederates were taken from the British mailboat *Trent*, 24 November 1861, but he does not record this story as told then.

245.   [Discussing a general who would not make a move without asking advice from Washington:] "This general reminds me," the President said one day while talking to Secretary Stanton, at the War Department, "of a story I once heard about a Tammany man. He happened to meet a friend, also a member of Tammany, on the street, and in the course of the talk the friend, who was beaming with smiles and good nature, told the other Tammanyite that he was going to get married.

         "This first Tammany man looked more serious than men usually do upon hearing of the impending happiness of a friend. In fact, his face seemed to take on a look of anxiety and worry.

         " 'Ain't you glad to know that I'm to get married?' demanded the second Tammanyite, somewhat in a huff.

         " 'Of course I am,' was the reply; 'but,' putting his mouth close to the ear of the other, 'have ye asked Morrisey yet?' " (Pages 353–354)

This story was prefaced with a note explaining that John Morrisey had been boss of Tammany Hall during the Civil War period, so despotic that Tammanyites would not enter business ventures without consulting him first.

246.   For a while during the Civil War, General [J. C.] Fremont was without a command. One day in discussing Fremont's case with George W. Julian, President Lincoln said he did not know where to place him, and that it reminded him of the old man who advised his son to take a wife, to which the young man responded: "All right; whose wife shall I take?" (Pages 401–402)

> This jestbook favorite was commonly told about the playwright R. B. Sheridan, as in *Ladies Literary Cabinet*, 6 (21 September 1822), 158: "I wish," said old Sheridan one day to his son Tom, "that you would take a wife." "I have no objection, Sir," replied Tom, reverently, "but whose wife shall I take?"

247.   [Filler paragraph in the Chicago *News*:] One day in the summer of 1857 Abraham Lincoln was sitting in his office when he was visited by one of his neighbors, an excellent farmer, but one inclined to increase the size of his crops even after harvesting. He had given on this particular morning a skillfully padded account of the hay he had put in. "I've been cutting hay, too," remarked Mr. Lincoln. "Why, Abe, are you farming?" "Yes." "What you raise?" "Just hay." "Good crop this year?" "Excellent." "How many tons?" "Well, I don't know just how many tons, Simpson, but my men stacked all they could outdoors and then stored the rest in the barn."

> Undated in Huntington Library scrapbook number 15, page 64. Carl Sandburg's treatment of this story in *AL: The Prairie Years* (1926), 2:81, is a representative creative paraphrase: "And it was told that once when Lincoln heard a farmer bragging too big about the size of a hay crop that year, he said that he had helped to raise hay one year, and when it came harvest time, 'We stacked all we could outdoors, and then we put the rest of it in the barn.'" Sandburg's version is made more credible by ignoring the statement that AL had been farming—which made the earlier story spurious.

1903

Entries 248–250 are from James Grant Wilson, *Washington, Lincoln, and Grant* (1903), the published version of a talk

given before the New York Society of the Order of the Founders and Patriots of America, 6 April 1903.

248.   Lincoln's story was that he was going down the Mississippi. The wood was getting low and the captain told the pilot to steer in to the nearest wood pile. When they reached it the captain said to the man on the shore, "Is that your wood?" "Certainly." "Do you want to sell it?" "Yes." "Will you take wild-cat currency?" [i.e., Confederate money] "Yes." "How will you take it?" "Why," he said, "cord for cord." (Page 12)

> In *Harper's Monthly*, 16 (February 1858), 426, the story, uncon-nected to AL, is about worthless currency by the Gallipolis (Ohio) bank. In *Fun of War* (1897), p. 17, it is about Confederate money but still unconnected to AL.

249.   Lincoln told a very droll story about going to a meeting of the Board of Trustees of the State Lunatic Asylum, which was situated near Springfield. He said it was rather chilly and the long hall was rather draughty, and as he walked through he thought it would be well to wear his hat. As he passed along, about mid-way, a little lunatic darted out in front of him, swelled out his chest, and looking very indignant, said: "Sir, I am amazed that you should presume to wear your hat in the presence of Christopher Columbus." "I beg your pardon, Christopher Columbus," Mr. Lincoln removing his hat and passing on to the meeting. Returning half an hour later, having for-gotten the incident, and having his hat on, the little lunatic darted out from the same passage and drew himself up as before and said: "Sir, I am astounded that you should dare to wear your hat in the presence of General Washington." "Excuse me, General," and Mr. Lincoln took off his hat, "but it seems to me that about half an hour ago you said you were Christopher Columbus." "Oh, yes; that is correct, but that was by another mother." (Page 12)

250.   Another day the President with the Secretary of State and accompanied by a young officer, attended a review. There was an ambulance provided, and four mules. The ambulance reached the Virginia side of the Potomac where the roads were very badly cut up by the army trains, and the driver had so much difficulty with the mules that his patience gave out and he began to swear, and the worse the roads became the more he swore. Finally the President leaned over and said, in his sweet way, "Driver, my friend." The driver looked

around and the President asked, "Are you an Episcopalian?" Naturally the driver looked very much astonished. "No," he said, "Mr. President, I ain't much of anything. If I go to church at all, I generally go to the Methodist church." "Oh, excuse me," said the President, "I thought you must be an Episcopalian, for you swear just like Seward, and he is a church warden." It was a noticeable circumstance among Mr. Seward's intimate friends that after he indulged a little less in profanity, and that, of course, was the President's purpose. (Page 14)

> Horatio C. King, telling this story at the Lincoln Fellowship Dinner, 11 February 1911, says it happened in May 1863 (stenographic transcript, Huntington Library, 2037, p. 33). King told another often confused with this one: General Oliver Howard, a religious man, cautioned his muledriver, "Don't you think you should be thinking sometimes about your soul's salvation?" The muledriver admits he does worry some but adds, "If I get religion who in hell is going to drive these mules?" (pp. 32-33). General King did not attribute that story to AL.

251.   [A law student of AL's, 1845-1847, Gibson W. Harris, recalls how he neglected his personal appearance:] One anecdote that passed current in those days derived almost as much point from his disregard of style in dress as from his well-known character as a humorist. A friend, passing him on the sidewalk one day, exclaimed, "Abe, your coat is too short in the waist!" Lincoln looked up with a twinkle in his eye, and quick as a flash, retorted, "Never mind; it will be long enough before I get another!"

> "Recollections of AL," *Woman's Home Companion*, December 1903, in Huntington Library scrapbook number 15, p. 10. This is a simple switch from a jestbook favorite that John Wardroper, *Jest Upon Jest* (1970), pp. 115, 184, traces back to the early seventeenth century.

1904

252.   [In the second year of the war, commenting on "highly-colored reports of a victory just gained at the West, and of the flight of the panic-stricken enemy":] "There was an Eastern chap," he said, "who came out to Illinois on a speculating trip, bringing with him a lot of notions to sell, which didn't go off as well as he expected. About all he could do while his stock lasted was to pay his expenses from day to day. Finally getting strapped, he had some handbills posted up in one

of the larger towns, announcing that on a certain evening would be exhibited a living specimen of that wonder of animated nature, the great Guyasticutus. Curiosity was so excited that at the appointed time enough money was collected at the entrance to handsomely fill his pockets. The next thing was to get rid of the crowd and off with the spoils. After a little speech about his wonderful beast, he retired behind the curtain. Pretty soon there was the rattling of a heavy chain, then a terrible crash, and the job was done when the showman stuck out his head, shouting: 'Run, run for life! The great Guyasticutus is loose!' "

Joseph H. Barrett, *AL and His Presidency*, 2 vols. (1904), 2:376. The story was fancifully attributed to AL in the anonymous, *Letters of Major Jack Downing* (1864), pp. 64–66, but in a more elaborate, dialect version. The "guyuscutus" tradition is discussed by B. Jere Whiting, "Guyuscutus, Royal Nonesuch and Other Hoaxes," *Southern Folklore Quarterly*, 8 (1944), 264–274.

1906

253.   He related the following story to illustrate that he perfectly well knew what was at stake. He saw that while Douglas, a "trimmer," might win the lesser office, he would damn himself for the prospect of being the next President. It so fell out. The story runs in this guise:

"There was an old farmer out our way, who had a fair daughter and a fine apple tree, each of which he prized as 'the apple of his eye.'

"One of the courters 'sparking' up for her hand was a dashing young fellow, while his rival next in consequence was but a plain person in face and speech, whom, however, the farmer favored, no doubt from 'Like liking Like.' (The dashing young chap was afterwards hanged, by the way.) One day, the two happened to meet at the farmer's fence. It enclosed his orchard where the famous Baldwin flourished. That year was the off-year, but, as somewhiles occurs, the yield, though sparse, comprised some rare beauties. There was one, a 'whopper,' on which the farmer had centered his care as if for a human pet. He looked after it well, and saw it heave up into plumpness with joy. When Dashing Jack came up, he saw his fellow-beau just hefting a stone.

" 'What are you going to do with that rock?' asked he, careless-like, though somehow or other interested, too, as we are in anything a rival does in the neighborhood of our sweetheart.

" 'Why, I was just a-going to see if I could knock off that big red apple, that is all.'

" 'You can't do it in the first try!' taunted the dasher.

" 'Neither can you. Bet!'

"Jack would not make any bet with plain John, but he took up a pebble and, contemptuously whistling through his fine regular teeth, shied, and, sure as fate! knocked the big Baldwin in the girth and sent it hopping off the limb. Then, as the victors are entitled to the spoil, he went in, picked up the fruit, and was walking up to the house when whom should he run up against but the old man! Now, to see *that* apple off, and to see any man munching it like a crab, was too much for his nerves. He did not stop to say 'Meal or Flour?' but, wearing these here copper-toed boots such as were a novelty in that section 'bout then, he raised the young man so that he and the apple, to which he clung, landed on this side of the fence together, in two-two's.

"Then? Well! then, the plain John swallowed a snicker or two, and went right in, condoled with the old fellow on his loss of the pet Baldy, and asked for the girl right slick.

"Dashing Jack got the apple, but it was t'other *who got the gal.*"

Henry L. Williams, *Lincolnics* (1906), pp. 85–87.

1907

Entries 254–256 are from Henry L. Williams, *The Lincoln Story-Book* (1907) in which the sources are appended to the stories.

254.   It is related that the ushers and secret service officials on duty at the Executive Mansion during the war were prone to congregate in a little anteroom and exchange reminiscences. This was directly against instructions by the President.

One night the guard and ushers were gathered in the little room talking things over, when suddenly the door opened, and there stood President Lincoln, his shoes in his hand.

All the crowd scattered save one privileged individual, the Usher [Thomas] Pendel, of the President's own appointment, as he had been kind to the Lincoln children.

The intruder shook his finger at him and, with assumed ferocity, growled:

"Pendel, you people remind me of the boy who set a hen on forty-three eggs."

"How was that, Mr. President?" asked Pendel.

"A youngster put forty-three eggs under a hen, and then rushed in and told his mother what he had done.

" 'But a hen can't set on forty-three eggs,' replied the mother.

" 'No, I guess she can't, but I just wanted to see her spread herself.' " (By Thomas Pendel, still usher, in 1900.)

> Page 120. In the *Nasby Papers* (1864), p. 35, a "spritely boy wunst put 200 eggs in a nest fer a hen to set on. Sez his maternal mother. 'My son why puttist thou so many eggs under the hen. She canst not kiver em.' 'Certainly she canst not, but thunder, I want to see her spread herself.' "

255.   [Speaking of a soldier accused of sleeping on sentry duty:] "This soldier's life is as valuable to him as any person's in the land. It reminds me of the old Scotch woman's saying about her laird going to be beheaded for participation in a Jacobite rebellion:

" 'It waur na mickle of a head, but it is the only head the puir body ha' got.' " (Assured, in substance, by L. E. Chittenden.)

> Page 196. *Harper's Monthly*, 5 (September 1852), 558, has this without dialect as a story of Sir Walter Scott's concluding: "It was no great thing of a head, to be sure," said the good old lady; 'but na'theless it was a sad loss *to him!*' "

256.   [Responding to a suggestion that he replace a general:] "Gentlemen, your request and proposition remind me of two gentlemen in Kentucky.

"The flat lands there bordering on the rivers are subject to inundations, so the fordable creek becomes in an instant a broad lake, deep and rapidly running. These two riders were talking the common topic— in that famous Blue Grass region where fillies and *fill-es*, as the *voyageur* from Canada said in his broken English, are unsurpassable for grace and beauty. Each fell to expatiating upon the good qualities of his steed, and this dialogue was so animated and engrossing they approached a ford without being conscious of outer matters. There was heavy rain in the highlands and an ominous sound in the dampening air. They entered the water still arguing. Then, at midway, while they came to the agreement to exchange horses, with no 'boot,' since each conceded the value of the animals, the river rose. In a twinkling the two horses were floundering, and the riders, taken for once off their balance, lost stirrup and seat, and the four creatures, separated, were struggling for a footing in the boiling stream. Away streaked the horses, buried in the foam, three or four miles down, while the men scrambled out upon the new edge.

"Gentlemen," concluded the President, drawing his moral with his provoking imperturbability, "those men looked at each other, as they dripped, and said with the one voice: 'Ain't this a lesson? Don't swap horses crossing a stream!'" (Heard by Superintendant [Charles] Tinker, war telegrapher.)

Pages 246–247.

Entries 257–260 are from *Lincoln in the Telegraph Office* (1907) by David Homer Bates who, along with Albert Brown Chandler and Charles A. Tinker, served in the War Department telegraph office during the war.

257.   [Speaking of his story-telling:] He said his case was like that of the old colored man on the plantation, who neglected his work in order to preach to the other slaves, who often idled their time away listening to the old man's discourses. His master admonished him, but all to no purpose, for the good old man had the spirit of the gospel in him and kept on preaching, even when he knew the lash awaited him; but finally he was ordered to report at the "big house," and was berated soundly by his master and told that he would be punished severely the very next time he was caught in the act of preaching. The old man, with tears in his eyes, spoke up and said, "But, marsa, I jest cain't help it; I allus has to draw infrunces from de Bible textes when dey comes into my haid. Doesn't you, marsa?" This reply interested his master, who was a religious man, and who said, "Well, uncle, I suspect I do something of that kind myself at times, but there is one text I never could understand, and if you can draw the right inference from it, I will cancel my order and let you preach to your heart's content." "What is de tex', marsa?" "'The ass snuffeth up the east wind.' Now, uncle, what inference do you draw from such a text?" "Well, marsa, I's neber heerd dat tex' befo', but I 'spect de infrunce is she gotter snuff a long time befo' she git fat." (Pages 184–185)

> This is a switch of an old favorite about two Scotch clergymen, as in *Ladies Literary Cabinet*, 6 (14 December 1822), 206.

258.   Many of Lincoln's stories were in couples, like man and wife, one complementing the other; for instance, some one spoke of

Tom Hood's spoiled child, which, as I recall, was represented in a series of pictures. First, the nurse places baby in an arm-chair before the fire and covers it with a shawl to shield it from the heat; next the fussy aunt comes into the room and, being near-sighted, fails to observe the sleeping baby and flops into the easy chair when, of course, there is a scream; then the nurse enters and rescues the baby from the heavy weight of the aunt and holds it in her arm edgeways so that when the father of the now *spoiled child* comes in the baby is mashed so flat that he does not perceive it. A reference being made to Hood's story, Lincoln produced its counterpart as follows:

Scene, a theater; curtain just lifted; enter a man with a high silk hat in his hand. He becomes so interested in the movements on the stage that involuntarily he places his hat, open side up, on the adjoining seat without seeing the approach of a fat dowager who, near-sighted, like the fat aunt of the spoiled child, does not observe the open door of the hat. She sits down, and there is a crunching noise, and the owner of the spoiled hat reaches out to rescue his property as the fat woman rises, and holding the hat in front of him says: "Madam, I could have told you that my hat would not fit before you tried it on." (Pages 197–198)

> Bates misremembers Thomas Hood's Shandyan sketch, "The Spoiled Child," about "my Aunt Shakerly" who, enthralled by reading about child murder in the sensational press, accidentally sits down on the baby in its nursing chair. There is neither maid nor father. The sketch appeared in *Hood's Own*, 2d series, 1861, pp. 415–417.

259.   [Charles A.] Tinker records that one day Secretary Seward, who was not renowned as a joker, said he had been told that a short time before, on a street crossing, Lincoln had been seen to turn out in the mud to give a colored woman a chance to pass. "Yes," said Lincoln, "it has been a rule of my life that if people would not turn out for me, I would turn out for them. Then you avoid collisions." (Page 204)

260.   At the annual banquet of the Military Telegraph Corps at the Arlington Hotel, Washington, on the evening of October 11, 1906, Mr. Tinker said: "I think I had the pleasure of hearing what in all probability was the last anecdote ever told by Mr. Lincoln in the telegraph office. Early on the morning of April 13, 1865, the day before his assassination . . . I was copying a despatch . . . couched in very

laconic terms. He read over the despatch, and after taking in the meaning of the terse phrases, turned to me and, with his accustomed smile, said: 'Mr. Tinker, that reminds me of the old story of the Scotch country girl on her way to market with a basket of eggs for sale. She was fording a small stream in scant costume, when a wagoner approached from the opposite bank and called: "Good morning, my lassie; how deep's the brook, and what's the price of eggs?" "Knee deep and a sixpence," answered the little maid, who gave no further attention to her questioner.' " (Page 206)

1908

Entries 261–262 are from the speech by General James Grant Wilson at the banquet of the Lincoln Fellowship in New York, 12 February 1908, which was printed in *Proceedings at the First Annual Meeting.* . . . The second item, however, was deleted from the stenographic transcript now at the Huntington Library, accession number 40000, to which the page numbers below refer.

261.   [Recalling an evening at Ford's Theatre when AL seemed bored, sitting with his eyes closed:] Suddenly I felt his heavy hand on my shoulder, and in place of the worn and wearied man who looked so haggard as if soul and body might part then and there, I saw the President sitting upright, his eyes full of fun, and with the well-remembered sweet smile he said, "Colonel, did I ever tell you the story of Grant at the circus?" "No, Mr. President, I am sorry to say you never did." "Well, when Grant was about ten years old, a circus came to Point Pleasant, Ohio, where the family resided, and the small boy asked his father for a quarter to see the circus. The old screw would not give it to him, so Ulysses crawled in under the canvas as I used to do, for I never saw a quarter when I was a little chap. The ring-master announced that any one who would ride a mule that was brought in, once around the ring without being thrown would be presented with a silver dollar. A number tried for the dollar, but all were thrown over the mule's head. Finally the ring-master ordered the mule taken out of the ring when in walked Master Grant, saying, 'I will try that mule.' The boy mounted, holding on longer than any of the others till at length the mule succeeded in throwing the boy into his father's tan bark, for" said Lincoln, "the old man was a tanner. Springing to his feet and throwing off his cap and coat Ulysses shouted

with a determined air, 'I would like to try that mule again.' This time he resorted to strategy. He faced to the rear, took hold of the beast's tail instead of his head, which rather demoralized the mule, the boy went around the ring and won the dollar. Just so," added the President, "Grant will hold on to Bob Lee." (Pages [6–7])

262.   When Lincoln was asked, during a visit of William M. Thackeray to America, if he was going to hear him; he replied, "Not if there is a good negroe minstrel show in town that night." (Page [9])

1909

 Entries 263–265 are from James Grant Wilson, "Recollections of Lincoln," *Putnam's Monthly and the Reader*, 5 (February, March 1909), drawn from his diary, 1865.

263.   Something led Mr. Lincoln one evening to mention the fact that David Tod, the war Governor of Ohio, who declined his invitation to succeed Chase as Secretary of the Treasury, had occasion to visit Washington in 1863, on government business. During an interview the President remarked: "You are perhaps aware, Governor, that my wife is a member of the Todd family of Kentucky, and they all spell their name with two *d*'s. How is it that you use but one?" "Mr. President, God spells his name with one *d*, and one is enough for the Governor of Ohio." (Page 524)

264.   It has ever since been a source of regret that I omitted at the time to jot down some of the delightful sayings and amusing anecdotes related by Lincoln in Leonard Volk's studio in Chicago in mid-April in 1860. A single Southern story is, after almost half a century, the only one I can recall, and I cannot remember what led Mr. Lincoln to relate the incident, for he rarely told a story without a purpose. A balloon ascension occurred in New Orleans "befo' de wa'," and after sailing in the air several hours, the aeronaut, who was arrayed in silks and spangles like a circus performer, descended in a cotton field, where a gang of slaves were at work. The frightened negroes took to the woods— all but one venerable darkey, who was rheumatic and could not run, and who, as the resplendent aeronaut approached, having apparently just dropped from heaven, said: "Good mawning, Massa Jesus; how's your Pa?" (Pages 671–672)

Wilson repeated this story to the Lincoln Fellowship, New York, 1911. The stenographic transcription now in the Huntington Library, accession number HM 2037, shows the difference between his written style and oral delivery, which probably echoed Lincoln's:

I do not remember what led up to it, but something, for he never told a story, or very rarely [without a purpose]—something led him to speak of New Orleans. He said when he was there—it was many years before the war, the days of slavery, when he was there there was a man making an ascent in a balloon, which created a great deal of excitement in New Orleans. He went one day to see the man go up; the wind was rather too strong, for this fellow instead of coming down as he intended to, he was blown away some miles into the country, and finally he affected landing in a cornfield, where there was a gang of slaves at work, and when they saw this thing coming apparently from heaven, these darkies all took to the woods, except one rheumatic old darky, who could not run, and could hardly walk, so he stood his ground, and this figure, gorgeous in spangles and so forth, and the old circus clothes, as General [Daniel] Sickles remembers, climbed out of the balloon, and came towards the old darky, who thought he would try to do the best he could for himself, so he said, "Good morning, good morning, Master Jesus, how is your papa?" (Page 42)

265.   [Referring to his diary for 15 March 1865:] "Among several 'good things,' the President told of a Southern Illinois preacher who, in the course of his sermon, asserted that the Saviour was the only perfect man who had ever appeared in this world; also, that there was no record in the Bible, or elsewhere, of any perfect woman having lived on earth. Whereupon there arose in the rear of the church a persecuted-looking personage who, the parson having stopped speaking, said: 'I know a perfect woman, and I've heard of her about every day for the last six years.' 'Who was she?' asked the minister. 'My husband's first wife,' replied the afflicted female." (Page 673)

266.   [From *Leslie's Weekly*, 4 February 1909:] In July 1864, upon Lincoln's return to the War Department after the battle of Fort Stevens, in which the total number of killed and wounded on both sides was nearly one thousand, he gave us a pretty full account of the fighting, and then told two stories, both relating to applications for letters patent. The first device, called a "hen walker," was intended to prevent

hens from scratching up the garden, and consisted of a movable brace attached to the hen's legs so that at each scratch the hen was propelled forward, and so by successive scratches all the way out of the garden. The other device was called a "double-back-action hen persuader," which was so adjusted under the hen's nest that as each egg was laid it fell through a trap door out of sight of the author, who would then be persuaded to lay another egg.

> David Homer Bates, "L as He Was," *Leslie's Weekly*, 8 (4 February 1809), 106. The hen-walker was in *Harper's Weekly*, 1 (6 June 1857), 366.

267.   [From a speech of Richard Price Morgan, Pontiac, Illinois, 12 February 1909:] Speaking of the relative merits of New England rum and corn juice, as he called it, to illuminate the human mind, he told me this story of John Moore, who resided south of Blooming Grove, and subsequently became state treasurer: Mr. Moore came to Bloomington one Saturday in a cart drawn by a fine pair of red steers. For some reason he was a little late starting home, and besides his brown jug, he otherwise had a good load on. In passing through the grove that night, one wheel of his cart struck a stump or root and threw the pole out of the ring of the yoke. The steers, finding themselves free, ran away, and left John Moore sound asleep in his cart, where he remained all night. Early in the morning, he roused himself, and looking over the side of the cart and around in the woods, he said: "If my name is John Moore, I've lost a pair of steers; if my name ain't John Moore, I've found a cart." After a good laugh together, Lincoln said: "Morgan, if you ever tell this story, you must add that Moore told it on himself."

> Isaac N. Phillips, ed., *AL by Some Men Who Knew Him* (1910), pp. 99–100. AL must have been fooling Morgan, for this is a perennial favorite of the jestbooks, from at least 1617 when it appeared in a temperance tract by Thomas Young, *England's Bane: or the Description of Drunkennesse*, sig. F2, as about John Lawrence who "being at Windsor, and drunke so hard, that having a Cart and three Horses, he was not able to stand to drive them out of towne, but some of his company helpt him up into the Cart, thinking the horse would bring him home. (But so it chanced he fell a sleepe in the Cart) and the Horse going in the middest of the Forrest, and there stayed feeding, came a good fellow by, and stole away two of the Horse: The Filhorse making after his fellowes, drew the man in the Cart so farre that it was out of his

knowledge where he was: and either by the braying of the horse, or some Jut of the Cart, hee by chance awaked before hee was come to himself: (which being) and he seeing but one Horse in the Cart, cried out, Lord, where am I? Or who am I? If I am *John Lawrence*, then have I lost a Cart and three Horses: But if I am not *John Lawrence*, then have I found a Cart and one Horse."

268.   [In the same speech, Morgan recalls a day in 1856:] I stood next to Mr. Lincoln and heard him say: "You can fool some of the people all of the time, and all of the people some of the time, but you can't fool all of the people all of the time." He was addressing an assemblage of three or four hundred people from the raised platform of the entrance to the Pike House, in Bloomington, upon the subject of the Kansas-Nebraska Act, and reviewing the arguments of Douglas in support of it. His application of his epigram was so apt and so forcible that I have never forgotten it, and I believe that no verbal modification of it would be accurate.

> Ibid., pp. 102–103. Morgan's emphasis on witnessing the event was necessary because J. G. Nicolay and John Hay, *Complete Works of AL* (1905), 3:349n reported that the combined efforts of the Chicago *Tribune* and the Brooklyn *Eagle* could not discover whether AL had said this oft-quoted remark, printed, for example, in A. K. McClure, ed., *"Abe" Lincoln's Yarns & Stories* (1901) as: "It is true that you may fool all the people some of the time; you can even fool some of the people all the time; but you can't fool all the people all the time" (p. 124). Nathaniel W. Stephenson, *An Autobiography of AL* (1926), p. 159, follows Nicolay and Hay in saying the talk was given at Clinton, Ill., 8 September 1858, but otherwise gives Morgan's version.

> Entries 269–270 are from an anonymous article, "The Sad Humorist," *Collier's*, 13 February 1909, p. 16.

269.   Senator Charles Sumner of Massachusetts called at the White House early one morning. He was told that the President was downstairs; that he could go right down. He found the President polishing his boots. Somewhat amazed, Senator Sumner said: "Why, Mr. President, do you black your own boots?" With a vigorous rub of the brush the President replied: "Whose boots did you think I'd black?"

> Thomas Lowry, *Personal Reminiscences of AL* (1910), p. 24, says it was Secretary Chase who complains, "Gentlemen don't black their own boots in Washington." AL asks, "Whose boots do they

black?" And Esme Howard, *Theatre of Life* (1935), 1:43, quotes Lord Lyons's secretary, Edward Malet, giving a different version: "Lord Lyons, who was a stickler for etiquette, held up his hands in horror, and said: 'Mr. President, do you think it right that the President of the United States should polish his own boots?' Lincoln looked at him, with his curious humorous twinkle in his eyes, and said: 'Mr. Minister, if he doesn't polish his own boots, whose boots, in the name of all that's holy, should he polish?' "

270.   While walking along a dusty road in Illinois in his circuit days, Lincoln was overtaken by a stranger driving to town. "Will you have the goodness to take my overcoat to town for me?" asked Lincoln.— "With pleasure; but how will you get it again?"— "Oh, very readily. I intend to remain in it," was Lincoln's prompt reply.

> This is a simple switch of an old jestbook favorite which, in *Sam Weller's Jest-Book* (1837), p. 227, is told of a Frenchman who makes the same request to a gentleman "travelling in his cabriolet from Paris to Calais."

1910

271.   [David Homer Bates talking to the Lincoln Fellowship, New York, 1910:] The only one of Lincoln's witticisms which I do not recall having seen in print. . . . In the War Department telegraph office adjoining one of the cipher operator's desks, there was, at one time, an old-fashioned haircloth lounge, on which the President sometimes reclined while waiting for news from the front. On one occasion he was seen to get up from the old lounge and flick from his vest a small brown bug known to entomologists as belonging to the species "cimex lectularius." As he did so, he looked around with his usual smile when emitting humor, and said: "Well, I have always had a great fondness for that old settee, but now that it has become a little buggy I shall have to give it up."

> *Proceedings at the Second and Third Annual Meetings of the Lincoln Fellowship* (1910), pp. 34–35.

 Entries 272–277 are from Thomas Lowry, *Personal Reminiscences of AL*, privately printed in Minneapolis, 1910.

272.   [Visiting AL with his father about 1856–1857:] He received us very cordially, and among other things told us of his last visit to David F. Lowry, my uncle in Pekin, Illinois, where he usually stopped

when "travelling the circuit." Mr. Lincoln said: "As I was going up the path from the street to the house, some boys were playing marbles near the walk. I stopped and put my hand on the head of Mr. Lowry's boy and said: 'My boy, you're playing marbles!' The urchin looked up and replied: 'Any d——n fool ought to see that.' " (Pages 11–12)

273.   A story was told of Lincoln to the effect that he was driving a two-horse wagon along a muddy road when he met a man coming in the opposite direction. The roads were almost impassable, and when a team got out of the trodden route it was almost sure to get stuck. Both teams were heavily loaded. The fellow called out to Lincoln and demanded that he turn out. Lincoln replied: "Turn out yourself." The fellow refused. It was near sunset, and Lincoln was between the other fellow and the setting sun. He began to rise from his seat in the wagon, at the same time saying: "If you don't turn out, I'll tell you what I'll do," and as he continued to rise and his tall form expanded between the man and the setting sun, showing his enormous proportions, the fellow called out: "Don't go any higher, I'll turn out." After he had passed Lincoln's wagon, he called out: "Say, what would you have done if I hadn't turned out?" Lincoln replied: "I'd 'a' turned out myself." (Pages 20–21)

> Another simple switch, this was a jestbook favorite, as in the *Chaplet of Comus* (Boston, 1811), p. 231. More recently, *Leslie's Illustrated Newspaper*, 2 (19 July 1856), 91, had a more elaborate version: Nooks tells Snooks, "If you don't turn out, I'll serve you just as I did a man I met half a mile back here in just such a place as this"— and so on to the conclusion— "When I found as how that he wouldn't turn out for me, why— hem— I jist turned out for him— that was all!"

274.   In [William E.] Curtis's "Life of Lincoln," he tells the story of Lincoln's answer to the question: "How long should a man's legs be in proportion to his body?" He omits the names of other prominent men connected with the story. It was when Lincoln, Stephen A. Douglas, and Owen Lovejoy were travelling in a stage coach on their way to attend Court at Bloomington, Illinois. Douglas had a *very* long body and very short legs, being only five feet high; Lovejoy had a short body, and long legs proportionately, and all know Lincoln's build. Douglas "chaffed" Lovejoy about his long legs and "pot belly" and Lovejoy retorted as to his very short legs, etc. One of them asked Lincoln: "How long should a man's legs be in proportion to his body?"

and Lincoln replied: "I have not given the matter much consideration, but on first blush I should judge they ought to be long enough to reach from his body to the ground." Owen Lovejoy told me this story in Galesburg, Illinois, in the winter of 1863–4, where I was at school. (Page 23)

> The story in Curtis's *Life of Lincoln* (1902, 5th ed. 1905), pp. 367–368, seems to derive from Gibson W. Harris, "Recollection of AL," *Woman's Home Companion*, December 1903 (Huntington Library scrapbook number 15, p. 10) where the scene is given thus: "Loafing on one of the street-corners next to the public square, several men were wrangling one day over the ideal length, in proportion to the body, for a man's leg."

275.   [Quoting a story told by John B. Alley in 1883–1884:] The celebrated engineer [John] Erics[s]on, who had tried long to get a hearing at the War Department, finally got an interview with President Lincoln. After going over the plans [for the *Monitor*] and discussing them freely, Lincoln said: "I feel like the girl who said when she put on her stocking, 'There's something in that worth looking at.'" (Page 24)

276.   Another story which was attributed to Lincoln in those days and afterwards diverted to others, was that of Lincoln riding on horseback and coming to an overturned load of hay. The boy driving the team was quite "upset," and striving hard to right the load. Lincoln asked the boy to a farmhouse with him where he could get some help. After much persuasion the boy consented, and after lunch he said: "Dad won't like my being away so long," and started back to his load of hay. Lincoln said: "Don't hurry; I'll send some help back to aid you." The lad replied: "Don't you know that dad's under that hay?" (Pages 24–25)

277.   Lincoln told my father about his first speech in Congress. He said he was always embarrassed when he got up to talk, and he felt in Congress about as elsewhere. He illustrated it by saying he felt like the boy whose teacher asked him why he didn't spell better. The boy replied: "Cause I hain't just got the hang of the school-house, but I'll get on better later." (Page 25)

278.   [From a typical school book of readings:] A lawyer, opposed to Lincoln, was trying to convince a jury that precedent was superior

to law, and that custom made things legal in all cases. Lincoln rose to answer him. He told the jury he would argue the case in the same way. He said: "Old 'Squire Bagly, from Menard, came into my office and said, 'Lincoln, I want your advice as a lawyer. Has a man what's been elected a justice of the peace a right to issue a marriage license?' I told him he had not; when the old 'squire threw himself back in his chair very indignantly, and said, 'Lincoln, I thought you was a lawyer. Now, Bob Thomas and me had a bet on this thing, and we agreed to let you decide; but, if this is your opinion, I don't want it, for I know a thunderin' sight better, for I have been 'squire now for eight years and have done it all the time.'"

> Stanley Schell, *Lincoln Celebrations*, Werner's Readings and Recitations, no. 46 (1910), pp. 144–145.

1911

Entries 279–281 are from the stenographic transcript of speeches made at the Lincoln Fellowship Dinner, New York, 11 February 1911. The transcript made by Edmund J. Murphy is now in the Huntington Library, HM 2037.

279.   [General Horatio C. King:] They say that Mr. Lincoln was never so happy as when some of his old chums from Illinois with whom he had sat around the cabins there in Illinois, swapping stories in his early days, came to Washington. He was delighted to see them. He used to invite them to the White House and have them swap stories about the old periods, and such newer ones as would come to him in the later period. As this particular gentleman was about to leave he said to Mr. Lincoln, "I want you to be honest with me. How do you like being president of the United States?" Well, Mr. Lincoln smiled and looked at him and then said, "You have heard the story, haven't you, about the man as he was ridden out of town on a rail, tarred and feathered, somebody asked him how he liked it, and his reply was if it was not for the honor of the thing, he would much rather walk." (Pages 33–34)

280.   [James Grant Wilson:] I heard a new story quite recently within a few weeks, of Lincoln. I hardly expected to hear a new story after the lapse of forty-five years, but I believe this will be new to everyone present. During the early part of the war, soon after Mr. Lincoln became president, it was his hobby [habit] to go about Washington

wearing a long linen duster, which was by no means fresh, very often soiled, wrinkled, and so forth. In that duster he would occasionally present himself at General Scott's headquarters. Going there one day, there being a new door-keeper, he was told to wait in a room and there he sat for about twenty minutes, until finally General Scott had occasion to come out into this room for some purpose, and discovered Mr. Lincoln and took him in, and he said with very great courtesy and politeness, to him, he said, "Mr. President, you will pardon me, but you must permit me to say that it is not quite becoming for the president of the United States to be seen going about and in coming to these headquarters so that he is mistaken by my door-keeper, as you were, for a Virginia woodchuck [woodchopper]." After that, Mr. Lincoln was never seen in the streets of Washington with his linen duster. (Pages 35–36)

> Words in brackets are corrections made on the transcript, probably by General Wilson.

281.   But before that event occurred he was out one morning, as it was his habit to take a walk always before breakfast.— he was out one morning, and he came upon a great throng of people gathered about a regiment that had just arrived, and was about to cross over into Virginia, and as he passed through the crowd he addressed one person, saying to him, "What men are these?" meaning of course, what regiment. Someone looked at him with the greatest contempt possible, and turned his back to him, and then said to those standing in front of him as he turned around, "Here is an infernal long-legged old fool that don't know a soldier when he sees one." He went home toward the White House and sat down to the breakfast table. At the breakfast table he related that story, which was told to me by his son Robert. (Pages 36–37)

282.   On another occasion Mr. Lincoln said that the claim that the Mexican War was not aggressive reminded him of the farmer who asserted, "I ain't greedy 'bout land, I only just wants what jines mine."

> Dorothy Lamon, ed., *Lamon's Recollections*, 2d ed. (1911), p. 285.

1912

283.   Then there were the stories in which subjects considered either too sacred or too profane were introduced. One described a rough frontier cabin, with children running wild, and a hard-worked

wife and mother, slatternly and unkempt, not overhappy perhaps, but with a woman's loyal instinct to make the best of things before a stranger. Into this setting strode an itinerant Methodist, unctious and insistent, selling Bibles as well as preaching salvation. She received him with frontier hospitality, but grew restive under questioning she deemed intrusive, and finally answered rather sharply that of course they owned a Bible. He challenged her to produce it. A search revealed nothing. The children were called to her aid, and at last one of them unearthed and held up for inspection a few tattered leaves. Protest and reproaches on the part of the visitor, but on her own stanch sticking to her colors. "She had no idea," she declared, "that they were so nearly out."

> Helen Nicolay, *Personal Traits of AL* (1912), pp. 21–22. In "The Editor's Drawer," *Harper's Monthly*, 16 (February 1858), 423, the basic story is about an old man, concluding: "The old man searched the house through, and at last produced a few stray leaves, saying he 'had no *idee* they were so near out of Bible.' " The editor calls it "old but good."

Entries 284–288 are from Anthony Gross, *Lincoln's Own Stories* (1912).

284.   [Rebuffing Know-Nothing supporters in 1854 because of their bias against immigrants:] "I had some time ago an Irishman named Patrick cultivating my garden. One morning I went out to see how he was getting along. 'Mr. Lincoln, what do yez think of these Know-Nothings?' he inquired. I explained what they were trying to do, and asked Pat why he had not been born in America. 'Faith,' he replied, 'I wanted to, but me mother wouldn't let me.' " (Page 49)

285.   [David K. Carter recounted how AL showed that tact and diplomacy could solve political problems:] Lincoln told a story of James Quarles, a distinguished lawyer of Tennessee. Quarles, he said, was trying a case, and after producing his evidence rested; whereupon the defense produced a witness who swore Quarles completely out of court, and a verdict was rendered accordingly. After the trial one of his friends came to him and said: "Why didn't you get that feller to swar on your side?"

"I didn't know anything about him," replied Quarles.

"I might have told you about him," said the friend, "for he would swar for you jest as hard as he'd swar for the other side. That's his business. Judge, that feller takes in swarin' for a livin'." (Page 84)

286.   Noah Brooks relates that when he had been at some pains, one day, to show the President how a California politician had been coerced into telling the truth without knowing it, Lincoln said it reminded him of a black barber in Illinois, notorious for lying, who, hearing some of his customers admiring the planet Jupiter, then shining in the evening sky, said: "Sho, I've seen that star afore. I seen him 'way down in Georgy." The President continued: "Like your California friend, he told the truth, but thought he was lying." (Pages 92–93)

287.   One of the telegraph operators at the War Department relates that the President came over there at night during the war and remarked that he had just been reading a little book which some one had given to his son Tad. It was a story of a motherly hen who was struggling to raise her brood and teach them to lead honest and useful lives, but in her efforts she was greatly annoyed by a mischievous fox who made sad havoc with her offspring. "I thought I would turn over to the finis and see how it came out," said the President. "This is what it said: 'And the fox became a good fox, and was appointed paymaster in the army.' I wonder who he is!" (Pages 169–170)

288.   Robert Dale Owen, the spiritualist, once read the President a long manuscript on an abstruse subject with which that rather erratic person loved to deal. Lincoln listened patiently until the author asked for his opinion, when he replied with a yawn:

"Well, for those who like that sort of thing I should think it is just the sort of thing they would like." (Page 96)

> In the *Lincoln Herald*, 67 (1965), 102, David Means suggests that the source of this is a mock testimonial by Artemus Ward: "For people who like the kind of lectures you deliver, they are just the kind of lectures such people like." And in the *Lincoln Herald*, 70 (1968), 137–141, Richard Hanser offers delightful and persuasive reasons for the anecdote's authenticity.

1918

289.   [Singer Lillie de Hegermann-Lindencrone in a letter, July 1864:] Mr. Lincoln said, "I think I might become a musician if I heard you often, but so far I know only two tunes." "*Hail Columbia?*" I asked. "You know that, I am sure." "Oh, yes; I know that, for I have to stand up and take off my hat." "And the other one?" "The other one? Oh, the other one is the other when I don't stand up."

Charles A. Shriner, *Wit, Wisdom and Foibles of the Great* (1918), p. 352.

1922

Entries 290–294 are from Russell H. Conwell, *Why Lincoln Laughed* (1922), based largely on events in December 1864 when, as a young captain, he visited the President seeking a pardon for a Vermont neighbor sentenced to death.

290.   One day when I was at the White House in conversation with Lincoln a man bustled in self-importantly and whispered something to him. As the man left the room Lincoln turned to me and smiled.

"He tells me that twelve thousand of Lee's soldiers have just been captured," Lincoln said. "But that doesn't mean anything; he's the biggest liar in Washington. You can't believe a word he says. He reminds me of an old fisherman I used to know who got such a reputation for stretching the truth that he bought a pair of scales and insisted on weighing every fish in the presence of witnesses.

"One day a baby was born next door, and the doctor borrowed the fisherman's scales to weigh the baby. It weighed forty-seven pounds." (Page 4)

291.   [Reminded that during the Cooper Union speech he'd forgotten to remove the pencil he had placed behind his ear:] He said that his absent-mindedness on that occasion recalled to him the story of an old Englishman who was so absent-minded that when he went to bed he put his clothes carefully into the bed and threw himself over the back of his chair. (Page 16)

292.   [Artemus] Ward once stated that Lincoln told him that he was an expert at raising corn to fatten hogs, but, unfortunately for his creditors, they were his neighbor's hogs. (Page 52)

293.   [Commenting on a lady's objections to Ward's humor as "out-and-out" lies:] "That makes me think of a colored preacher who worked here on the grounds through the week, and who loved the deep waters of theology in which he floundered daily. One evening I asked him why he did not laugh on Sunday, and when he said it was because it was 'suthin' frivlus,' I told him that the Bible said God

laughed. The old man came to the door several days after that and said, 'Marse Linkum, I've been totin' dat yar Bible saying "God larfed," and I've 'cluded dat it mus' jes' tak' a joke as big as der universe ter mak God larf. Dar ain't no sech jokes roun' dis yere White House on Sunday.' " (Page 72)

294.   "Ward told Mr. [Salmon P.] Chase that his father was an artist who was true to life, for he made a scarecrow so bad that the crows brought back the corn they had stolen two years before." (Page 74)

> Ward must have been fooling Chase, for in *Porter's Spirit of the Times*, 2 (2 May 1857), 135, the same thing was told of "Uncle Ben": "One of the boys tells of a scare-crow made by Uncle Ben. It not only scared off every crow that saw it, but one crow was so frightened that he brought back the corn he stole three days before."

1923

295.   [In an article in the *Cincinnati Daily Gazette*, 14 February 1861:] He avoided discussing the political questions of the day. The nearest he would come to it was to illustrate with quaint humor and simplicity the demands of the South upon the North by a little home story. He said it reminded him of a dispute that once occurred between his two younger boys, Tom and Bill, a pair of mischievous rogues of eight and ten years. One of them had a toy that the other wanted and demanded in terms emphatic and boisterous. At length he was told to let his brother have it in order to quiet him. "No, sir," was the sturdy response, "I must have it to quiet myself." Lincoln was of the opinion that the quiet of the South at the expense of the North did not amount to much.

> Daniel J. Ryan, "Lincoln and Ohio," *Ohio Archaeological and Historical Society*, 32 (1923), 146.

1924

296.   [George Shaw recalls 1856:] In that year he canvassed the state for Fremont. I was then living in Tazewell county, and heard him at Tremont and Pekin. His ideas were clearly and forcibly expressed. He said: "They tell me that if the Republicans prevail, slavery will be abolished, and whites and blacks will marry and form a mongrel race. Now, I have a sister-in-law down in Kentucky, and if any one can

show me that if Fremont is elected she will have to marry a negro, I will vote against Fremont, and if that isn't an argumentum ad hominem it is an argumentum ad womanum." This joke never failed to bring down the house.

George W. Shaw, *Personal Reminiscences of Lincoln* (1924), p. 18.

1926

297.   [A member of his bodyguard remembers the President:] I can recall only one instance where he made use of a story to illustrate his point. This was at the Soldier's Home, when one of the boys, speaking for the Company and encouraged by Mr. Lincoln's evident interest in their welfare, expressed the belief that the Company was of no use there and was needed at the front. Mr. Lincoln prefaced a kindly admonition as to a soldier's duty to obey orders without question, by saying: "You boys remind me of a farmer friend of mine in Illinois, who said he could never understand why the Lord put the curl in a pig's tail. It never seemed to him to be either useful or ornamental, but he reckoned that the Almighty knew what he was doing when he put it there. I don't think I need guards, but Mr. Stanton, Secretary of War, thinks I do, and as it is in his Department, if you go to the front he will insist upon others coming from the front to take your place." Then he added, with a twinkle in his eye— "And boys, I reckon it is pleasanter and safer here than there."

> Robert W. McBride, *Personal Recollections of AL* (1926), pp. 54–55. Virtually the same episode is reported in a book by another member of the bodyguard, Smith Stimmel, *Personal Reminiscences of AL* (1928), pp. 26–27.

298.   Of old man Krone at the Macon House in Decatur, he had a tale of a man riding up one night and asking, "Landlord, can I stay here tonight?" And the old man gazed off into the sky, rubbed his chin thoughtfully, and gave no answer. On the rider again asking his question and getting no answer, he rode on into the next county, came back the next day, and again pulled in on his horse and was going to ask the landlord if he could stay that night, when the landlord spoke and said, "I reckon so"— in reply to the question of the day before.

Carl Sandburg, *AL: The Prairie Years* (1926), 2:80.

299.   Lincoln had stood with two umbrellas at an imaginary rat hole, impersonating Sam'l, the Quaker boy whose father wanted to stop the boy's using swear words. The two umbrellas were blacksmith tongs. Sam'l's father had said, "Now, Sam'l, thee will sit here until thee has a rat. If I hear thee swear, thee sit here till thee has another." And Sam'l had sat there for hours, snipping the tongs a few times, but no rat caught. At last one came out from the rat hole, the whiskers peeping up, then the black nose, and the eyes blinking. And the two umbrella tongs snapped together in a flash. And Sam'l yelled, "By God, I have thee at last!" And Lincoln with a shaking, swaying frame let out a squeal and stood holding an imaginary wriggling rat between the two umbrellas. He had told this in Illinois towns during the debates with Douglas. And Robert R. Hitt, the phonographic reporter, said he forgot himself and politics and business and nearly believed there was a live squeaking rat caught between the two umbrellas.

Ibid., 2:298–299.

300.   [A Chilean admiral, an Englishman, comes to Washington asking permission to purchase two contraband vessels:] President Lincoln received him with his usual affability, and while Seward was reading the Chilean state paper Abraham Lincoln said: "Admiral, I must tell you a little story. When a young man I was anxious to read a book which belonged to a neighbor of mine. 'Neighbor,' I asked, 'could you lend me this book?' 'Certainly,' he replied, 'you can come here and read it whenever you like.' As the book was rather a bulky one I thought this was rather an odd way of lending it to me, but I let that pass. A short time afterwards he came to me. 'Lincoln,' he asked, 'can you lend me your bellows?' 'Certainly,' I replied, 'here they are; you can come here and blow away as much as you like.' And that is exactly the case now, Admiral; you can come here and blow away as much as you like, but we cannot let you take the ships away."

> *Magazine of History*, 32 (1926), extra number 125, p. 43, reprinting "a letter from Panama which appears in the London Athenaeum." The story is a simple switch of an old jestbook favorite; e.g., in the *American Jest Book* (Philadelphia, 1833), p. 153, it is told about "Master Mason of Trinity College" who sends his pupil to borrow a book from another don.

301.   President Lincoln once said that the best story he ever read in the papers of himself was this:

Two Quaker ladies were traveling on the railroad, and were heard discussing the probable termination of the war. "I think," said the first, "that Jefferson will succeed." "Why does thee think so?" asked the other. "Because Jefferson is a praying man." "And so is Abraham a praying man," objected the second. "Yes, but the Lord will think Abraham is joking," the first replied, conclusively.

Ibid., p. 44.

1927

302.   Mr. Ed Thayer, Springfield's old bachelor dry-goods merchant, used to tell a story coming from Lincoln, which he said was a true one. It concerned the occasion of the birth of one of his children, I think the oldest. Mr. Thayer, who was familiar with the conditions of the story, relates that he met Mr. Lincoln who was on his way to church one Sunday morning, and they talked together. Mr. Lincoln said: "Well, the affair is all over, and both mother and child are doing well. I may consider myself fortunate in this matter. Only think of it. If the child had been born with a long leg like mine and a short one like Mary's, what an awful thing that would have been!"

I. M. Short, AL: *Early Days in Illinois* (1927), p. 65.

1939

 Entries 303–316 are from Emanuel Hertz, *Lincoln Talks* (1939, rpt. 1941), the most comprehensive of collections, with sources sometimes indicated at the end of the anecdotes.

303.   I [E. L. Baker] remember very distinctly hearing him tell a story to three or four gentlemen sitting around Mr. Baker's editorial table [of the *Illinois State Journal*], in reference to some plan of the Democrats, in which they had ingloriously failed, owing to their over-confidence in not reckoning on what had been planned by the Republicans.

Mr. Lincoln said: "This situation reminds me of three or four fellows out near Athens (Menard County), who went 'coon hunting one day; after being out some time, the dogs treed a 'coon, which was soon discovered in the extreme top of a very tall oak tree; they had only one gun, a rifle, and after some discussion as to who was the best shot, one was decided on, who took the rifle and, getting in good position, the 'coon being in plain view, lying close on a projecting limb, and at times moving slowly along, the man fired, but the 'coon was still on the limb; a small bunch of leaves from just in front of the 'coon fluttered down.

"The surprise and indignation of the other fellows was boundless; and all sorts of epithets were heaped on the best shot. 'Well,' he said, 'you see, boys, by gum, I sighted just a leetle ahead and 'lowed for the durn'd thing crawling.' "—E. L. Baker. (Pages 124–125)

304.   Something was said about the absurdity of the Breckinridge followers in holding fast to the old party name, when Democratic principles had long been thrown overboard. Upon this hint Mr. Lincoln spoke, relating how an ancient colored lady, dwelling upon the line of one of the old Missouri highroads, had acquired considerable fame as a manufacturer of game pies. In the natural course of events her "ole man," who provided the chief ingredient of these delightful pasties, grew feeble and rheumatic, and failed to keep up the supply but the business was too profitable to be stopped, and the sales went on for a while as briskly as ever. Presently, however, customers began to grumble, and at last Aunt Jenny was called to account.

"What is the matter with these pies of yours, Aunt Jenny?"

"Well, what is the matter, they're good pies, isn't they?"

"But there's no game in them."

"Lor, child, prayer hen (prairie hen) ain't suitable to these times. My ole man, he do the best he can, but they're too quick for his rheumatiz. You jest wait a while."

"But you shouldn't let on to sell game pies when there's nothing but crust and old pork to them. What do you call them game pies for anyhow?"

Aunt Jenny thought this unreasonable, and her patience gave way. "Bless you, child, I call 'em game pies 'cause that's their name. Game pies always was the name, and game pies is always a-going to be the name. That's all they is about it."—Charles A. Dana, in the New York *Daily Tribune*, 1860. (Pages 157–158)

305.   One evening during the last week of his life, when extremely busy and weary as well, Lincoln was called to the reception room to see Mr. [James] Speed, then Attorney-General. He had called to introduce a friend and, seeing the weary look on the President's face, began to apologize.

"I am very sorry, Mr. President," said Mr. Speed, "to disturb you."

"Speed," he replied, "you remind me of a story of Henry Ward Beecher. One Sunday as he was going to preach, he saw some boys playing marbles in the street. He stopped and looked at them very hard. 'Boys,' he said, presently, 'boys, I am scared at what I see.' 'Then,' replied one of the boys, 'why the hell don't you run away?' "— Chicago *Tribune*. (Page 200)

306.   "My opinion as to who will be the next President," said Mr. Lincoln, "is very much the opinion that Pat had about the handsome funeral. You see, Pat was standing opposite the State House in Springfield, with a short black pipe in his mouth and his hands deeply buried in his empty breeches pockets.

" 'Pat, whose funeral is passing?' inquired old Jake Miller, who seemed impressed with a belief that an Irishman must know everything.

" 'Plaize your honor,' replied Pat, removing his pipe for a moment, 'it isn't myself can say for sartin, but to the best o' my belief the funeral belongs to the gintleman or lady that's in the coffin.'

"Now, it's very much the same," continued Mr. Lincoln, "about the Presidency. I can't say for certain who will be the people's choice; but to the best of my belief it will be the successful candidate." —New York *Herald*, February 21, 1863. (Page 303)

> This jestbook favorite is found even in the *Philogelos*, a collection of jests in Greek, popular in the fifteenth century: Someone asks a native of Cumae at a funeral, "Who is the departed?" The Cumaean points at the corpse— "He who is lying upon the bier." (Charles C. Bubb, tr., *The Jests of Hierocles and Philagrius* (1920), p. 64.)

307.   During an interview with Mr. Lincoln in the fall of 1862, I [anonymous] told him that almost every prominent man I had met since my arrival in the city had desired me to urge upon him a certain line of policy in regard to the prosecution of the war, adding that I supposed he was in great need of advice.

"Yes," said he, "I am suffering for it. I remember a clock-peddler in Marshall County, Illinois, who told the people that they were actually suffering for clocks."—*Gospel Banner*. (Page 338)

308.   The conversation afterwards turned upon the Emancipation Proclamation, and he referred to the Southern objection that it was an interference with the rights of property, and said it reminded him of an affair which happened near St. Louis a few years before:

A ruffian made an unprovoked assault in the street upon a quiet citizen, at the same time drawing his revolver, but the assaulted party made a sudden spring and wrested the weapon from the hands of the would-be assassin. "Stop!" said the latter. "Give me back that pistol; you have no right to my property." (Ibid.)

309.   Bishop [Matthew] Simpson recently delivered his great lecture in Wesley Chapel, Washington, to a large audience [?5 March 1865], among whom were President Lincoln and Secretary Stanton. The bishop told an anecdote about a Kentuckian asked by an Englishman what were the boundaries of our country. The Kentuckian replied that the United States were "bounded on the East by the rising sun, on the West by the precession of the equinoxes, on the North by the aurora borealis, and on the South by the day of judgment." This reminded the President of the following story, which he told sub voce to those around him:

"John Bull met with a North American Indian, and in the course of conversation was very anxious to impress him with the greatness of the British Empire. 'The sun,' said Mr. Bull, 'never sets on English dominion. Do you understand how that is?' 'Oh, yes,' said the Indian, 'that is because God is afraid to trust them in the dark.' "— Bishop Simpson. (Page 355)

> Since this is a personal favorite, I regret not having been able to track down Hertz's source. I assume the reference is to the bishop's delivering his patriotic lecture, "Our Country," but an eyewitness, Thomas Bowman, says he watched Lincoln closely during the talk: "I happened to be near him, and could see his every movement." Yet Bishop Bowman says nothing about the story, alas. (George R. Crooks, *Life of Bishop Matthew Simpson*, [1890], p. 372.)

310.   The confidence reposed in Lieutenant-General Grant by President Lincoln was illustrated by a characteristic anecdote related recently by the President in reply to a question in regard to the present military prospect: "Well, sir, your question reminds me of a little anecdote about the automaton chess-player, which many years ago astonished the world by its skill in that game. The automaton was

challenged by a celebrated player, who, to his great chagrin, was beaten twice by the machine. At the end of the second game, the player, significantly pointing his finger at the automaton, exclaimed in a very decided tone: 'There's a man in it!' And this, sir, is just the secret of our present success."—Maj. Gen. E. D. Townsend. (Page 562)

311.   Lincoln used to tell a story about a school teacher who said to his pupils one day:

"If each child will bring an egg to school tomorrow I will show you how Christopher Columbus made the egg stand on end. Those who cannot bring an egg kindly bring a piece of ham."—Pres. Batsell Baxter, Abilene College. (Page 608)

312.   I [John Cochrane] recall the forcible illustration with which President Lincoln characterized the fatal facility of the Rapahannock transit, when I subsequently described to him the particulars [of the defeat at Fredericksburg].

"Well," he said, "I thought the case was suspicious. It reminded me of a young acquaintance out in Illinois, who, having secured the affections of a lass, was proceeding to her father for his permission to marry her, when he saw him plowing in a field.

" 'Hallo,' cried the impatient youth, 'I want your darter.'

" 'Take her,' said the old man as, without turning, he trudged after the plow.

" ' 'A little too easy,' exclaimed the prudent swain, scratching his head, 'a little too darned easy.' "—Maj. Gen. John Cochrane. (Page 470)

313.   [After tapping telegraph lines, the War Department uncovered widespread correspondence with the enemy:] The Secretary of War said: "Bring them all to justice; let no one escape." Others said anxiously: "These are but a few of the hundreds known to us before. We have before us the results of only one hour's work." At last the Secretary turned to Mr. Lincoln, who had been thus far thoughtfully silent, saying: "Mr. President, what shall we do? The country is threatened with betrayal and destruction by enemies in our own camp."

Mr. Lincoln, putting himself in a favorite attitude, remarked: "I have a story which I think applicable to this case, and which is expressive of my feelings. When I was out West, I knew an old farmer who had moved there, and settled in a dense forest not far from my house. He cleared about an acre of land, built him a log cabin, brought his wife and children there, bought a cow, a pig, and some fowls, and seemed to be living very happily and doing finely. He had a truck-patch on most of the cleared ground, on which he was growing his winter store of vegetables. All the trees had been cut down except one old monarch, which he had left to shade his house.

"It was a majestic-looking tree, and apparently perfect in every part— tall, straight, and of immense size— the grand old sentinel of his forest home. One morning, while at work in his garden, he saw a squirrel run across the ground before him. Thought he, that fellow would make me a nice dinner. So he picked up a stick and sent it flying after him; but squirrel-like, he dodged it, and went up the great pine tree. The woodman went into the house and got his gun to shoot him. After looking a long time he spied a hole, and thought the tree might be hollow. He proceeded to examine it carefully and, much to his surprise, he found that the stately monarch that he had spared for its beauty and grandeur to be the pride and protection of his little farm was hollow from top to bottom. Only a rim of sound wood remained, barely sufficient to support its weight; all the inside was punky or rotten. What was he to do? If he cut it down, it would spoil nearly all his truck-patch with its great length and spreading branches. If he let it remain, his family was in constant danger. In a storm it might fall, or the wind might blow it down, and his house and children be crushed by it. What should he do? As he turned away, he said, sadly: 'I wish I had never seen that squirrel'; and" said Mr. Lincoln, "I wish we had never seen what we have today."—*Beecher's Magazine.* (Pages 363–364)

314.   President Lincoln, while refusing to grant a request to some House members, related the problem of some orthodox ministers who wished to get rid of a Universalist minister in their midst. It was resolved to "preach him down," and the pastor appointed to "take the first shot," exclaimed: "Why, the impertinent fellow declares that all shall be saved, but, my dear brethren, let us hope for better things."— Luther E. Robinson, quoting Sen. Cornelius Cole. (Page 583)

315.   Some politicians had called on President Lincoln, to urge the appointment of some of their friends to positions in a certain department. By way of refusal the President told the following story:

"Gentlemen, the conditions in that department put me in mind of the time that a young friend and myself tried to court the two daughters of a peppery widow living near our homes. The old lady kept a lot of hounds.

"We had not been in the house long before one of the hounds came into the room, and lay down by the fire. In a little while another one came to the door. He didn't get in, for the old lady gave him a kick, saying: 'Get out of here! There's too many dogs in here now!'

"We concluded to court some other girls."—Sen. James Harlan. (Page 242)

316.   Mr. Lincoln gave the following account of the first announcement of the Emancipation Proclamation in a Cabinet meeting. He said he read it through, and there was a dead silence. Presently Mr. Chase spoke. He said he liked all but so and so, instancing a clause; then someone else made an objection, and then another, until all had said something. Then the President said: "Gentlemen, this reminds me of the story of the man who had been away from home, and when he was coming back was met by one of his farm hands, who greeted him after this fashion: 'Master, the little pigs are dead, and the old sow's dead, too, but I didn't like to tell you all at once.' "—Springfield *Republican*. (Page 337)

 Entries 317–322 are from the third volume of Carl Sandburg, *AL: The War Years* (1939).

317.   In the White House Lincoln philosophized no less than in earlier days, in the same manner as when, after hearing many theories and noisy wranglings in a big law case, he had walked out on the Rock Island bridge, coming on a boy with a fishing-pole whose legs dangled idly from the ties above the water. "I suppose you know all about this river," he ventured. The boy, brightly: "I guess I do. It was here when I was born, and it's been here ever since." And Lincoln smiled. "I'm mighty glad I walked out here where there is not so much opinion and a little more fact." (Page 321)

318.   Grown-up men and women, even nations, at times were like the little girl Lincoln told Gustave Koerner about. She asked her mother if she could run out and play. The mother refused, and the girl begged harder, kept teasing till the mother gave her a whipping. When that was over the girl said, "Now, ma, I can surely run out and play." (Page 322)

319.   To illustrate a shifting political policy, Lincoln told of a farm boy whose father instructed him in plowing a new furrow. "Steer for that yoke of oxen standing at the further end of the field." The father went away. The boy followed instructions. But the oxen began moving. The boy followed them around the field, furrowed a circle instead of a line! (Page 324)

> On the back cover of *The American Comic Almanac* (Boston, 1837) the story is told of Cuffee, whose master tells him to plow up to a cow: "Whilst the cow stood still he made straight furrows; but as she ran about the field and changed positions, he made his furrows crosswise, in all directions."

320.   [In a meeting with Ben Wade and James Sanks Brisbin, recalled by the latter in the Philadelphia *Times*, the President is told that Kentuckians are sometimes loyal and sometimes not, varying with the Union's victories, which reminds him of this story:] "When I was a youngster out in Kentucky there was a chap who had a high-combed cock that could lick all the roosters in the country. One day an emigrant came in to settle who said he had a low-combed cock he reckoned could thrash anything in them parts, the high-combed cock included. The interest became intense, and the chickens were examined by all the boys. Both looked well, and seemed to be genuine game-cocks. A meeting was arranged to come off between the cocks, and the whole neighborhood was excited over it. Squire C—— was a noted man and very sharp. The Squire was always right, but no one could ever find out exactly what his beliefs were, his reserved opinions being the correct ones. The Squire was consulted about the roosters, as he was about everything else, and putting his spectacles on his nose, he examined both roosters carefully. He said the high-combed cock had 'pints' about him which indicated he would win, but the low-combed cock was much the heaviest rooster of the two, and by sheer weight might beat his antagonist. The young fellows who wanted to bet questioned the Squire closely, but they could not get any nearer to his opinion of the real merits of the chickens. The day came for the battle, and with it a great crowd. The Squire presided, for in those days more than now, racing, fighting and betting were the height of a Kentuckian's glory. Close attention was given to the Squire's position on the fight, as he was both oracle and judge.

" 'I propose,' said the Squire, 'this yere shell be a fare fite, and tharfore we will give three cheers for both roosters.' It was done with a will, and the fight began. At every turn in the battle the Squire would cry out: 'Hurrah for the high-combed cock! Hurrah for the low-combed cock!' Once he made a bet on the high-combed cock, but immediately hedged by betting on the low-combed cock. At last, after a bloody contest, the low-combed cock got the worst of it, and turned tail and ran. 'Hurrah! hurrah! hurrah for the high-combed cock! Gentlemen, I knew that rooster would win in the end, but it is always unfair to express an opinion in a contest like this in advance of the rale issoo. Now, gentlemen, you have had all the fun, but you see that high-combed cock was bound to win. Why, look at his comb! Any man can see with half an eye he is a real game chicken, while that other one is only a dunghill fowl!'

"Now," cried Uncle Abe, "that is the way it is with those fellows out in Kentucky. They want to be on both sides of this fight and hurrah for the high-or the low-combed cock as policy dictates." (Page 327)

321.   One story James M. Scovel said Lincoln told to illustrate the petty jealousies and bickerings among Congressmen and army generals. Lincoln was reminded of two Illinois men, one Farmer Jones, a churchman gifted in prayer, the other Fiddler Simpkins, welcome at every country merrymaking. At one Wednesday evening prayer meeting Brother Jones made a wonderful prayer which touched the hearts of all. And Brother Simpkins felt called on to rise and say, "Brethring and sistring, I know that I can't make half as good a prayer as Brother Jones, but by the grace of God I *can* fiddle the shirt off of him." (Page 337)

322.   "The great West is with you," Ralph Emerson of Rockford, Illinois assured him.

"Yes— but I am sometimes reminded of Old Mother Partington on the sea beach. A big storm came up and the waves began to rise till the water came in under her cabin door. She got a broom and went to sweeping it out. But the water rose higher and higher, to her knees, to her waist, at last to her chin. But she kept on sweeping and exclaiming, 'I'll keep on sweeping as long as the broom lasts, and we will see whether the storm or the broom will last the longest.'" (Page 383)

> Sydney Smith speaking at Taunton, England in October 1831, about the House of Lords trying to prevent reform said the attempt: "reminds me very forcibly of the great storm of Sidmouth, and of the conduct of the excellent Mrs. Partington on that

occasion. In the winter of 1824, there set in a great flood upon that town— the tide rose to an incredible height— the waves rushed in upon the houses, and every thing was threatened with destruction. In the midst of this sublime and terrible storm, Dame Partington, who lived upon the beach, was seen at the door of her house with mop and pattens, trundling her mop, squeezing out the sea-water, and vigorously pushing away the Atlantic Ocean. The Atlantic was roused. Mrs. Partington's spirit was up; but I need not tell you that the contest was unequal." (Sydney Smith, *Works*, 4 vols. [1839–40], 4:392–393.)

1958

323.　　Sometimes he told his stories, and cracked his jokes, for the pure spontaneous fun of it, like any natural-born humorist. Once he was looking idly out of the window of his Springfield law office at the muddy, rain-soaked street below. Along came a stately matron wearing a many-plumed hat, and in picking her way in precariously she slipped and fell.

　　"Reminds me of a duck," said Lincoln to a companion.

　　"Why is that?"

　　"Feathers on her head and down on her behind," said the future President of the United States.

> Richard Hanser, "The Laughing Lincoln," *Saturday Review*, 41 (8 February 1958), 12.

324.　　In a comic piece Lincoln wrote out and gave to Arnold Robinson, he used the elementary device of transposing the first letters of various words, and partly of transposing words themselves. "He said he was riding bass-ackwards on a jass-ack, through a patton-cotch, on a pair of baddle-sags, stuffed full of binger-gred, when the animal steered at a scump, and the lirrup-steather broke, and throwed him in the forner of the kence, and broke his pishing-fole. He said he would not have minded it much, but he fell right into a great tow-curd. . . . He said about bray-dake he came to himself, ran home, seized up a stick of wood and split the axe to make a light, rushed into the house, and found the door sick abed, and his wife standing open. But thank goodness, she is getting right hat and farty again."

> Mort R. Lewis in *Lincoln: a Contemporary Portrait*, ed. Allan Nevins and Irving Stone (1962), pp. 180–181. This must have been an early transaction, since Arnold Robinson, Springfield contemporary, deserted to the Locofocos in 1848 (*W* 1:490n).

1980

325.   Lincoln sent General [Joe] Hooker to take over the Army; Hooker rushed headlong into action, sending his dispatches from "Headquarters in the saddle." Grinning to an aide, Lincoln said: "The trouble with Hooker is that he's got his headquarters where his hind-quarters ought to be."

> Richard Wolkomir, "Political Insult Ain't What It Used to Be," *Smithsonian*, 11 (June 1980), 176. In the August issue, p. 14, an editorial note said: "A number of sources associate this story with General Hooker, but we are convinced by authoritative historians that it was of General [John] Pope" that President Lincoln made the remark. The "authoritative historians" remain nameless.

SOURCES
Main Entries

Abbott, John S. C. *History of the Civil War in America*. 2 vols. Springfield, Mass.: Gurdon Bill, 1863–1866. [23]

Anonymous. Unidentified newspaper paragraph in Judd Stewart scrapbook, Huntington Library accession 151179. [224]

Arnold, Isaac N. *Abraham Lincoln*. A paper read before the Royal Historical Society, London, June 16, 1881. Chicago: Fergus, 1881. [157]

Barrett, Joseph H. *Life of Abraham Lincoln*. New York: Loomis National Library Association, 1888. [80–82, 252]

Barton, William E. *The Soul of Abraham Lincoln*. New York: Doran, 1920. [158]

Bates, David Homer. "Lincoln as He Was Day by Day." *Leslie's Weekly*, 108 (4 February 1909), 106. [266]

———. *Lincoln in the Telegraph Office*. New York: Century, 1907. [22ln, 257–260]

———. Address. *Proceedings at the Second and Third Annual Meetings*. New York: Lincoln Fellowship, 1910. [271]

Brandegee, Augustus. "Abraham Lincoln." New York *Tribune*, 23 January 1887, in Judd Stewart scrapbook, Huntington Library accession 151179. [186]

Brooks, Noah. "Personal Reminiscences of Lincoln." *Scribner's Monthly*, 15 (1878), 4–5, 561–569, 673–681, 884–886. [149–155]

Brown, Christopher C. Interview with W. H. Herndon. Herndon papers, Huntington Library accession LN 2408. [110–111]

Browne, Francis F. *The Every-Day Life of Abraham Lincoln.* New York: N. D. Thompson, 1887. [64n, 115n, 181–185]

Carman, Caleb. Interview with W. H. Herndon. Herndon papers, Huntington Library accession LN 2408. [105]

Carpenter, Frank B. "Anecdotes." In Henry J. Raymond, *Life and Public Services of Abraham Lincoln.* New York: Derby and Miller, 1865. [58n, 82n, 87–88]

————. *Six Months at the White House.* New York: Hurd and Houghton, 1866. [33n, 78n, 87n, 88n, 109n, 120–138]

————. Unidentified newspaper clipping in Huntington Library scrapbook 15. [143]

Chicago *News.* Undated paragraph in Huntington Library scrapbook 15. [247]

Clark, Philip. Interview in Chicago *Times-Herald,* ca. 1897, in Judd Stewart scrapbook, Huntington Library accession 151179. [223]

Colliers. "The Sad Humorist." Volume 42 (13 February 1909), 15–16, 24. [269–270]

Congressional Globe. Thirtieth Congress, 1st Session. Appendix. [4]

Conwell, Russell H. *Why Lincoln Laughed.* New York: Harpers, 1922. [290–294]

Dawes, Henry Laurens. "Recollections of Stanton under Lincoln." *Atlantic Monthly,* 73 (February 1894), 162–169. [209]

Ellis, Abner Y. Letter to W. H. Herndon, 1 February 1866, in Herndon papers, Huntington Library accession LN 2408. [97–103, 110n, 189]

Evening Star (?Washington, D.C.). Undated paragraph, in Huntington Library scrapbook 15. [179]

Friend, Charles. Letter to W. H. Herndon, 20 August 1889, in Herndon-Weik papers, Library of Congress microfilm 10: 2535, 2537. [200–201]

Gillespie, Joseph. Letter to W. H. Herndon, 31 January 1866, in Herndon papers, Huntington Library accession LN 2408. [96]

Grigsby, Nat. Interview with W. H. Herndon in Herndon papers, Huntington Library accession LN 2408. [94]

Gross, Anthony. *Lincoln's Own Stories.* New York: Harpers, 1912. [193n, 284–288]

Gross, William L. Journal entry. In Harry E. Pratt, *Concerning Mr. Lincoln.* Springfield, Ill.: Abraham Lincoln Association, 1944. [17]

Hanser, Richard. "The Laughing Lincoln." *Saturday Review,* 41 (8 February 1958), 11–13, 37–38. [323]

————. "Old Abe v. Incomparable Max." *Lincoln Herald,* 70 (1968), 137–141. [228n]

Harper's Monthly. "Editor's Drawer." Vols. 5 (1852) 69 (1884). [13n, 22, 88, 99n, 125n, 136–138, 140n, 144–145, 159n, 204n, 223n, 248n, 255n, 283n]

Harper's Weekly. Vols. 1 (1857) – 9 (1865). [1n, 2l, 4ln, 69n, 107n, 130n, 168n, 179n, 200n, 232n]

Harris, Gibson W. "Recollections of Abraham Lincoln." *Woman's Home Companion,* December 1903. In Huntington Library scrapbook 15. [251, 274n]

Hart, Charles F. Letter to W. H. Herndon, 3 May 1866, in Herndon papers, Huntington Library accession LN 2408. [104]

Hay, John Milton. "Diary." Brown University Commemorative Catalogue. Providence: Brown University, 1935. [34]

———. Letter to Charles Graham Halpine, 22 November 1863, Huntington Library manuscript HP 119. [26]

———. Letter to W. H. Herndon, 5 September 1866, in Herndon papers, Huntington Library accession LN 2408. [35n]

———. *Lincoln and the Civil War in the Diaries and Letters of John Hay.* Ed. Tyler Dennett. New York: Dodd, Mead, 1939. [32–33, 35–41]

Hegermann-Lindencrone, Lillie de. "Anecdote." In Charles A. Shriner, *Wit, Wisdom and Foibles of the Great.* New York: Funk and Wagnalls, 1918. [289]

Herndon, John R. Letters to W. H. Herndon, 25 June, 3 July 1865, in Herndon papers, Huntington Library accession LN 2408. [89–92]

Herndon, William H. Letters to J. W. Weik, 1887–1889, in Herndon-Weik papers, Library of Congress microfilm 9: 1906-1909, 11: 2876, 2879–2880, 2887–2889, 2898, 2935–2936. [56n, 189–201]

Herndon, William H. and Jesse W. Weik. *Abraham Lincoln: the True Story of a Great Life.* 3 vols. Chicago: Belford, Clarke, 1889. [90n, 97n, 203]

Hertz, Emanuel. *Lincoln Talks.* New York: Viking, 1939; rpt. Halcyon House, 1941. [31n–32n, 186n, 229n–230n, 303–316]

King, Horatio. Address to Lincoln Fellowship, New York, 12 February 1911. Stenographic transcript, Huntington Library accession HM 2037. [250n, 279]

Kyle, Otto R. "Mr. Lincoln Steps Out: the Anti-Nebraska Editors' Convention." *Abraham Lincoln Quarterly,* 5 (March 1948), 25–37. [9–10]

Lamon, Ward H. "Administration of Lincoln." Typescript. Huntington Library accession LN 2418A. [23n, 39n, 81n, 123n, 175–178]

———. Manuscript notes. Huntington Library accession LN 2405 (6). [78n]

———. Unidentified newspaper articles, copyright 1887–1888. In Huntington Library, Judd Stewart scrapbook, accession 151179. [78n, 187]

———. *Recollections of Abraham Lincoln.* Ed. Dorothy Lamon Teillard. Chicago: A. C. McClurg, 1895. Second ed.: Washington: by the Editor, 1911. [78n, 112n, 137n, 214–217]

Legacy of Fun. London: Frederick Farrah, 1865. [83–86]

Leslie's Illustrated Newspaper. Vols. 2 (1856) – 16 (1863). [24, 25, 71n, 108n, 168n, 273n]

Lewis, Mort R. "Lincoln's Humor." In *Lincoln: a Contemporary Portrait,* ed. Allan Nevins and Irving Stone. Garden City, N.J.: Doubleday, 1962, pp. 163–183. [240n, 244n, 324]

———. "Were It Not for This Occasional Vent." *Lincoln Herald,* 60 (1958), 87–90. [63n, 87n]

Lincoln, Abraham. *Collected Works.* Ed. Roy P. Basler. 9 vols. New Brunswick, N.J.: Rutgers University Press, 1953–1955. [1–3, 7–9, 14–16, 18, 20, 35n, 187n]

Lincoln's Anecdotes. New York: American News Company, 1867. [2n, 139–142]

Lincolniana, or the Humors of Uncle Abe. New York: J. F. Feeks, copyright 1864. [19n, 52n, 61–71]

Littlefield, John H. Letter to W. H. Herndon, 11 December 1866, in Herndon-Weik papers, Library of Congress microfilm 8: 1284. [108]

Lowry, Thomas. *Personal Reminiscences of Abraham Lincoln.* Minneapolis: Edmund D. Brooks, 1910. [269n, 272–277]

McBride, Robert W. *Personal Recollections of Abraham Lincoln.* Indianapolis: Bobbs-Merrill, 1926. [297]

McClellan, George B. *McClellan's Own Story.* New York: Webster, 1887. [188]

McClure, Alexander K. *"Abe" Lincoln's Yarns and Stories.* Philadelphia: Winston, copyright 1901. [231–246]

———. *Lincoln and Men of War-Times.* 4th ed. Philadelphia: Times Publishing Co., 1892. [208]

———. Symposium. *Success Magazine,* February 1904. In Huntington Library scrapbook 15. [38n]

Magazine of History. "Mint of Lincoln's Wit." Volume 32 (1926), extra number 125, 43–45. [300–301]

Matheny, James H. Interview with W. H. Herndon in Herndon papers, Huntington Library accession LN 2408. [113]

Means, David C., ed. *Lincoln Papers.* 2 vols. Garden City, N. J.: Doubleday, 1948. [5–6]

Mitgang, Herbert. *Abraham Lincoln, a Press Portrait.* Athens: University of Georgia Press, 1989. [13,19]

Moore, Frank. *Anecdotes, Poetry and Incidents of the War.* New York: for Subscribers, 1866. [114–119, 152n]

New York *Post.* Wednesday, 17 February 1864, p. 1. [42–60]

New York *Tribune.* Sunday, 21 May 1899, sec. 3, p. 2. [230]

Nichols, Clifton M. *Life of Abraham Lincoln.* New York: Mast, Crowell, and Kirkpatrick, 1896. [218–220]

Nicolay, Helen. *Personal Traits of Abraham Lincoln.* New York: Century, 1912. [240n, 283]

Old Abe's Joker, or, Wit at the White House. New York: Robert M. DeWitt, copyright 1863. [27–31, 52n]

Old Abe's Jokes, Fresh from Abraham's Bosom. New York: T. R. Dawley, copyright 1864. [31n, 36n, 52n, 72–79]

Oldroyd, Osborne H. *Lincoln Memorial: Album Immortelles.* New York: G. W. Carleton, 1882. [141n, 158n, 159–162]

Palmer, John. Interview in undated Washington *Post.* In Judd Stewart scrapbook, Huntington Library accession 151179. [228]

Paris, Comte de, Louis Philippe Albert d'Orleans. *History of the Civil War in America.* 4 vols. Philadelphia: Joseph H. Coates, 1876–1878. [146]

Phillips, Isaac N. *Abraham Lincoln by Some Men Who Knew Him.* Bloomington, Ill.: Pantagraph Printing, 1910. [10n, 131n, 267–268]

Porter, Horace. Address. *Addresses Delivered at the Lincoln Dinners of the Republican Club of the City of New York.* New York: privately printed, 1909. [46n]

———. *Campaigning with Grant.* New York: Century, 1897. [225–227]

Raymond, Henry J. *Life and Public Services of Abraham Lincoln.* New York: Derby and Miller, 1865. [82n, 87–88]

Rice, Allen Thorndike. *Reminiscences of Abraham Lincoln by Distinguished Men of His Time.* New York: North American Publishing Company, 1886. [29n, 64n, 66n, 124n, 165–174]

Richardson, James C. Interview with W. H. Herndon in Herndon papers, Huntington Library accession LN 2408. [95]

Ryan, Daniel J. "Lincoln and Ohio." *Ohio Archaeological and Historical Society Publications,* 32 (1923), 1–281. [295, 58n]

Sandburg, Carl. *Abraham Lincoln: The Prairie Years.* 2 vols. New York: Harcourt-Brace, 1926. [14n, 247n, 298–299]

———. *Abraham Lincoln: The War Years.* 3 vols. New York: Harcourt-Brace, 1939. [317–322]

Schell, Stanley. *Lincoln Celebrations.* Werner's Readings and Recitations, no. 46. New York: Werner's, 1910. [278]

Shaw, George W. *Personal Reminiscences of Lincoln.* Moline, Ill.: Carlson Printing, 1924. [17n, 296]

Short, Isaac M. *Abraham Lincoln: Early Days in Illinois.* Kansas City, Mo.: Simpson, 1927. [302]

Speed, James T. Interview with W. H. Herndon in Herndon papers, Huntington Library accession LN 2408. [109]

Speed, Joshua Fry. *Reminiscences of Abraham Lincoln.* Louisville, Ky.: R. T. Durrett, 1884. [147–148]

Stanton, Henry B. *Random Recollections.* 2d edition. New York: Macgowan and Slipper, 1886. [180]

Stuart, John T. Note to W. H. Herndon in Herndon papers, Huntington Library accession LN 2408. [112]

Thompson, Richard W. Interview in Detroit *Free Press,* 9 January 1898. In Judd Stewart scrapbook Huntington Library accession 151179. [229]

Viele, Egbert. "A Trip with Lincoln, Chase and Stanton." *Scribner's Monthly,* 16 (October 1878), 813–822. [156]

Ward, William H., ed. *Abraham Lincoln: Tributes from His Associates.* New York: Crowell, 1895. [210–213]

Wartman, J. W. Letter to W. H. Herndon, 21 July 1865, in Herndon papers, Huntington Library accession LN 2408. [93]

Weber, John B. Letter to W. H. Herndon, 5 November 1866, in Herndon papers, Huntington Library accession LN 2408. [106]

Weed, Thurlow. *Autobiography.* Ed. Harriet A. Weed. Boston: Houghton-Mifflin, 1883. [163–164]

Weik, Jesse W. "Personal Recollections." *Outlook,* 13 February 1909, p. 348. [195n]

———. "The Real Lincoln." Unidentified newspaper article copyright 1896, in Judd Stewart scrapbook, Huntington Library accession 151179. [221–222]

Welles, Gideon. *Diary.* Ed. Howard K. Beale. 3 vols. New York: Norton, 1960. [165n, 171n]

Whitney, Henry Clay. Letters to W. H. Herndon, June-September 1887, in Herndon-Weik papers, Library of Congress microfilm 10: 2154, 2184, 12: 386. [190–193]

———. *Life on the Circuit with Lincoln.* Boston: Estes and Lauriat, 1892. [204–207]

Wickizer, John H. Letter to W. H. Herndon, 25 November 1866, in Herndon papers, Huntington Library accession LN 2408. [107]

Williams, Henry L. *Lincoln Story Book.* New York: Dillingham, 1907. [254–256]

———. *Lincolnics.* New York: Putnam's, 1906. [253]

Wilson, James Grant. Address to Lincoln Fellowship, New York, 12 February 1911. Stenographic transcript. Huntington Library accession HM 2037. [280–281]

————. Address. "Proceedings at the First Annual Meeting of the Lincoln Fellowship, New York." Stenographic transcript. Huntington Library accession 40000. [261–262]

————. "Recollections of Lincoln." *Putnam's Monthly and the Reader*, 5 (February, March 1909), 515–529, 670–675. [183n, 263–265]

————. *Washington, Lincoln and Grant*. New York: New York Society of the Order of the Founders and Patriots of America, 1903. [248–250]

Wilson, William B. *A Glimpse of the United States Military Telegraph Corps and of Abraham Lincoln*. Holmesburg, Pa.: privately printed, 1889. [202]

Wolkomir, Richard. "Political Insult Ain't What It Used to Be." *Smithsonian*, 11 (June 1980), 176. [325]

RESOURCES:
Notes

Aesop. *Aesop's Fables*. Tr. Thomas James. London: John Murray, 1848. [142n, 148n]

American Comic Almanac. Boston: Charles Ellms, 1837. [319n]

American Jest Book. Philadelphia: M. Carey, 1789. [66n]

———. Philadelphia: Hogan and Thompson, 1833. [61n, 157n, 300n]

American Magazine of Wit. New York: H. C. Southwick, 1808. [138n]

Andersen, Hans C. "The Tinder Box." *Classic Fairy Tales*. Ed. Iona and Peter Opie. New York: Oxford University Press, 1974. [172n]

Baldwin, Joseph G. *Flush Times of Alabama and Mississippi*. New York: D. Appleton, 1853. [129n, 145n]

Bonham, Jeriah. *Fifty Years' Recollections*. Peoria, Ill.: J. W. Franks, 1883. [2n]

Book of Anecdotes and Joker's Knapsack. Philadelphia: John E. Potter, 1871. [202n]

Brown, David Paul. *The Forum*. 2 vols. Philadelphia: Robert Small, 1856. [37n]

Bunn, John W. Interview with W. H. Herndon in Herndon-Weik papers, Library of Congress microfilm 14: 1366–1367. [199n]

Burton, William E. *Cyclopaedia of Wit and Humor*. 2 vols. New York: D. Appleton, 1858. [159n, 227n]

Chandler, Albert B. "Abraham Lincoln in the War Department." In William H. Ward, *Abraham Lincoln: Tributes from His Associates*. New York: Crowell, 1895. [63n, 136n]

Chaplet of Comus. Boston: Munroe and Francis, 1811. [273n]

Chittenden, Lucius E. *Recollections of President Lincoln.* New York: Harpers, 1891. [87n]

Conant, Alban J. "A Portrait Painter's Reminiscence of Lincoln." *McClure's,* 32 (1909), 512–516. [13n, 240n]

Conway, Moncure D. *Autobiography.* 2 vols. London: Cassell, 1904. [88n]

Cooper, James Fenimore. *Gleanings in Europe.* Ed. Robert E. Spiller. 2 vols. New York: Oxford University Press, 1928–1930. [187n]

Court Jester. London: A. Hamilton, 179–. [27n, 172n]

Cowen, Benjamin Rush. *Abraham Lincoln, an Appreciation.* Cincinnati: Robert Clarke, 1909. [78n]

Crook, William B. "Lincoln's Last Day." *Harper's Monthly,* 115 (1907), 519–530. [109n]

Crooks, George R. *Life of Bishop Matthew Simpson.* New York: Harper, 1890. [309n]

Dickson, W. M. "Abraham Lincoln at Cincinnati." *Harper's Monthly,* 69 (1884), 63. [13n]

Doig, Ivan. "The Genial White House Host and Raconteur." *Illinois State Historical Journal,* 62 (1969), 307–311. [159n]

Eaton, John. *Grant, Lincoln and the Freedmen.* New York: Longmans, Green, 1907. [63n]

Franklin, Benjamin. *Ben Franklin Laughing.* Ed. P. M. Zall. Berkeley, Los Angeles, London: University of California Press, 1980. [65n, 85n]

Fry, Smith D. *Lincoln and Lee.* Washington: privately printed, 1922. [141n]

Fun of the War. National Tribune Library, no. 15. [73n, 248n]

Funny Stories, or the American Jester. Worcester, Mass.: Worcester Book Store, 1795. [3n]

Haycroft, Samuel. Letter to W. H. Herndon, 5 July 1861, in Herndon papers, Huntington Library accession LN 2328. [17n]

Hoddeson, John. *History of Sir Thomas More.* London: E. Cotes, 1652. [86n]

Hood, Thomas. *Hood's Own.* Second series. London: Edward Moxon, 1861. [258n]

Howard, Esme. *Theatre of Life.* 2 vols. Boston: Little, Brown, 1935. [269n]

Humourist's Own Book. Philadelphia: Key and Biddle, 1834. [16n, 192n]

Johnson, Byron. *Abraham Lincoln and Boston Corbett.* Waltham, Mass.: Byron Johnson, 1914. [87n]

Joke Upon Joke. New Haven, Conn.: Maltby, Goldsmith, 1818. [46n, 69n]

Ladies Literary Cabinet. Volume 6 (1822). [246n, 257n]

Lamar, John W. Letter to W. H. Herndon in Herndon-Weik papers, Library of Congress microfilm 9: 1464–1465. [93n]

LeStrange, Nicholas. *Merry Passages and Jeasts*. Ed. H. F. Lippincott. Salzburg: Institut für Englische Sprache und Literatur, 1974. [159n]

Lincoln, Abraham. *Complete Works*. Ed. John G. Nicolay and John Hay. 12 vols. New York: Century, 1905. [268n]

Lippincott, Sara Jane. *Records of Five Years*. Boston: Ticknor and Fields, 1867. [210n]

Locke, David Ross. *Nasby Papers*. Indianapolis: C. O. Perrine, 1864. [254n]

Means, David. Note. *Lincoln Herald*, 67 (1965), 102. [288n]

Merry Fellows Companion. Philadelphia: M. Carey, 1789. [211n]

Miller, Joe. *Family Joe Miller*. London: William S. Orr, 1848. [188n]

———. *Joe Miller's Jests, or the Wit's Vade Mecum*. London: T. Read, 1739. [204n, 232n]

New Ben Johnson's Jester. London: R. Bassam, ?1800. [30n]

New York *Mail and Express*. Undated paragraph in Judd Stewart scrapbook, Huntington Library accession 151179. [205n]

New York *Tribune*. December 20, 1903, p. 13. [38n]

Newell, Robert H. *Orpheus C. Kerr Papers*. 1st series. New York: Carleton, 1866. [149n]

———. *The Palace Beautiful and Other Verses*. New York: Carleton, 1865. [165n]

Old American Comic Almanac. Boston: S. N. Dickinson, 1842. [71n]

Philagrius. *Jests of Hierocles and Philagrius*. Tr. Charles C. Bubb. Cleveland, Ohio: Rowfant Club, 1920. [306n]

Porter's Spirit of the Times. Vols. 1 (1856), 2 (1857). [41n, 294n]

Royal Court Jester. London: J. Sudbury, 179–. [106n, 84n]

Shakespeare's Jests. London: R. Sharpe, 1767. [211n]

Smith, Goldwin. *Life and Opinions of Goldwin Smith*. Ed. Theodore Arnold Haultain. London: Laurie, 1913. [66n]

Smith, Seba. "My First Visit to Portland." In William E. Burton, *Cyclopaedia of Wit and Humor*. 2 vols. New York: D. Appleton, 1858, pp. 231–232. [159n]

Smith, Sydney. *Works*. 4 vols. London: Longman, Orme, 1839–1840. [322n]

Stephens, Alexander. *Recollections*. Ed. Myrta Lockett Avary. New York: Doubleday, Page, 1910. [82n]

Stephenson, Nathaniel W. *Autobiography of Abraham Lincoln*. Indianapolis: Bobbs, Merrill, 1926. [268n]

Stimmel, Smith. *Personal Reminiscences of Abraham Lincoln*. Minneapolis: W. H. M. Adams, 1928. [297n]

Stoddard, William O. *Lincoln's Third Secretary: Memoirs of William O. Stoddard.* Ed. W. O. Stoddard, Jr. New York: Exposition Press, 1955. [125n]

Tarbell, Ida. *Early Life of Abraham Lincoln.* Ed. Paul M. Angle. New York: A. S. Barnes, 1974. [93n]

Wardroper, John. *Jest Upon Jest.* London: Routledge and Kegan Paul, 1970. [251n]

"Weller, Sam." *Sam Weller's Jest Book.* London: Orlando Hodgson, 1837. [270n]

White, Andrew D. *Autobiography.* New York: Century, 1907. [131n]

Wilson, Rufus Rockwell. *Intimate Memories of Lincoln.* Elmira, N. Y.: Primavera Press, 1945. [74n]

Wit and Wisdom. London: J. Smith, 1826. [125n]

Young, Thomas. *England's Bane.* London: William Jones, 1617. [267n]

Zall, P. M. *A Nest of Ninnies and Other English Jestbooks of the Seventeenth Century.* Lincoln: University of Nebraska Press, 1970. [152n]

Indexes

The following indexes serve two distinct purposes. Those who may wish to review the stories Lincoln told on some general topic—say, inebriation—should consult the immediately following Topical Index, where they will find a heading, "Drinking and Eating," with twenty-two entries and another, "Drunks," with ten. Those who may wish to track down a particular Lincoln story—say, Lincoln on General Grant's drinking—should consult the Subject Index, where they will find a heading, "Grant, Ulysses S.," and a subheading, "his brand of whiskey." The Subject Index is by far the longer of the two, with hundreds of entries. The Topical Index contains only sixty categories, reflecting Lincoln's concerns measured by how frequently his stories touch upon specified topics. Thus among the fourteen entries from his own writings, seven topics appear at least twice: *Boys, Politics, Wild Animals* (e.g., bears, coons, skunks), *Conmen, Irishmen, Senior Citizens,* and *Wives.* Of these, *Boys, Politics,* and *Wild Animals* repeat with twice the average frequency in the remaining entries, indicating that they were his favorite topics. By the same measure, he had these other favorites—in order of declining frequency: *Foibles, Hogs & Other Domesticated Animals* (e.g., bulls, chickens, cats), *Drinking & Eating, Soldiers & Officers,* and *Conmen & Criminals.* Altogether the topics generally reflect a distinctive combination of the traditional and the timely: Like conventional humorous stories these favor fools and knaves in a rural setting but now applied to timely national issues respecting politics and the war. This feature supports the repeated assertion by those who knew him well that Lincoln seldom told a story for its own sake.

Topical Index

References are to entry numbers

Subject Index

Only stories are indexed, not contexts in which they were told. References are to entry numbers not pages.